THE UNCERTAIN ART
OF MANAGEMENT

To Nikki, once more with feeling.

THE UNCERTAIN ART
OF MANAGEMENT

HARRY ONSMAN

MANAGEMENT
TODAY SERIES

AUSTRALIAN
INSTITUTE OF
MANAGEMENT

Series Editor
Carolyn Barker

Associate Editor
Robyn Coy

Sydney New York San Francisco Auckland Bogotá Caracas
Lisbon London Madrid MexicoCity Milan Montreal New Delhi
SanJuan Singapore Tokyo Toronto

McGraw·Hill Australia

A Division of The McGraw·Hill Companies

National Library of Australia Cataloguing-in-Publication data:
Onsman, Harry.
The uncertain art of management

Includes index.
ISBN 0 074 71107 5.

1. Management – Australia. I. Barker, Carolyn.
II. Australian Institute of Management.
(Series : Management today (McGraw-Hill)).

658.00994

Published in Australia by
McGraw-Hill Australia Pty Ltd
Level 2, 82 Waterloo Road, North Ryde NSW 2113, Australia
Acquisitions Editor: Javier Dopico
Production Editor: Sybil Kesteven
Editor: Jo Rudd
Designer (cover and interior): Lucy Bal
Cover Illustration: gettyimages
Typeset in 11/12 pt Bembo by Post Pre-Press Group
Printed on 80 gsm woodfree by Pantech Limited, Hong Kong.

CONTENTS

PREFACE

This is the third book in AIM's Management Today Series. Each book in the series tackles contemporary management and leadership issues, but the thread that runs through is: *people, people, people.* Whether you think management is an art, a craft, a science or voodoo . . . people, and how well you interact with, motivate, challenge and lead them, will determine your success or failure as a manager.

That is why at times management can seem so difficult and perplexing, but also why it can be so gloriously satisfying for all concerned when it works in an organisational context.

Throughout the world there are libraries full of books, dissertations and research about management and leadership. The problem is, there is no way that any one manager can access, consume, prioritise and implement this huge body of knowledge—let alone determine which theory will work best for what situation, especially when the situation is constantly changing (as are the findings and the theories). So as a manager, how can you possibly know which approach to use, how to do it and when, let alone why? And when you do apply a theory, why is it that it doesn't always work?

When faced with an issue or crisis, people (regardless of position in the hierarchy) often choose the fastest or easiest way through, the 'quick or the dead' option. And often the big stuff, the underlying causes and the deep-seated problems, don't get fixed. But what to do? We don't always have the time and space to undertake a thorough investigation of the issue, neatly lay out alternative solutions, ponder the pros and cons, check back with the literature, and then progress in an orderly and documented fashion to the outcome (not forgetting to do the follow-up afterwards).

So often in day-to-day management we need to just get on with it—and hope to do the best by our people and organisational resources in the process. In other words, we must do the job in the best way that we know how, using experience and intuition to guide us. But which manager has not lain awake in the early morning, pondering the ceiling, and thought, 'Perhaps there was a better way'?

Which brings us back to where we started. What an interesting dilemma. On one side, a daunting, constantly growing and changing body of knowledge . . . and on the other, the realities of day-to-day management and, above all, the practical implications of people being people in the workplace.

And that is where this book comes in. It is an attempt to provide some signposts to guide you through the maze of everyday management. Each chapter tackles a management issue and provides background information to help you understand its dimensions and complexities—historical context, research and conflicting theories, gurus, myths, misunderstandings, sources of confusion, even strange philosophies! Current best practice and new directions in thought are also included. And to help you put it all in perspective, the chapter then provides practical guidelines to help you 'cut through' when decisions need to be made.

The underlying philosophy of this book was not to provide the total management solution or definitive answers, but to provide a tool for those who plan, implement, control, evaluate and lead (or in other words, manage) at all levels. It is not totally comprehensive . . . after all, how could it be? Management is, and always will be, an uncertain art. And mastery of any art is ephemeral at best. We delude ourselves if we think otherwise, and such arrogance can only lead to hubris. What works one day can be overturned the next by the vagaries of fortune or the unpredictability of human behaviour, factors beyond our control and sometimes beyond our understanding.

In reality, in life as well as in management, the only thing you can control is yourself and your attitude. But for how many of us does this remain unexplored or ignored territory? The key is to have the flexibility and strength of character to keep searching for a better way, and to be willing to constantly learn, develop and grow. It is about developing a capacity for emotional resilience in the face of setback. And it is about having a knowledge of self that allows you to remain true to yourself and what you value when faced with ambiguity and uncertainty.

So, perhaps it is time for us to 'grow up' and acknowledge that there is no panacea for management and no short cut to mastery. But there is always a better way to do things if we are prepared to look.

No one person can ever find all of the solutions. But whether you are an aspiring or new manager, or perhaps an old dog looking to learn new tricks, we hope that this book will provide a commonsense frame of reference for your personal and ongoing search for 'a better way'.

Carolyn Barker, FAIM
Series Editor and National Director
Australian Institute of Management

ABOUT THE AUTHOR

Harry Onsman (MA, LittB, BEd)

Harry Onsman is a management consultant, management educator and writer who works with organisations on issues of strategy, structure, and performance management. He has held senior management positions in the private and public sectors in various Human Resource Management capacities.

The author of *Taking Control of Training* (1989, ABC Books), Harry has also written extensively on management issues for *Business Review Weekly*, *Management Today*, and *The Manager Online*.

Harry is a member of the Institute of Management Consultants, and a Fellow of the Australian Institute of Training.

INTRODUCTION

Most of us who are practising managers are doing exactly that: *practising*. If you speak with experienced and senior managers, you typically hear stories about how they face difficult and complex situations with only a slight and often intuitive notion about how to deal with them. Some worry about this. Some revel in the challenge of 'making it up as you go along'. And others deny the complexity.

With other professional activities, seniority usually bestows a depth of understanding and sometimes wisdom. Management is different. Perhaps this is because people become managers first and then start to learn how to do it. And while I would not recommend this approach for a cardiac surgeon, it probably is not a bad model for management.

One reason for this unusual approach to professional development is that managers do not have a body of theory that is universally accepted by the practitioners, or even by those who teach the practitioners. Despite some reasonable attempts by a few thinkers, there is no coherent body of thought that sums up the field of management.

In most fields of human endeavour, it is easy to list the pre-eminent thinkers that have shaped the field and provided consistency of approach. In management, however, we quickly run out of contemporary names after Peter Drucker. A few names from the last one hundred years (such as Henri Fayol, Mary Parker Follett or Frederick Taylor) may be added. But that's about it. Of course, many managers can rattle off the names of the current gurus who fill the gap created by the lack of sound theory by providing a swag of 'how-to' ideas and quick cure-alls.

Many managers do seek to study theory and practice, but it is usually after they have started their managerial careers. Typically it is taught as part of a postgraduate qualification, following an undergraduate degree in other areas. Many complete technical qualifications in areas such as finance, engineering or IT, and seek a management qualification to add to their name. Many are also disappointed that the certainties that generally prevail in their technical areas of expertise do not carry over into the practice of management.

There are many possible explanations as to why management has benefited less from the scientific method than other areas of human endeavour. The main one is that management is quintessentially a human activity, and so defies the rigidities of scientific experimentation. In that sense, it is more akin to an art or craft than a science. Often in management, relationships matter more than data, intuition more than rationality, and attitude more than everything else put together.

Critically, management is about dealing with others. You manage your staff, your peers, and (as often as not these days), your boss. This often leaves little time for the other person in the equation: you.

For many managers, ignoring their own needs as they focus on everyone else around them and thereby neglecting themselves, simply stores up trouble. Sometimes this leads to a crisis point when experienced and senior people suddenly decide that the whole management malarkey is something they can do without. A few make sudden career diversions, others just burn out.

No wonder we have a younger generation coming along for whom promotion to management is not the most important thing in life. In fact, working is not the most important thing in their lives. This trend suggests that in the future we may well have trouble attracting the best and the brightest to the managerial role. Why should they be attracted to it when managers don't necessarily earn as much money as, and are likely to work much harder than, those who are in non-management jobs?

All of which suggests to me that we need to look after our managers. Which in turn makes me think that if you are a manager, you had better look after yourself, because I don't believe anyone else will look after you! This is not because no one cares, but simply because in the scheme of things nurturing managerial talent in all its many dimensions is no one's job, so it doesn't happen.

If you're lucky, you may find a mentor or coach who can provide some assistance. But this kind of support often has a career development focus, which is not the whole of it. There is more to being a manager than just becoming a better manager. And as managers become better at managing, they tend to realise that the job is much more uncertain, ambiguous, complicated and perplexing than anyone ever told them.

As collaborative partners, both AIM and I have a strong view about the need to put into perspective some of the issues that managers face on a day-to-day basis. That perspective is based on an acceptance that management will never be a precise practice, that learning as you go along is OK, and that some problems cannot be figured out to the solution stage by the time you need to act.

Of course, we do know some things about the practice of management. In some instances we can act from a basis of knowledge. But, there is much more that we don't know. Often the best we can do is guess, while firmly ignoring those who claim to have the full and complete answer.

In management there is never one best way, but there are some suggestions that may help avoid the worst of the wrong ways. I hope you find some of them in this book.

Harry Onsman

Creating
a better workplace

TRUST IN THE WORKPLACE 1

There are some key words in management that are used by many people as if their mere use explained something. One of those words is *trust*.

Trust is often used as a pseudo-explanation of what is wrong with an organisation. Senior managers are liable to proclaim gravely that the source of problems in their organisation is a 'lack of trust', that the 'level of trust' has to go up for things to improve and that the 'issue of trust' needs to be addressed.

Then the analysis stops. Questions such as 'Why is trust low?' and 'What can we do about it?' are rarely heard. Instead, the sad state of affairs is acknowledged, before moving on to more pressing issues such as considering the next downsizing project or some other rationalisation initiative.

Does trust matter in the workplace?

Background

As the level of turbulence inside and outside organisations increases, the intangible glue that helps to hold organisations together is dissolving. At the same time, the largely unmeasured impacts of downsizing, job change, relocation, product/service rationalisation, work redesign and the rest of the panoply of changes affecting workers and managers become apparent. Where once a manager could rely on at least a small measure of understanding, tolerance, flexibility, cooperation and discretionary effort from employees, today such expectations are laughable.

The changes that have been made in organisations in the last twenty years have created an overwrought workforce. We have used up whatever employee goodwill we might have had in the past. The bank account of trust and tolerance has been drawn down to the point where most employees have closed the account. In these situations, managers tend to look for recipes that will somehow turn back the clock. But the structural changes organisations have undergone are so irrevocable that any hope of bringing back the past is just foolish. The most significant structural elements of the workplace of the 1960s and 1970s have all gone.

- Careers have been replaced by *employability*.
- Jobs have been replaced by *roles*.
- Lines-of-command have been replaced by *matrix structures*.
- Job functions have been replaced by *accountabilities*.
- Salary has been replaced by *performance-based pay*.
- Offices have been replaced by *open-plan arrangements*.
- Management has been replaced by *team leadership*.
- Promotional ladders have been replaced by *career enhancement opportunities* (go back to the top of the list).

None of this can be undone. We have to live with it and make the best of it, even when there is a collective feeling of 'Let's find the bastards who did this and throttle them'.

It is unrealistic to try to replace what is gone, although many managers still seek to do so.

High on the list of 'what we need to put back into the workplace' is trust. This idea is one of the *big* ones, up there with 'We need to change the culture'; 'We need more leadership'; 'We need better communication'; and 'We need to empower the workforce'.

If it wasn't for the fact that the so called big ideas are so prevalent in management thinking around the globe, it would be funny. For most of those advocating these big ideas, every item on the list is typically ill defined or undefined, misunderstood or misconstrued, difficult or impossible to change. Sometimes they are just a complex consequence of many other elements.

Maybe it is all part of the phenomenon that anthropological linguist Malinowski called 'phatic communion'.[1] This is the speaking or chanting of meaningless mantras in order to create a sense of togetherness. The actual semantic value of the chanting is nil. So why do it, when it adds nothing to the daily chore of creating shared meaning? Maybe managers need to speak meaninglessly of things in order to retain a semblance of sane purpose.

Trust is starting to emerge from the scrum of big ideas, possibly because we have discovered that we are unable to easily do anything about the others: leadership is too confusing and those expensive leadership development programs we tried did not seem to have much impact; culture turned out to be something that you could not beat into shape on an anvil of reform; and communication is just too elusive and involves a lot of actual contact with the workforce. And so we turn to trust.

It's early days for trust as a management panacea. Only a few books have been written on the topic in the popular press, and most of them are either delightfully optimistic or hilariously unrealistic about something that is so intangible. Possibly the best so far is *Driving Fear out of the Workplace* by Ryan and Oestreich.[2] Also worth a look, though a little over-simplified, are Reina and Reina's *Trust and Betrayal in the Workplace*[3] and Marshall's *Building Trust at the Speed of Change: The Power of the Relationship-based Organisation.*[4]

To date, no serious training program or consulting group has focused on the idea of how to build or rebuild trust in organisations. But it's only a matter of time, if the progress of the other big ideas is any guide. Probably, what is needed to kick the idea along is a guru, a speaker of note, who will evangelise the idea on the international speakers' circuit. (If anyone out there is thinking of taking this up, I would suggest a title like, 'Building Profits by Building Trust: Seven Simple Steps'—the 'seven' is very important as it is the magical number for most management panaceas.)

What is trust?

In the meantime, the question of trust is being addressed in a more rigorous fashion by other disciplines. Both sociology and economics have a great deal to say on the subject. Interestingly (and maybe predictably), they say quite different things, each discipline bringing a different perspective to understanding what is going on in society. Economics treats society a bit like a mechanical device that generates outcomes that are measurable by indicators such as productivity, wealth, employment levels and so forth. Sociology is more interested in the internal forces and pressures that make the social machine what it is rather than what it produces.

An interesting example from economics of the concept of trust is provided by Williamson in the article 'Calculativeness, trust and economic organization'.[5] An equally interesting example from sociology is Giddens' *The Consequences of Modernity.*[6] While both claim to be talking about trust, a comparison of these two approaches illustrates that they might as well be speaking different languages.

This is where Marek Korczynski's recent article, 'The political economy of trust',[7] comes in handy. It provides not only a review of the issues about trust in an organisational (although largely economic) context but also some key observations about how to bridge the disciplinary divide. It is also readable.

Korczynski argues that the notion of economic cooperation (which includes the contract between labour and capital) is based on three key notions: trust, power and the market. Sociologists have tended to focus on trust and power, while economists focus on power and the market. Until now, no one has been interested enough to include all three in their analysis. Korczynski claims that combining all three gives us a powerful explanation for what happens in the real world.

Trust is usually defined as the confidence you have that the other party to an arrangement you have made will not exploit your vulnerabilities. The words may differ but the essential elements are:

- an *arrangement*, *exchange* or *agreement* of some kind;
- a *willingness to accept an element of risk* by one or more of the parties involved;
- the acceptance of risk is based on a *level of confidence* held by one or more of the parties.

When you have these three elements, you have trust. So, when an employee goes to work for an employer:

- the employment *arrangement* is agreed upon;
- the employee accepts the *risks* inherent in that arrangement (for example, whether she will actually get paid at the end of the week);
- the employee's willingness to accept risk is based on her *level of confidence* in the employer fulfilling his obligations to pay her at the end of the week (based on the reputation of the employer, legal frameworks and so on).

Economists and sociologists usually differ in their explanations of the last item: for economists, the level of confidence comes from the formal structures or from market forces; for sociologists, it is based on social relations and expectations deriving from social norms. Either way, *level of confidence* is the key intangible in the trust equation.

Unfortunately, workers' level of confidence that an employer will do 'the right thing' has been eroded over the last few years. Contributing factors to this decline in confidence range from a recent rollback in many countries of employment legislation that protects workers to the disempowerment of managers in 'de-layered' organisations.

When companies go broke and it is discovered that they have squandered employee accumulated leave and retirement entitlements, then the level of confidence declines. When corporate commitments are made to maintain local manufacturing facilities, only to be broken by a new management regime, confidence declines again. When jobs are slashed in pointless and profitless downsizing programs, then confidence hits rock bottom.

In this context, it seems futile to speak of rebuilding trust. And yet that is the challenge facing many organisations because we are finally realising that high-trust organisations are more productive, longer lasting and more profitable.

Why trust matters

Those most likely to discover the relationship between trust and productivity are the so-called *knowledge-based* organisations. Initially, the term 'knowledge-based' referred to those organisations that were highly dependent on their people. In these organisations, at the end of each day, the key assets of the company walk out the door. But lately even the leftovers from the industrial age, the manufacturers, are realising that much of the knowledge needed to run their organisations also walks out of their doors each night. Today, most organisations are knowledge-based, or are becoming so, and are therefore people-based.

The manifestation of trust in knowledge-based organisations has been called the *loyalty effect* and it has been estimated to add as much as 40 per cent to the productivity of a high-trust organisation compared with its low-trust counterpart.[8]

Trust provides a pay-off by enabling the organisation to do more with less. For example:
- trust can lead to less structure and bureaucracy, which saves operating costs;
- trust can increase empowerment, which speeds up responsiveness and flexibility, which in turn leads to higher levels of customer satisfaction;
- trust increases knowledge sharing, which generally improves productivity.

In short, trust pays off.

Trust leads to profits, but trust cannot be rebuilt on the old basis, because that is gone forever and we cannot turn back the clock.

Rebuilding trust

So, we must move forward and create a new basis for trust in organisations. It must be built on elements of the newly emerging employment relations—elements that are driven by employees as much as by employers.

Some of these elements are clearer than others. For example, many employees have responded to the structural changes in the workplace by treating their job as a temporary phenomenon. They now treat organisations as places to work from, not organisations to work for. Psychologically, the job has a different meaning for them. Employers (and managers) can use this sea change in employee attitudes by offering incentives such as personal, career or profile development opportunities. The objective is not to make the job appear permanent but to make it more rewarding.

Today, the employment deal is different; the world has changed. It means much more risk for managers as they deal with intangible benefits while having a tangible lack of security of tenure for themselves and their staff. No one is handing out road maps that tell you how to go about doing all this. There are no guarantees about who will survive and who won't. But that's part of the fun. And it beats trying to bring back the past—trust me.

Guidelines

There is no formula for creating trust in the workplace. But if you think of trust as the balance held in a bank account, there are some management actions that draw down on that balance and there are others that increase it. The following may help to increase the balance.

1 Undercommit and overdeliver

Don't commit yourself to delivering things that are out of your direct control.

The degree of trust that people will have in you depends in part on the extent to which you deliver on your promises. The fastest way to teach people to distrust you is by not delivering. Therefore, adopt a deliberate strategy of *undercommitting and overdelivering*.

Over time, you will be seen as a reliable manager who follows through on commitments and delivers. People will trust you to do the same in the future.

2 Treat everyone as a knowledge worker

Every job can be divided into those elements that can be controlled externally through direct supervision and control, and those elements that are discretionary. The latter are those bits that happen because the employee wants them to happen. Employees can't be forced to do them. For example, we can supervise employees to make sure they follow the correct procedure—but we can't supervise them to keep an eye out for quality problems. They have to *want* to do that. Such discretionary elements now make up an ever increasing part of any job.

By treating every employee as a repository of considerable knowledge about their job, you will accord them the respect they deserve, because most jobs are now knowledge-based or are rapidly becoming so.

You will get a return from managing people by gaining their respect and respecting them. Relationships based on mutual respect are relationships based on trust. The trust 'bank balance' goes up accordingly.

3 Find appropriate rewards

As the employment contract changes in nature from 'tenure' to 'contingent', retain people by creating opportunities for them to acquire new skills and develop new capabilities. Accept the fact that research suggests that most people are motivated more by intangibles (such as access to training) than by tangibles such as money.

So for each of your direct reports, *find out what matters to them*. For example:

- access to training;
- access to specialised knowledge;
- access to intellectual property;
- opportunities to work with acknowledged experts;
- equity in the organisation, such as shares;
- opportunities to experiment or be entrepreneurial;
- better pay (as long as it is now, because promises don't carry much weight in the fast paced world of business);
- flexible working arrangements controlled partly by the staff;
- non-monetary 'status rewards' such as special job titles.

In terms of professional development, there is a host of desirable 'mini' opportunities, such as visiting suppliers/customers, attending short training programs or leading a small project. Happily, such opportunities are usually far cheaper than promotion or pay increases.

For further exploration

Like many other topics in management, common sense and trusting your instincts will get you a long way. Trust in the workplace is no different from trust elsewhere in human society so most of you will have a pretty good idea of what is helpful and what is not. However, if you want to explore the issue more thoroughly, you could try:

- K. Ryan and D. Oestreich, *Driving Fear out of the Workplace*, Jossey-Bass, San Francisco, 1991.

Based on one of the 12 Deming principles for creating an effective and productive workplace, it was one of the first books to enter the field. It provides a number of useful concepts for understanding the fear issue and tackling the fear-filled workplace. It does not provide a panacea and is modest in its ambitions, but its scope is wide-ranging and it makes many practical suggestions.

EMPOWERMENT

Some management notions seem to take on a life of their
own, helped by the publications of a few enthusiasts.
Empowerment is one of those notions. It has tremendous face
appeal to managers as it promises a mix of less work (for the
managers) and greater effort (on the part of employees). Any
such mix is clearly powerful enough to sell itself.

However, it ain't that simple. The reality is that
empowerment is hard work for most managers and the returns
are often less than hoped for. As a result, the appeal diminishes
over time and, lately, the notion seems to be losing its shiny
and attractive image.

Empowerment can be made to work, however, if managers
are prepared to change themselves first before they set out to
change others.

Background

Workplace empowerment is a recurring theme in current
management thinking. This is largely because the illusion of
management control is gradually being stripped away by
technological changes, flatter hierarchical structures, and the
advent of virtual organisations and knowledge workers. The
bosses are no longer in control because they do not understand
the equipment that the workers are using, aren't there to call
the shots and don't know what the workers know.

In the face of these changes, managers are turning to the
gurus of empowerment to seek an intellectual justification for
a process that is already happening. It is almost as if the
decision to *empower* or *give power* to workers restores to
managers a psychological sense of control over a process that is
actually inevitable. Nothing like the semblance of control
when you're powerless!

The paradox of empowerment

Mary Parker Follett (1868–1933) was the first to identify the
fundamental paradox in all this. Although she came to
management from a practical background (she set up the
earliest vocational guidance centres in the United States), her
focus was on the dynamic interplay between the individual
and the organisation. She wrote about leadership, control,

authority, power and conflict at a time when her contemporary, Frederick W. Taylor, was lecturing the US Senate about the very static structure of work. To appreciate how ahead of her times she was, you need only look at her writings on the now fashionable topic of 'empowerment'. While the term was not in use in the first part of the twentieth century, Parker Follett's observations on the concept heralded an approach that still has not fully penetrated management thinking, let alone management practice. When it does, we will finally be able to move beyond the current facile preoccupations with what empowerment entails.

The paradox of empowerment, as explored by Parker Follett,[1] is that *you cannot give power to another*. Only others can empower themselves, and you may assist or resist that process. So when a manager decides to empower a worker, unless both parties set in place a process of self-empowerment, they are involved in a furphy. This furphy is based on the notion that the power game is a zero-sum game where, if your power goes down, mine goes up. When the worker's power increases, the manager must somehow have less of it.

This zero-sum metaphor misleads managers into thinking that the process of empowering others is somehow to managers' detriment. When you empower others, you lose power. Replace this metaphor, say, by the *knowledge metaphor* (as in knowledge shared is *not* knowledge halved) and the concept of empowerment becomes a positive and uplifting notion. Parker Follett calls this having 'power-with', as opposed to the notion of 'power-over' implicit in the zero-sum metaphor. (The universal importance of 'non-zero sumness' is superbly explored by Robert Wright in *Non-zero: The Logic of Human Destiny*.[2])

Parker Follett describes power-with as 'a jointly developed power, a co-active, not coercive power'.[3] In this way, the notion of power in empowerment becomes a self-developing capacity that is encouraged by the manager. It is more closely related to personal development than it is to authority.

With this concept of power-with, Parker Follett both predates and encapsulates the fundamental issue in the so-called 'empowerment programs' advocated today—that is, it is not about power but about enabling others to develop their abilities. By conceptualising empowerment as a process rather than an act, she cuts away most of the ground from beneath those who question empowerment as something that will undermine the authority of management. The power-with approach inevitably leads to considerations of context and of the structural and social elements in organisations that either facilitate or hinder the development of empowered employees.

By shifting from power-over to power-with, Parker Follett changes the empowerment debate from a competition to a joint development project. It is probably the most sensible contribution made so far to the discussion on empowerment. And it's a contribution from the 1920s, long before the debate was even conceived!

Parker Follett does not provide quick fixes or step-by-step formulas for implementing her ideas. She believed that it is hard work to create an organisation that thrives as a result of encouraging its people to thrive. Her prescriptions are for the long haul, not for the one-minute sprint. But her writings contain many of the notions that are now fashionable in management thinking, such as the 'win–win' approach to conflict resolution, the importance of respectful reciprocity, the concept of emergent strategy (as opposed to deliberately designed strategy) and the idea of creating synergies through cooperative endeavours.

In his introduction to a recent collection of Parker Follett's writings, Peter Drucker called her a 'prophet of management'.[4] So, for inspiration about the pressing management issues of today, it may be valuable to turn the clock back eighty years.

Why managers don't empower

Regrettably, there is little evidence that any of this is having an impact today out there in what is often called 'the real world'. Despite the truckloads of books, it is virtually impossible to detect any movement in the extent or degree to which managers are empowering their staff.

Sure, it is difficult to delineate just how we might measure whether there has been any movement or not. From my own point of view (and to the extent that my own visits to hundreds of organisations and discussions with thousands of managers over a 15-year period is any guide), there is no more empowerment to be seen today than one generation of managers ago. Empowerment may be a topic for discussion but it is not the subject of management action.

It is important to make one minor but significant exception here, if only to prove the general application of the 'no-change' view. A number of organisations have invested considerable time and effort in creating self-managing teams in a structured way, and in these organisations we do find examples of increased workforce self-management. Such examples are relatively rare, although they provide concrete illustrations of what can be achieved. In many of these instances, the teams involved (or their managers) are able to provide clear and accurate explanations of the extent of their autonomy and the limits to their self-management (see Chapter 20).

There are several possible reasons why empowerment works in the team context but not elsewhere. The collective nature of the self-management arrangements seems to provide management with the security that authority boundaries won't be exceeded. An alternative explanation is that the arrangements frequently grow out of structured and planned change processes. For example, self-managing work teams are typically the outcome of formal organisational change processes such as work redesign. Maybe the formality and structure of such processes provide management with the confidence to trust the outcomes.

Either way, the relative rarity of these examples demonstrates that management is far from ready to accept the notion of workforce empowerment. This conclusion sits uncomfortably with the level of interest in the subject. For example, Ken Blanchard's books (such as *The One Minute Manager*[5] and *Empowerment Takes More Than a Minute*[6]) have sold by the millions. Ricardo Semler's *Maverick*[7] was a runaway bestseller and still sells well even after eight years in print. A steady stream of new material on this topic is published every year, and academia continues to pour out research that links empowerment to corporate benefits.

Usually, when the interests of the promoters (consultants, authors, speakers, or academics trying to become one of these) coincide with the findings of the research establishment (universities, professional bodies or industry-backed research institutes), then you have a sure-fire management initiative. So, what's the problem with empowerment?

It probably has something to do with the fundamental nature of the boss–worker relationship. Most other successful initiatives are some distance removed from this relationship. An organisation can invest in 'strategy development' or 'balanced scorecards' or 'quality accreditation' without affecting the relationship between the boss and the bossed. All are about rational and logical changes to the way things are done in an organisation. They are unemotional things and, by their nature, are inanimate, dispassionate and not alive.

Empowerment is different. It touches a nerve that springs alive with emotions, especially fear and anxiety. For bosses unfamiliar with the realities of empowerment, there is the fear of loss of control, of being held accountable while not being in charge, of not knowing what might happen and even of losing their job. For employees, there is the fear of doing the wrong thing, of being asked to do more than they are capable of doing well or of being shown up as inadequate.

All this fear creates an atmosphere of anxiety, usually signalled by nervous behaviour from both parties. As a result, people react negatively when empowerment is first mooted as an organisational objective, to the extent that the word itself is now avoided by many in industry. The root causes of these fears are rarely addressed directly because the idea of dealing with emotion in the workplace is anathema to most managers.

The challenge for managers

And so empowerment languishes in a strange limbo where a few organisations thrive because of it and others stare in amazement at the crazy few. Study after study shows that people want to have greater control over how they do their job, while even more studies show that management is actually introducing more workplace controls. So our best management gurus and promoters get rich promoting something that no one in industry really wants to do.

The point about empowerment as a management strategy for getting exceptional results is that it actually starts with managers, and not with workers. Empowerment requires managers to change the way they do what they do. Making the necessary changes is difficult but there are no short cuts. A personal anecdote will illustrate why you can't 'fake' empowerment.

The father of the concept of Total Quality Management, W. Edward Deming, is famous for formulating *twelve* principles that will create a more productive workplace. During a recent visit to a large manufacturing plant, I was told proudly by one of the shop-floor employees that he had completed several days training on Deming's *seven* principles. I said that I thought there were twelve principles, not seven. He was quite sure there were only seven and showed me his course workbook to prove it. Sure enough, five of Deming's principles had been carefully excised from the usual list of twelve, including the one that urges management to drive out fear in the workplace.

Maybe we're not ready yet for empowerment in the workplace.

Guidelines

There are many philosophies and approaches about how to make empowerment work in the workplace. There is no easy way to decide which one is best. Empowerment is first about the manager, and only second about employees. It demands an approach to working with people that assumes that, if people are provided with a framework and the freedom to operate within that framework, the results can be exceptional. Here are some principles to guide what you do. Refer to the work of Ken Blanchard (see *For further exploration*) for more detail.

1 Share information widely

You cannot empower ignorant people—it's dangerous! You need to give people as much information as they can handle and increase their capacity to handle more complex information.

Invest in the 'business literacy' of your workforce. Educate them so that they understand the business as much as possible. If you want them to care about your business and help you drive it, then they must understand the business.

Share all information with everyone in the organisation unless there is a very strong reason to hold something back. For many organisations, this reverses the current paradigm (that is, they withhold everything unless there is a compelling reason not to do so).

2 Create autonomy through boundaries

Once you have informed people, you need to create the framework in which they can operate autonomously.

Your job as manager is to set the boundaries that limit what people are authorised to do. These boundaries should be clear, unambiguous and understood. Set the boundaries and check continually that your employees understand them. Monitor people to see that they operate within the boundaries.

Your slogan should be: *Freedom within a framework.*

3 Replace hierarchy with teams

In most organisations, people depend on each other to get work done. Use this mutual dependency to create a team approach.

Teams have been demonstrated to increase work satisfaction and productivity at the same time. And that's a very powerful combination. It will take some work on your part as a manager to create the level of teamwork that you need. But on almost every measure, teams are a smarter way of 'obtaining control' than hierarchy.

For further explanation

While many shudder at the notion of the 'industrial novel', you cannot argue with the sales numbers racked up by Ken Blanchard's books. He may not have invented this poor cousin of literary writing, but he sure made it popular with *The One Minute Manager*. The format is story-based, short and carries its main messages in LARGE PRINT. It has sold millions of copies. The fact is that the content of his material is meticulously researched and even complex topics are clearly presented. Let's face it: Blanchard's stuff is well done.

On empowerment, Blanchard is thorough and sound. Try the one listed below for a very practical but effective approach.

- K. Blanchard, J. Carlos and A. Randolph, *Empowerment Takes More Than a Minute*, Berrett-Koehler, San Francisco, 1996.

WORKPLACE SATISFACTION 3

Attracting and retaining staff is likely to become a bigger issue
for many managers than it may have been in the past. Several
factors (such as an ageing population, the changing work
preferences of younger generations of workers, and the
changing nature of work itself) suggest that in the future
getting the very best people is going to be harder.

The days of lifelong employment have long gone and
today's employees have no problem with flitting from one job
to another. They are more committed to their own career (and
life) than they will ever be to the goals of someone else's
business. All this has implications for employers. The cost of
replacing employees keeps rising, making it more important
than ever to hang on to your best people.

How can you create a workplace that will make the best
and the brightest stay with you?

Background

What makes a workplace a great place to work? Managers
hold widely different views about the key aspects of a
workplace that will attract and retain employees. Some
advocate the simple solution of higher pay, while others
believe that money is not the only thing that encourages
people to stay or go. Some have stopped thinking altogether
about what seems a painfully complex issue.

The debate is important, however, because it affects what an
organisation does when it is trying to hang on to its best
people. Some organisations chase the money route by upping
salaries whenever it seems necessary to keep their staff happy.
But are they wasting their money?

Why workers stay (and go)

Most management theorists argue that motivating people goes
way beyond money issues. Jeffrey Pfeffer, author of *The Human
Equation*, argues that current research quite clearly
demonstrates that 'pay rates are much less important than most
managers think, and even lower labor costs may not be the
basis for competitive success'.[1]

After reviewing hundreds of studies that explore the link
between pay and performance, author Alfie Kohn concluded in

Punished by Rewards that 'rewards usually improve performance only at extremely simple—indeed, mindless—tasks, and even then they improve only quantitative performance'.[2]

None of this explains the gap between what the research says and what managers and organisations actually do. The annual salary review creates more anguish on both sides of the managerial fence than almost any other activity in organisations. But it's a ritual dance that both sides seem locked into and unwilling to abandon. Why?

Possibly, what has been missing from the debate is some hard-nosed data. Despite various corporate efforts to obtain reliable information on what employees actually want, there is little indisputable evidence. Attempts to quantify the issue range from regular employee surveys to in-depth focus groups. At best, these efforts have told us what employees do *not* like about their workplace; data on what they *do* like is much harder to obtain.

Recent analysis by the US polling company, the Gallup Organization, provides data that may be the basis for an objective answer. Gallup has been in the polling business for almost thirty years, including polling workers to find out what makes them stay in their jobs. In what may well be the mother of all surveys, Gallup went back to all the millions of pieces of data it had obtained over a quarter of a century from thousands of workplace surveys involving hundreds of thousands of employees.[3]

The research by the Gallup Organization drew on interviews and questionnaires completed by over one million employees over a 25-year period. Using sophisticated statistical techniques such as factor analysis, regression analysis and concurrent validity studies, Gallup researchers identified a large range of questions that would measure whether employees were likely to stay with their employer. The examined factors were reduced to the 'core elements' that seem to attract and retain productive employees.

The research focused intentionally on more than just job satisfaction. Apparently, many employees think their jobs are great (high job satisfaction) but the workplace is lousy. Others have lousy jobs (low job satisfaction), but stay because the workplace is great. Gallup defined 'great workplaces' as those which performed well on four key measurable outcomes: employee retention, customer satisfaction, productivity and profitability.

The following twelve questions, devised by Gallup and based on their findings, concern the core elements that make a difference to workplace life.

1 Do I know what is expected of me?
2 Do I have the materials and equipment I need to do my work right?
3 At work, do I have the opportunity every day to do what I do best?
4 In the last seven days, have I received recognition or praise for good work?
5 Does my supervisor, or someone at work, seem to care about me as a person?
6 Is there someone at work who encourages my development?
7 At work, do my opinions seem to count?
8 Does the mission of my company make me feel like my work is important?
9 Are my colleagues committed to doing quality work?
10 Do I have a best friend at work?
11 In the last six months, have I talked with someone about my progress?
12 At work, have I had the opportunity to learn and grow?[4]

What makes a workplace great?

According to Marcus Buckingham, senior consultant at the Gallup School of Management: 'Great workplaces in different companies have a great deal in common.'[5] He claims that the research clearly shows a number of aspects of workplace life that really make a difference, especially to those employees most valuable to an organisation—the talented and the productive.

The answers to Gallup's twelve questions seem particularly important to the most productive and talented employees in an organisation, but less important to underperforming staff. Addressing these aspects, therefore, has the potential to encourage the best to stay without encouraging those that an employer is less interested in retaining.

For example, the findings show that employees' greatest need is for clarity regarding *what is expected of them*. This seems to back up other surveys that consistently show that most employees (up to 70 per cent) are not clear about what their bosses expect of them.

It is interesting to note that pay does not even make the list of core elements. While the level of remuneration obviously has an impact on employee satisfaction, it does not differentiate between those places where work life is great and those where it is not. Apparently, some very unhappy employees are paid very high salaries.

The importance of relationships

The Gallup results suggest that one reason why managers have not been able to figure out what employees want is that they have been looking in the wrong place. The Gallup research shows that most of the critical elements of a great workplace relate to the *workgroup* level (in other words, the group of people you work with), not the corporate level. In fact, according to Buckingham, 'Best practices in the best workplaces can only be observed at the workgroup level'.[6] The group level, however, is not where senior management typically focuses its attention. This is partly because it is actually easier to tackle corporate-wide policy matters such as pay, parking entitlements and the subsidised canteen than group-level issues. Looking at the Gallup findings, only two aspects can be controlled by management at the corporate level (Question 2—having the right equipment for the job; and Question 8—working for a company that does something useful). Senior management has an easy and ready influence over these aspects of work but creating a good work environment at the workgroup level is much harder.

For many managers, the research is a mixed blessing; it brings some clarity to a complex area of management but it also throws the spotlight on areas that many prefer to leave unmanaged.

Most of the twelve core elements that make a difference to work life involve *workplace relationships* with bosses, colleagues and workplace friends. It is the nature and quality of these relationships that makes a critical difference. So, it appears that constructive and supportive relations with those around you at work helps to make a workplace a great place to be. Yet many managers are neither skilled nor willing to tackle such 'soft' issues. Their reluctance may be costing their organisations dearly, as staff turnover and absenteeism (often used as indicators of employee satisfaction) translate quickly into bottom-line costs.

Part of the problem is that many managers will run a mile rather than sit down with their staff and sort out relationship-based issues. Many are simply not comfortable with the people management side of their job, preferring to concentrate on the technical side.

Managers need to learn to deal with the full range of workplace aspects that will attract and retain the best staff. The easy and traditional tools for motivating employees—higher pay, better perks, corner office—may not be enough to keep your most productive staff.

Guidelines

1 Use the checklist

Apply the Gallup checklist of twelve questions to your company and do an assessment of the workplace you are currently providing for your staff. If possible, involve your staff in obtaining some of the data. After all, it's their opinion that counts in this type of survey.
- How do you rate?
- Where are the highs and the lows?
- What stands out?

2 Improve where possible

As a manager, you have control or influence over most (although not all) of the factors in the list.
- Identify one or two areas where you, as a manager, can make a difference.
- Decide what you can do in that area to improve how your staff feel about their workplace.
- Define each action as precisely as you can by turning it into an action-oriented goal, such as: 'I will provide a 10–20 minute opportunity once every month to talk individually with employees about their current job performance and development needs'.

3 Focus on you

You are part of your workplace. The list applies as much to you as it does to the staff you manage. Is your workplace meeting your needs?

Review the list, this time with you as the focus.

- Which of your needs are not being met?
- Who can you talk this over with?
- What does your boss have to do differently to make your workplace a great place to work?

  And then talk to your boss about it.

For further exploration

It is always misleading to reduce complex topics (such as human satisfaction at work) to a simple formula. If you want to explore this topic and many others that arise from placing people in work situations in more depth, try:

- J. Pfeffer, *The Human Equation*, Harvard Business School Press, Boston, 1998.

  This book is written by an angry man! Pfeffer has been researching how management deals with people at work for decades and he's not very happy that today's managers are largely ignoring the findings of most of the research that he has uncovered. The book's subtitle is 'Building profits by putting people first' and that's really the theme of the book. Example after example shows that companies make more profit by investing in people.

  Pfeffer takes virtually every critical people-management issue and provides detailed, hard-nosed research to show that most organisations get it wrong. He turns much 'accepted wisdom' on its head simply by providing an overwhelming volume of research. Profitability is not possible if the workforce is unionised? Check out the mountain of research that shows the opposite and none that supports the proposition. Incentive payment systems work best to motivate staff? Ditto. Training is an expense, not an investment? Ditto. Offering employment for life to staff is corporate suicide? Ditto.

  This book will change your mind about many things. It is so contrary to conventional thinking and so well researched that many managers will prefer not to read it as it is too disturbing. Give it a go!

Encouraging performance

DISCRETIONARY EFFORT   4

The task of management continues to evolve. The command-and-control approach that has worked well in the past is giving way to other approaches. Although some may think these changes are driven by fads or fashions in management style, it is much more likely that some fundamental forces are at work, making changes in management style a necessity rather than a fashionable choice.

The forces that are driving the change arise from the changing nature of the employment contract between employer and employee. We now rely more than ever on the discretionary effort of employees. There will be some managers and some employees who do not like these changes, but they are real and probably lasting. What managers must now learn is how to manage the *discretionary effort* of employees in these changed circumstances.

How do you manage discretionary effort?

Background

Gazing into crystal balls about changing trends in management is a rather hazardous occupation. Mostly we get it wrong. But there is little harm in trying to foresee aspects of the workplace that may be subject to change in the near future. One that stands out is the changing nature of employment and the implications of these changes for the managerial role.

The new nature of work

Three strands have emerged recently suggesting that employees are starting to think about work in a different way. Pull all these strands together and we might just be seeing the new nature of work.

The outsourced workforce
As organisations continue to get leaner and leaner (some say meaner and meaner), more and more work is supplied to the organisation from outside—contractors, consultants, temps and fixed-term employment. The core of the organisation is shrinking and outsourcing is the dietary prescription driving it. It is difficult to nominate a single corporate activity that some organisation somewhere has not outsourced. While each

organisation may have a different view of what is core and what is not, the sum total is that for most organisations most functions are 'on the table' for discussion regarding outsourcing.

Process functions were the first to go. For example, for a service function such as Human Resources, what started as the outsourcing of a small component (for instance, recruitment) has grown to encompass the total function. Many organisations now do without their own facilities for payroll, training, occupational health, superannuation, leave, and almost everything else. And what has not been outsourced has been devolved to line managers.

Similar developments have occurred in finance and information technology. Small outsourcing projects have led to the wholesale abandonment of the total function. In many cases, you'd be lucky to find one person left in charge of the function.

Charles Handy predicted many of these changes over twenty years ago. It has taken the last decade to provide evidence that the Handy vision of 'doughnut structures' and the 'clover leaf organisation' was the way of the future. The 'doughnut principle' allows organisations to maintain flexibility and adaptability by retaining only the core expertise needed for the business. The organisation consists of a small core of 'permanent' people around which circulates a collection of stringers and temporary workers. Expertise and skills are brought in as required. The 'clover leaf structure' is a variation on this theme of permanent versus temporary employees.[1-4]

The uncontrollable workforce

Managers like to think they are in charge in the workplace. Yeah, right! Tell that to the twelve-year-old in charge of the computer network that is the backbone of all the company's commercial activities. And he's probably a contractor! Could most managers step in and fix the e-commerce function on their intranet if it went down? Even in traditional areas of work, the very leanness advocated by consultants and demanded by shareholders creates a span of control that makes the notion of 'control' a mere furphy.

Today, managers are not in control. At best, they can claim to have a significant *influence* over events in their organisation. The nature of work has changed to the point where the immediate boss is usually some distance removed (physically and/or knowledge-wise) from the work that is being done.

Of course, there are some notable exceptions. The call-centre environment is the pre-eminent example of a work environment where the boss does oversee (or is able to) every word and action of an employee. A space mission control centre is another example. But call-centre staff and astronauts aside, the nature of work has evolved to the point where managerial control is at best indirect.

Whether this evolution has driven us to find new management solutions or whether the new management solutions have changed the work is hard to decide. For example, the introduction of self-managing teams has forced managers to behave differently. Those who manage such teams manage for outcomes, not for process; they focus on developing the capability of others rather than solving daily problems themselves; they encourage the team towards independence rather than make decisions for them.

What matters is that the changes are now irreversible. Employees who have had a taste of a work environment where they make their own decisions, organise themselves and control their own work area rarely want to go back to the old 'command-and-control' environment. And when was the last time you saw an advertisement for a management job that indicated a preference for an autocratic style of people leadership, for someone with a 'kick-ass' attitude?

Again, Charles Handy is in the background somewhere, predicting the emergence of more democratic forms of organisations where the almighty power of the shareholder declines and employees gain an even greater say in what happens. We'll have to wait for the next instalments in this strand.

The un-loyal workforce

Whether we think of the ageing baby boomers, Generation X or the next lot (whatever they are called), the reality for employers today is that none of them cares very much about their employing organisation. Loyalty in the workplace is dead.

Its demise was brought about by organisational strategies like outsourcing and downsizing, as well as by changes in the priorities of the workforce. Together, these changes buried the concept of lifetime employment and, with it, the idea of company loyalty.

Today, employment is a disposable item. And any manager who wants to appeal to a sense of loyalty on the part of her staff is simply out of touch with reality. We can ask for commitment—commitment to a task, to a contract, to a project, to an outcome, to a customer. Just don't use the word 'loyalty', especially not to someone who has been downsized, part-timed, contracted out or made redundant.

The volunteer model

Where will these changes lead? There is one model that I think is the future writ large today. Imagine managers who work in a voluntary organisation such as the Red Cross or the Smith Family. As likely as not, these managers have a staff comprised of volunteers who do much needed work in the community. Each day, such managers go to work knowing that, unless they create the right work environment, an environment that will make 'staff' want to turn up, then they won't and don't. And there's nothing that the managers can do to force them to turn up for work.

In a voluntary organisation, the managerial job is to attract the volunteers to their daily work in the same way that flowers attract bees. The flower is not in control of the bees but it can evolve to the point where it offers an attractive environment. And then the bees come, again and again.

The best managers in voluntary organisations are very good at creating the best environment for their workers. Although the workers are motivated typically by wanting to serve a good cause, they always have a choice about which cause they will serve, and when and how.

So to motivate people to come to work, the ultimate challenge is to create an attractive environment (see Chapter 3, *Workplace satisfaction*). But what exactly motivates workers?

Motivating discretionary effort

Sometimes we get confused about what motivates people, especially in the workplace. We rarely worry about this stuff in other contexts. For example, in sport we generally assume that the participants will be motivated; they *want* to succeed. Only in the workplace is there someone else in the picture (the boss) who is concerned about motivation. There are as many theories about human motivation as there are philosophers, alive or dead! It is a subject that reaches far beyond management but comes back to haunt us whenever we think about motivating employees.

For my money, I like the approach of Australian researcher Fred Emery who spent his working life trying to figure out how to reconcile the need of the organisation for productive output with the needs of the employees who make productivity possible. Emery draws a distinction between what he calls *satisfiers* and *motivators*[5] (see Table 1.1).

Satisfiers are those factors that we need from work to ensure we are prepared to keep doing it. If any of the satisfiers are missing, it is unlikely that you will have a productive employee working for you. For example, consider the satisfier, due process (see Table 1.1). If employees are subject to arbitrary and inconsistent treatment by management they are much more likely to focus on matters other than doing a productive day's work.

Motivators are those factors that 'turn us on'. Motivators are the factors that make us want to go to work, and come back the next day. These factors hold the potential for superior performance.

Table 1.1 Why we go to work

Satisfiers	Motivators
1 Fair and adequate pay	1 Variety and challenge (optimise)
2 Job security	2 Room for decision making (optimise)
3 Benefits	3 Feedback and learning (optimise)
4 Safety	4 Mutual support and respect (maximise)
5 Health	5 Wholeness and meaning (maximise)
6 Due process	6 Room to grow and develop (maximise)

The contrast between the two lists in Table 1.1 is obvious. Satisfiers will keep us coming to work but it's the motivators that make us contribute that extra bit. Satisfiers are the bare minimum that any employee needs—but, if all you give to your employees is the bare minimum, then a bare minimum contribution is all you will receive in return. Satisfiers are *necessary* and essential but they are not *sufficient* for most people.

Motivators, on the other hand, extract *discretionary effort*. This effort is the bit that makes the difference between the bare minimum and the exceptional contribution. Management can always enforce compliance with a minimum standard, but managers cannot mandate exceptional contributions. Only the motivators can obtain that sort of contribution.

Emery's motivators fall into two categories. The first three should be *optimised* (or individualised)—that is, you need to find the level that is suitable for each individual employee. What may be welcome variety for one person may be stressful unpredictability for another. The level of power to make decisions in the workplace that is appropriate for one skilled person may be inappropriate and stressful for a less skilled employee. What is easily learned by one individual may be tantamount to the impossible for another.

The last three factors on the list of motivators should be *maximised*. There is no such thing as too much respect or too much room to grow. When you design the work of others, you should build as many of these factors into the jobs as possible.

Designing productive jobs and productive workplaces is another story, but the elements from which you build such things include the satisfiers and the motivators. We have argued for decades about the satisfiers. It is what the unions fought for and still do.

It is now time to focus on the motivators because that is where you will find discretionary effort, the wellspring of productivity.

Guidelines

1 Manage your volunteers

Try to picture your current staff as if they were working for a volunteer organisation. What would you have to do differently to make them want to come to work? How would you change the way you manage them if they were volunteers?

Some areas to consider:
• Understand better what motivates each individual.

- Deliver some benefits to each individual that are linked to their motivators.
- Ensure you deliver the benefits and outcomes to which you commit.
- Review your people management (or leadership) behaviours.
- Get input from other people on how you manage others. Test how others see you managing people and compare this with how you rate yourself as a people manager (for example, through the use of a multi-rater 360-degree feedback survey).

2 Redesign jobs

It is unlikely that you can change the jobs of your people wholesale but it is often possible to build in some more motivational aspects.

Review the list of motivators (I'm assuming that you don't need to review the satisfiers!) and rate each job in terms of the six factors. Is each job structured to optimise the first three factors for the individual? And maximised for the last three? Make changes as appropriate.

3 Manage your own career

Use the list of motivators to review your own job as well as the next job to which you aspire.
- What can you change in your job to make it more motivating?
- What should your next job be like to be optimally and maximally motivating?
- Draw up a list of job elements based on the six motivators and be prepared to structure them into your next job.

Be ready to have a conversation with your current or future boss about the job elements for which you are looking.

For further exploration

No one writes books about discretionary effort. The idea that managers should invest in how to make people want to do more for the organisation is not in fashion! To explore this topic in more depth, you may have to move a little sideways. One direction is to look at why organisations seem almost designed to discourage discretionary effort. Marvin Weisbord's wonderful book on this is still pertinent after fifteen years in print:

- M. Weisbord, *Productive Workplaces: Organizing and Managing for Dignity, Meaning and Community*, Jossey-Bass, San Francisco, 1987.

The subtitle gives away its angle on the issue of how you create workplaces where people want to come to work. Terms like 'dignity', 'meaning' and 'creating community' do not readily roll off the lips of many managers! But that is what discretionary effort requires.

Another direction you can take is the leadership route. This suggests that you create the sort of workplace where people are prepared to go the extra yard because of the leadership you provide. Try:

- Max De Pree's *Leadership is an Art*, Dell, New York, 1989.

As CEO, De Pree ran Herman Miller, one of the most successful companies in the United States, and one that was consistently voted year after year one of the best twenty-five companies to work for. He is no academic and no theorist. He just writes it as he sees it. To give you the flavour:

Leadership owes a covenant to the corporation or institution which is after all a group of people. Leaders owe the organization a new reference point for what caring, purposeful, committed people can be in the institutional setting. Notice I did not say what people can do—what we can do is merely a consequence of what we can be. Corporations, like the people who compose them, are always in a state of becoming. Covenants bind people together and enable them to meet their corporate needs by meeting the needs of one another.

FEEDBACK 5

If management is about getting things done through other people, it is undeniably important that those other people do things well—hence the focus on performance. For some managers, management is about obtaining performance and nothing else. This seems a very limited view but nevertheless it is at least grounded in reality. All managers depend on getting a certain level of performance from their staff. Indeed, this is what they are held accountable for.

One critical part of the performance-management process is the act of giving feedback to others. Performance and feedback go hand in hand. But how does feedback work in improving performance? What exactly is feedback?

Background

While there is much debate about what works in management and what does not, in some areas there is a considerable degree of consensus. One area of apparent consensus is that managers should provide feedback to their direct reports and others in order to improve performance in the workplace. We *know* this works. Or do we?

What do we know about feedback?

It is commonly accepted that feedback can affect behaviour and thereby increase performance. But what exactly is meant by feedback? How does it work and why? Does it work in isolation from other factors? Does it work with complex tasks? And does it work in the workplace?

A brief incursion into the research literature reveals less consensus than is suggested by some popular writers on management. The heart of the problem is the word 'feedback', which turns out to be a recent addition to the field of behaviour modification. Until 1943, the discussion centred on what was called *knowledge of results*.[1]

Knowledge of results has been around for a while as a concept and management tool. For example, the workplace experiments of social reformer Robert Owen in the early nineteenth century included placing painted blocks of wood near each worker's station, informing the workers of their previous day's output. He hoped the information would increase their output. It did!

Owen attributed the improvement to knowledge of results, specifically that provided by external sources (an objective source providing *information* to a person about that person's *behaviour*). The behaviour was then modified, presumably as a consequence of gaining knowledge of results. In Owen's experiments, the information was about work output and the behaviour was about the level of work performed.

In the flurry of research on knowledge of results in the first half of the twentieth century, it was confusingly combined with other elements such as rewards and/or punishments. That is, instead of just providing the person with information about, say, level of output produced, it was also linked to information about the consequences of that level of output. For example, workers might be told that they had reached a certain level of output and this would be rewarded. Or, if output failed to reach a certain level, there might be a consequence such as punishment awaiting them.

These additional elements complicated matters in terms of explaining the cause of performance improvement. The most influential researchers of the times, the behaviourists, thought that the rewards/punishments were enough to change behaviour in their own right, without the mediation of consciousness. To them, the knowledge of results factor was only relevant in letting people know they were getting close to being rewarded or punished. Some denied that 'knowledge' was even involved in the process and wanted nothing at all to do with the notion of consciousness.

Other researchers threw a spanner in the behaviourist works when it was demonstrated that goal setting (surely a conscious activity) had a significant impact on behavioural change, including human performance. What may seem silly now (to ignore the fact that people have minds that have some impact on their behaviour) was standard practice in many experiments, until the goal-setting experiments showed that, by giving people goals to strive for, performance could improve.

Elsewhere, developments in communication technology led to a different view of human behaviour, one that drew on engineering concepts rather than psychology. The most important of these was the concept of 'feedback' in the acoustic sense. Anyone who has held a microphone too close to an amplifier will have experienced the consequences of a feedback loop! These engineering models were applied to human information processing. The human equivalent is when the human brain takes account of what is happening and modifies behaviour accordingly. When this is done repeatedly, we create a feedback loop.

As a result of all this different research, we have ended up with three distinct concepts: knowledge of results (whether external or internal), rewards/punishments and goal setting. All three may be and are described as 'providing feedback'.

Progressively, research has led to more and more complex cognitive processes being incorporated in the various feedback models. And, over time, research has drawn on more and more complex tasks, some of which simulate what actually happens in the workplace. The theories and models that have evolved over time are becoming more complex, and have moved a long way from the simple concept that Robert Owen had in mind 200 years ago.

There is still significant disagreement between theorists.[2] The research is incomplete and many aspects of how feedback affects human behaviour remain unexplained. No single theory is accepted as generally true—for example, the role of rewards in influencing human behaviour is problematic with much contradictory evidence. But the research is continuing.

Managing feedback

So, from a practical management viewpoint, a hundred years or more of research has not delivered the certainty that most of us would want. Yet we continue to use the concept of feedback almost on a daily basis, never really knowing which of the three distinct concepts we or others are using.

Some points, however, have emerged from the research mist and can be claimed as generally accepted and useful:

1 Goal setting, on its own, can affect performance positively.
2 Goal setting is most effective if the goals are specific and difficult.
3 Knowledge of results, on its own, can impact positively on performance.
4 The source of the information fed back to us (whether it comes from ourselves, from others or from the task environment) can have differing impacts depending on the situation.
5 Information fed back to us that is *perceived* as accurate has a greater impact on performance than information that is not perceived as accurate.

6 The perception of accuracy is largely determined by the *credibility* of the source of the feedback and by its timing (sooner is better).

That's about it. That's what we know so far. Anything outside this is mere belief and/or speculation. The task for managers is to translate these findings into their actions and systems.

First, as a manager, if you can do nothing else, *help your staff to set goals*. Make sure the goals are specific and difficult but achievable; they should have an element of 'stretch' in them. Easy goals are not motivating; impossible goals demotivate.

Second, make it easy for people to find out how they are travelling in terms of their performance. People generally want to know how they are doing and this knowledge has an impact on their performance. The information should be accurate and believed to be so by the other person. We know that immediate supervisors are most trusted by employees to tell the truth (as opposed to senior management or computers) so be part of the feedback mechanism. And give the feedback as soon as possible.

People need feedback to help them learn about themselves and their performance. So what's the best way to give feedback (whether it is praise for goals achieved or information about shortfalls in performance)? Try the following:

1 *Provide feedback on a continuing basis.* Ongoing feedback is essential to good management. Whether the feedback takes the form of informal, on-the-run comments or formal performance reviews, continuity of communication is vital.

2 *Provide immediate feedback whenever possible.* Feedback is most effective if it is given immediately. Delays should only occur if it would embarrass the employee to give the feedback immediately or if further information is required.

3 *Be specific and descriptive.* For greatest impact, feedback, whether positive or negative, must be specific in nature. For example, it would be inadequate to say to an employee, 'Your manners leave a lot to be desired'. However, if the employee is told, 'I was quite upset at this morning's committee meeting because you kept talking while I was speaking', then the employee will be able to take purposeful action to address this behaviour.

4 *Focus only on those things that can be changed.* There are some things about an employee that can't be changed, such as personality or physical features, so don't focus your feedback on those aspects. Concentrate instead on those areas where change can be made.

5 *Adjust feedback to individual needs.* Individuals differ in their approach to feedback. Most people appreciate positive feedback. High performers usually like a lot of feedback while some employees are wary of negative feedback. You must match the content and timing of feedback to the individual and the situation.

6 *Focus on achievements rather than errors.* If you accentuate the positive aspects of your employees' behaviour, you will influence performance more than if you provide only critical feedback.

7 *Try not to mix positive and negative feedback.* People *learn* from negative feedback but are *motivated* by positive feedback. Provide both separately for maximum impact. (They are often mixed together because it makes the job of giving feedback easier for the manager.)

8 *Ensure feedback is always constructive.* It should never be used as a weapon. Rather it is a valuable tool for improving employee performance. Both parties should see negative feedback as a critical component of performance improvement and of the review process.

Guidelines

Giving feedback to people to help them improve their performance can never be entirely reduced to a formula (everyone is different) but the following steps will help.

1 Set goals

Goal setting is one of the most powerful techniques available to managers to obtain improved performance from others. The goals must be specific and achievable or it is likely to have the opposite effect to what is intended.

Involve your staff in the process of setting goals by letting them nominate possible performance goals (see Chapter 6). The reason for doing this is that people are more likely to be motivated by the goals they set rather than those set for them by other people, including you. Your job then becomes one of 'quality inspector'. Ask yourself, is the nominated goal realistic and achievable, and will it stretch the employee a little?

2 Provide feedback about performance levels

Once the goal or target has been set, make sure that there is a flow of information back to the employee about progress. This will enable the employee to do a 'gap analysis' and decide whether the progress is adequate to ensure ultimate achievement of the goal.

The information provided has to be accurate and trusted. The easiest way to ensure this is to set regular review sessions in which progress is discussed.

3 Be involved in the feedback process

You can't delegate the feedback process.

You are the person most trusted by your staff (or, at least, that's what the surveys suggest; there are always exceptions!). This means that you must be involved in the feedback process. You add 'gravitas' to the process and your approval of their efforts and achievements will be an additional powerful motivating factor.

For further exploration

Feedback is generally treated as part of performance management so most books on that topic will carry a section on feedback. As with many management texts, it can be hard to pick personal opinion from evidence-based opinion. Here are some books that at least make the effort to explain the basis for the author's opinion:
- G. Ferris and K. Rowland (eds), *Performance Evaluation, Goal Setting and Feedback*, JAI Press, Greenwich, 1990.
- C. Thor, *Designing Feedback: Performance Measures for Continuous Improvement*, Crisp Management Library, Menlo Park, 1998.
- J. Harbour, *The Basics of Performance Measurement*, Quality Resources, New York, 1997.
- R. Hodgetts, *Measures of Quality and High Performance: Simple Tools and Lessons Learned from America's Most Successful Corporations*, AMACOM, New York, 1998.

SHARED GOAL SETTING 6

Goal setting is a powerful motivator for most people. We can make the goal-setting process even more powerful by making it a *shared* process, whether between an employee and a manager, a student and a teacher, or an athlete and a coach.

Thankfully, there are few organisational barriers to shared goal setting. While many other management techniques depend on a supportive context (or at least one that allows a manager to do things), shared goal setting can be conducted anywhere. If, for example, you work to a highly prescriptive performance management system that requires you to fill in boxes with headings such as 'Annual Goals' or 'Performance Targets', you can still use shared goal setting to generate those outcomes.

How does shared goal setting make a difference to performance?

Background

The quintessential activity of management is interaction with other people. This activity defines the managerial role in a way that no other component does. Whether the role is described as people management, supervision or leadership, the common element is always the human one. Managers deal with people. How they do so will have an impact (positive or negative) on performance.

The way managers deal with people has been of critical interest to researchers. Both academic models and popular writings have focused on the elements that impact on the relationship between the manager and the managed. Well known efforts include:

- The psychology of the relationship—for example, the transactional analysis approaches described in *The Games People Play* by Eric Berne[1] and *I'm OK—You're OK* by Thomas Harris.[2]
- The style of management—for example, the situational management approaches described in *The One Minute Manager* by Ken Blanchard and Spencer Johnson.[3]
- The behaviour of the manager—for example, the behaviourally based approaches to leadership described in *The Leadership Challenge* by Barry Posner and James Kouzes.[4]

- The behaviour of the managed—for example, the reward-focused approaches described by Michael LeBoeuf in *How to Motivate People*.[5]
- The context of the relationship—for example, approaches based on organisational dynamics, such as described by Chris Argyris and Donald Schon in *Organizational Learning II*.[6]

But there is something missing in most of the equations presented in these respected management publications: *the managed*. Obviously, they are there in the sense that the various prescriptions involve doing something that will affect the other individual in the relationship. But it generally seems to be a one-way relationship—the manager does something and then the other person responds. Much of this is because of the general requirement that managers *do* things.

Performance goals

Generally, we actively select managers for their action orientation rather than for other characteristics such as their reflective capabilities. The general principle is that managers are expected to do something, not just stand there. There are times, however, when the reverse is more constructive: 'Don't just do something—stand there.'

One of the most effective versions of the 'just stand there' approach is the idea of *letting your employees nominate their own performance goals*. The idea is based on the fact that people are more likely to be committed to an objective such as a performance target if they have set the target themselves. Mandated objectives are often resisted by employees simply because they are set by someone else. Many managers will ask for a contribution from their staff to the goal-setting process but this is usually tokenism because, in reality, the objectives are unchangeable. This creates a justifiable degree of cynicism about an invitation to contribute to the development of objectives.

When employees set their own goals there is an almost in-built sense of ownership. The psychological pressure to succeed is immense. The responsibility of management then becomes one of ensuring that the goals are set, they are realistic and there is a follow-up process. This is a far easier role than the traditional one of ensuring commitment to imposed objectives.

Of course, it is possible that employees will propose goals that are significantly lower than or different from those that the organisation believes are necessary to achieve corporate goals. In practice, however, it is often the case that employees propose more difficult targets than the manager might impose. Sometimes their targets are quite unrealistic. This is why the manager must mediate the goal-setting process to ensure balance is maintained. Setting unachievable goals is not only pointless, it is counterproductive—demotivating rather than motivating.

Care is required to ensure that the management mediation of the nominated goals does not become a substitute for the employee's contribution. The process relies on a questioning technique rather than on a 'command-and-control' technique. The only measure of whether the manager has mediated the goal-setting process effectively is whether the final and agreed objective truly comes from the employee.

The manager's task is largely an educational one, not dissimilar to that of a coach. The job of a sports coach in athletics is to help the athlete set achievable but challenging targets. The conversation concerns what is needed and what is possible, as well as what needs to change for the goal to be realised. But, ultimately, the athlete decides because the coach works for the athlete and not the other way round. Only the athlete can make it happen.

Managing for performance

In most organisations, a manager's performance ultimately depends on other people. While today technology drives much of the routine work, it is people who drive the technology. As technology changes the workplace more and more, the balance between those who manage and those who are managed is changing. Where once the manager was the technical expert, now the manager may know less than the workers about technical aspects of their job. Where once the manager could closely monitor the workers, now they may not even live in the same city. Management is no longer about control but about achieving results through others because those others want to achieve those goals.

So, managing people for performance now means a change in style for some managers. More than anything else, however, it means a change in approach—research demonstrates quite clearly that some managerial behaviours help employees perform better and other behaviours actually lead to worse performance.

While nothing is simple in the world of management, there are some clear principles that will generate improved performance. Possibly the single most powerful technique is also one of the simplest: *use written performance objectives.*

Time and again, research shows that the use of written performance objectives leads to a better and shared understanding of what needs to be achieved, when it needs to be achieved and how it will be measured. This virtually guarantees improved performance.

Yet a recent survey I conducted of some 800 employees showed that:

- fewer than 60 per cent of employees said they understood the measures used to judge their performance;
- fewer than 57 per cent said the judgment was fair;
- less than half (47 per cent) said their managers were clear about expressing goals and tasks;
- 42 per cent reported regular performance reviews;
- 39 per cent said the reviews were helpful in improving their performance;
- 19 per cent reported a compelling link between their performance and their pay.[7]

This data suggests that there is a lot of room for improvement! The situation is made even more interesting by research suggesting that more than 80 per cent of managers think they do a good job at managing the performance of their staff.

While the use of written objectives will make an immediate difference, managers need to use a range of techniques to get the best out of people. Start by:

- using feedback to greatest effect;
- tapping into the magic of self-appraisal;
- focusing on improvement rather than shortcomings;
- agreeing on 'stretch' targets.

Most of these techniques require just a little knowledge, a little practice and lots of application on the job. In an era where managerial performance is closely linked to employee performance, the investment in learning such techniques is worthwhile.

The conclusion: managers should encourage, persuade, cajole, demand, support and coach their employees to set their own performance objectives.

Assessing performance

At some point, performance has to be followed up and assessed. This process can be simplified if the original performance goals are structured in such a way that follow-up is easier rather than harder.

The following (much quoted) SMARTER criteria provide a useful structure for assessing the effectiveness of performance objectives. As the purpose of a performance objective is to create an opportunity for success, each objective should be:

- *Specific*—it must explain either a *specific task* that must be performed ('You must state your name, the company name, and offer assistance when you answer the phone') or a *specific result* that must be produced ('You must produce this report each month by the last working day of the month').
- *Measurable*—the *expected standard* must be made explicit, either how the task should be done (required behaviour) or the expected level of achievement (required results).
- *Achievable*—it must be *within the reach* of the employee. Setting excessively high standards of achievement is inviting failure, which can be very demotivating. Reaching agreement on what is achievable involves two points of view, so make it a mutual decision.
- *Relevant*—it must be *understood* by the employee and put in the *context* of organisational goals. If employees cannot see the link between the performance target you have set and their overall job, then they are unlikely to do the task well.
- *Timed*—ensure the employee knows by *when* the task or the result is to be achieved. The absence of explicit agreement on a time frame causes more disagreement between managers and employees than almost any other omission.
- *Extending*—it must *stretch* the employee. The achievement of the task or result should be something of a challenge. This is highly motivating but it requires clear and mutual agreement on its achievability.
- *Required*—it must be explained as a requirement. It should contain such words as 'I expect you to . . .'. It must clearly establish that it is not optional for the employee to meet the objective.

Guidelines

1 Invite employees to nominate their own performance goals

This involves managers doing something that doesn't come easily to many: shutting up. The task is to *facilitate* a conversation about what has been achieved in the past, what could be achieved in the future and what needs to change in order to realise future achievement.

Use questions to elicit answers rather than feeling obliged to spoon-feed information to employees about a matter they understand only too well—their own performance. Coach-and-coax rather than command-and-control.

2 Moderate the goal-setting process

Make sure the goals are achievable and involve a degree of stretch.

Employees often nominate goals that are unrealistic and to agree to such goals is to set them up for failure. Others nominate goals that are too easily achieved, so the task is one of coaxing a more appropriate level of performance.

Ask questions to assess whether the nominated goals really are achievable.

Make sure all performance goals are in writing.

3 Follow up meticulously

There are so many reasons for following up on the agreed goals that it borders on a sin for managers not to do so. Regular and joint reviews of progress towards the goals have the following benefits:

- The manager is kept informed.
- The employee is aware of progress achieved.
- Corrective action is possible by either party.
- The employee remains motivated.
- The manager emphasises the importance of achievement.

Find ways to follow up meticulously—use diary reminders or other systematic methods.

For further exploration

Shared goal setting is not the sort of topic that is well published. It is such a small part of the overall management process that it tends to escape attention. This is a pity because its impact can be huge if it is done well. To explore this topic in more detail, you need to move up one level and look at how managers can transform themselves into *facilitators* of a management process (including goal setting) rather than controllers.

One excellent effort to describe this emerging management role is:

- R. Weaver and J. Farrell, *Managers as Facilitators*, Berret-Koehler, San Francisco, 1977.

This book provides a very practical approach to what some may fear is a 'touchy-feely' subject. Topics include:

- clarifying the work that needs to be done;
- improving group dynamics to improve performance;
- building effective work processes;
- creating change;
- managing boundaries.

MEASURING PERFORMANCE 7

Performance management is driven by performance measurement. So it seems surprising that most organisations only discovered the measurement idea recently. People who have more than ten years employment with one organisation (presumably a rapidly declining percentage of the population) will recall the day that management started to speak of performance indicators. Before that time, the talk was of 'financial results' or, more typically, 'end-of-year results'.

These days, the time frame is much shorter. Management effectively wants continuous results and the nature of those results has changed, and continues to change, in response to new management demands. So the measurement systems have had to meet these new demands. Measurement systems based on key performance indicators have stepped in to fill this need. But it is possible to take them too far.

So how should we be measuring performance?

Background

The point of measuring performance is to get better performance. As a goal, 'high performance' is something of a Holy Grail, as witnessed by the continuing efforts of most organisations to measure themselves against competitors (for example, through benchmarking) or at least against their own previous performance.

The urge to perform accounts for much of the 'short-termism' in organisations that is criticised by many observers. Today, managers are constantly urged to believe that organisational change needs to happen at lightning speed. The payback time frame for a new management approach is measured in months. Results are needed now, not tomorrow.

No wonder so much organisational change that is supposed to improve business performance fails: '. . . as many as three quarters of re-engineering, total quality management (TQM), strategic planning, and downsizing efforts have failed entirely or have created problems serious enough that the survival of the organisation was threatened'.[1]

All this is well known to managers, which only increases the pressure to get it right fast. Which just makes them more nervous about failing. Which, of course, leads to more quick-fix fads, which leads to more failures. Worst of all, it often leads to seriously muddled thinking by managers about the management techniques on offer.

While performance indicators have been around a long time under various descriptions, adding the simple word 'key' turned the notion of using performance measures from an accounting tool into a strategic management tool.

By having a few indicators rather than a truckload of different measures, organisations suddenly started prioritising what they measured. By elevating some measures to 'key', others get downgraded. Clearly, this means choosing. And making a choice is always a strategic activity. And so the key performance indicator (KPI) was born.

Key performance indicators

In the 1990s organisations and managers all over the developed world adopted the language of KPIs. This in turn had implications for focusing the attentions of employees, based on the old notion of 'that which gets measured gets done', which in practice also means that what does not get measured gets done less—and less—and less. The price of focus is narrowness of vision and effort. Still, in the right circumstances, it can pay off.

The *Dictionary of Business*[2] defines KPIs as:

The key measures of the performance of a company, which are monitored and assessed to ensure its long-term success. These indicators help to pinpoint the company's strengths and weaknesses.

Clearly, there is a strategic intent behind these words.

Interestingly, the KPI phenomenon has not been driven by any explicit theory, book or guru. It slipped quickly into day-to-day management language without any overt marketing campaign. The KPI approach has achieved enormous acceptance all on its own. No one writer is associated with the concept and no one consultant or consulting group has become famous through advocating it.

The idea of focus seemed so natural in a competitive world that the KPI tool swept all before it. Even a brief glance at the management literature on performance management shows its impact on industries as diverse as manufacturing, hospitals and universities.

As the approach drilled down into the organisation, functional units such as sales, human resources and even research and development came to be driven by sets of KPIs. Many organisations developed multi-level and neatly interlocking systems of KPIs.

The KPI approach travelled beyond the boundaries of the organisation so that suppliers were judged on the KPIs that were at the heart of their service agreements. This infected the thinking back inside the organisation so that internal service providers (for example, HR, finance and IT) came to have their performance assessed on the basis of KPIs and their attendant targets.

The drilling down did not stop there. Soon, individual jobs were affected and KPIs started to take pride of place in job descriptions, individual performance plans and even project briefs. Where once these job statements related largely to inputs into the work process, the focus is now on outputs, results and achievements. KPIs seemed an ideal way to handle this change.

To make them a little easier to use, KPIs are typically incorporated into a framework that comprises some area of focus (often called key results areas or KRAs). KRAs lead to KPIs, which then lead to numerical targets. The language varies from organisation to organisation. KRAs may be called key effectiveness areas and KPIs may be called performance measures. But the overall structure is the same, regardless of the actual descriptions used. KRAs lead to KPIs that lead to targets.

Many organisations use the KRA/KPI format to structure their corporate plans. The senior managers of the organisation create the top-level version of the KRA/KPI structure, which is then used by the level below to develop their versions. And so on down the organisation, level by level. They call it cascading the KPIs down.

Today, KPIs are everywhere. There is only one problem: no one has actually bothered to define the notion in any substantive way. There seemed no need to define it as the underlying concepts—a select group of indicators that measures performance in certain areas—seemed too intuitive to need defining. It was obvious.

But it wasn't. For a start, not all KPIs are the same.

As KPIs evolved it become apparent that there was more than one type of KPI. Some KPIs provide only historical data.

An example from the area of safety is where organisations use an indicator such as 'Lost Time Injuries'. This KPI is very common in manufacturing organisations and indicates how many times somebody took time off from work because of injury. The actual measure unit may be days lost or hours lost; sometimes the unit used is the number of incidents recorded.

Because a KPI such as 'Lost Time Injuries' measures what has happened in the past, such KPIs came to be called 'lag' indicators. A 'lag' measure tells us what has already happened in the area of safety in the recent past. Over time, the data from this KPI can suggest trends (that is, the figures trend up or down) but they are always historical results. Once they go up on the board outside the factory gate, no one can do anything about the data.

This is quite different from another group of indicators called 'lead' indicators. These KPIs tend to measure what is happening right now in respect of a specific crucial activity. Once that activity has occurred, it is the turn of the 'lag' indicator to measure what the ultimate outcome was.

In the area of safety, 'lead' measures might be 'On-time Safety Audits' (measuring whether safety audits are being carried out when they should be) or 'Personal Protective Equipment Adherence' (whether people are wearing the correct safety gear). These measures measure the things that ultimately impact on a KPI such as 'Lost Time Injury'. That's what makes them 'lead' measures. They have a predictive capability.

The difference between lag and lead indicators is that the first can only give you trends about what has already happened in the organisation; the second can indicate what is happening right now, which will eventually show up in results of the first. Many argue that this makes the second type of indicator more valuable from a management viewpoint because it points out what will happen rather than what has happened.

Most organisations are now trying to design and build more lead measures, mainly because it is a better use of management time to work with such measures. Looking at pages of lag indicators at the end of the month is just contemplating history. Lead measures are simply more useful.

One drawback is that lead measures are much harder to create. Most organisations are well equipped with systems that generate lag information such as last month's sales figures or how much was paid out to creditors. But the systems for measurement of lead indicators are often not there. In many organisations, there is little experience in how to go about developing and using lead measures. But over time, as experience is shared, better measures are starting to become available.

Balanced KPIs

What really pulled all this into some perspective was the publication of the book *Balanced Scorecard: Translating Strategy into Action*[3] by Robert Kaplan and David Norton in 1996. This book elegantly put the case for adding logic to your collection of KPIs. Kaplan and Norton argued that KPIs are not independent elements but are *connected*. That is, a KPI in one area (such as maintenance) is connected to KPIs in other areas (such as production performance), which in turn impacts on further areas (such as financial performance).

Kaplan and Norton shaped this connectivity into a scorecard based on four major areas of performance measurement:

1 capability
2 internal processes
3 customer satisfaction
4 financial performance.

Each area of the scorecard has a number of key performance indicators, and each area cascades *upwards* to impact on the area above it. The notion of cascading is important because it links the areas into a dynamic whole. Instead of having a grab bag of indicators, the links between them create a structure where all the parts of the scorecard are connected.

For example, measuring your investment in developing the capabilities of your people and the systems they work with is a 'lead area' for the effectiveness and efficiency of your internal processes. This can predict what your customers think about your performance, which in turn will predict your overall financial performance. More specifically, training your staff to respond more quickly to customer inquiries (for example, by giving them decision-making powers supported by effective IT systems) will make your internal processes work more effectively. This is almost guaranteed to please your customers who will return for more. This will generate the most valuable business you can get (return buyers) and that will make you more profitable.

The task of management is to ensure that there is progress in all four areas of the scorecard (creating a balanced organisational effort) rather than just focusing on one area or the other. For example, in the past organisations have focused too much on financial indicators only (most of which were lag indicators).

The concept of creating a balanced approach to driving the performance of the organisation has probably been the most powerful management idea of its time. It is estimated that over 40 per cent of Fortune 1000 US companies have installed versions of the scorecard in their organisation in the last fifteen years.[4] This is a phenomenal rate of penetration for a management concept.

Why KPIs aren't for individuals

Although Kaplan and Norton sorted out some of the conceptual confusion surrounding KPIs as measures of organisational performance, the balanced scorecard did little to stop the infiltration of KPIs into individual performance management. If anything, simply by association, their work added impetus to the idea that we could also measure human effort by using KPIs. On the surface, the logic seems impeccable. If a balanced set of KPIs can be used to focus organisational effort, why not use it to focus individual effort?

And so KPIs were built into the performance-management systems that focused on individual effort. Before the arrival of 'personal performance plans' based on KPIs, most organisations used simple devices such as position descriptions and role definitions to focus the efforts of individual employees. Such devices all share one characteristic: they focus on *inputs* to the work activities.

Even today, many job descriptions tell you what you have to *do* and role definitions tell you where your activities *fit* in the organisation. But neither tells you what you have to *achieve*. Some grudgingly include a reference to standards (for example, 'Answer the phone promptly and courteously'). It seems inevitable that someone would put these together with KPIs to manage individual employee performance.

Especially favoured for individual evaluation was the use of lag indicators. By using lag KPIs, judging the performance of an employee became truly simple: yes (you achieved your KPI-based target) or no (you did not achieve the target).

Some notable extremes of this practice are those firms that each year simply sack those employees who fail to reach their KPI targets. Or those who are in the bottom 10 per cent of KPI performance get the boot. Softer versions abound, especially in results-focused functions such as sales.

There is only one huge problem. It does not work.

Organisational results are achieved by people employed by the organisation doing certain things. We call that 'working'. The work of individual employees should be judged on whether or not they are doing the activities they are supposed to be doing. We can do that by agreeing on objectives with employees and then giving them feedback on whether they are meeting those objectives.

Sometimes objectives for individuals need to have standards of achievement incorporated into them. In fact, to be a really useful performance objective, it is essential that some element of measurability be incorporated, whether that relates to a time frame ('complete within three months') or a quality standard ('with 98 per cent accuracy') or a financial standard ('within budget'). Such standards are very helpful in guiding employees and allowing managers to make a judgment about the level of performance of employees.

But because such performance standards look a bit like KPIs, managers think they are the same. They are not.

- Individual performance standards are about ensuring that an *individual* achieves a desired *standard of work.*
- Organisational KPIs are about measuring the *organisation*'s progress towards a desired *standard of organisational performance.*

Organisational performance measurement is not the same as employee performance planning. It is quite possible for all the individuals in an organisation to achieve their individual performance standards and for that organisation to fail miserably on its own overall measures of performance. There are many organisations in which everyone does the right thing in terms of their personal work standards but the company makes no profit.

So, using KPIs for managing individual performance is what is called a 'category mistake'.

Does it matter? Well, just ask any employee struggling to complete an annual planning process that is written in the language of KPIs rather than in the language of performance objectives. For example, in writing this book I am writing to a deadline and to a quality standard. These provide useful standards in gauging my performance as a writer. If you ask me to explain how this will contribute to the profitability of McGraw-Hill Australia, I have no idea and nor does it matter to me. KPIs do not motivate me; performance objectives do.

Although an organisation's performance can be summed up by a handful of KPIs, try doing the same with your job. In fact, if you do not provide employees with any formal structure or framework at all, and just ask them how they would like to have their performance judged, the answer is likely to be that it should be based on how they do their work. 'Judge me on whether I have done the things I am supposed to do and how well I have done those things.' And KPIs are not very useful in doing that.

Guidelines

1 KPIs are for organisations

Key performance indicators (KPIs) have a marvellous capacity to focus organisational effort on a few critical areas of performance.

They can be structured (lead versus lag) so that there is a shared focus on outcomes and on the processes that lead to outcomes. They can be used to create balance by ensuring that some KPIs come from each of the different stakeholder areas (shareholders, customers, staff, the community, etc.).

But they are not useful in guiding people to achieving higher standards of performance.

2 Performance objectives are for people

To manage, guide or drive the performance of people, use performance objectives. They may bear some similarities to KPIs but that is only superficial.

Performance objectives (or goals, targets, outcomes, etc.) are an agreement between a manager and an employee about what is to be achieved by that employee. It usually involves elements such as 'what', 'how' and 'by when'.

Don't confuse things by using the same language to describe organisational performance measures (KPIs) and individual performance measures (performance objectives).

3 Keep it simple

If you are unfortunate enough to have to work to a mandated corporate performance and a management system that uses KPI language, subvert the dominant paradigm!

Use the system as if it were there to suit you. Live with whatever crazy language the HR department has dreamt up but conceptually use performance objectives. It's not worth arguing with the HR department; they always win because they created the system to suit them.

Instead, abuse the system by making it one that is based on you and your staff agreeing performance objectives. You can do this by using a shared goal-setting process (see Chapter 6) and by creating trust between you and your staff (see Chapter 1).

For further exploration

With the balanced scorecard, there seems no reason to look further than the originators of the concept, Robert Kaplan and David Norton. (I can only assume that in their darker moments these fellows kick themselves for allowing it into the public domain free of proprietary control!)

The first book tells you everything you need to know for building a balanced scorecard for your organisation:

- R. Kaplan and D. Norton, *Balanced Scorecard: Translating Strategy into Action,* Harvard Business School Press, Boston, 1996.

The follow-up book is less successful in creating practical value. It seems to be an 'extension' work that is interesting rather than valuable.

- R. Kaplan and D. Norton, *The Strategy-Focused Organization: How Balanced Scorecard Companies thrive in the New Business Environment,* Harvard Business School Press, Boston, 2000.

For briefer descriptions, try:

- R. Kaplan and D. Norton, 'Putting the balanced scorecard to work', *Harvard Business Review,* September–October 1993, pp. 134–47.
- R. Kaplan and D. Norton, 'The balanced scorecard: measures that drive performance', *Harvard Business Review,* January–February 1992, pp. 71–79.

ON-THE-JOB TRAINING 8

The training function occupies an unusual place in business. It is grudgingly recognised as necessary but is often underfunded. In times of stress, the training budget is often the first to be cut, and it is treated as if it were discretionary expenditure. In addition, many employers are reluctant to train employees because they believe they are investing in a resource that will walk out of the door inevitably.

Training just doesn't have the standing it used to have in industry. There are probably many explanations for this. In recent years, the Australian Government sullied training's reputation by making training expenditure compulsory for a while (that really inspired confidence!). When that didn't work, next came replacing the compulsory payroll levy with a huge and growing federal bureaucracy that is supposed to look after training matters (yet more confidence inspiring).

By limiting training, however, organisations also limit the development of their most valuable resource. Many organisations also overlook the potential for less structured and more informal approaches to learning. The classroom is not the answer to every training problem. And it is often a lot easier to implement the less formal approaches.

Does informal training work?

Background

Informal approaches to training are making something of a comeback. Research suggests that informal, on-the-job training accounts for most of the learning that happens in the workplace—around 70 per cent. Yet most organisations spend most of their training efforts on formal learning opportunities. Some organisations are now trying to redress that imbalance, placing a new emphasis on encouraging and promoting informal training. Early signs suggest that informal training can be managed effectively.

The informal option

As temporary and part-time work becomes the basic form of work in many organisations (for example, the fast-food industry, the retail industry, the hospitality industry), finding opportunities to train employees becomes more difficult. If an employee is not going to be around for long, and is only on the job for a few hours each day, most employers are unlikely to want to invest in formal training as this usually involves time away from work.

One answer is to re-examine the role of informal training in the organisation. Most on-the-job learning comes from other workers through informal processes such as the sharing of knowledge. This can be managed—for example, McDonald's is now training its managers to encourage the process of knowledge sharing by employees.

One barrier to doing this is that the informality of the learning process leads to a belief that learning is not happening. People talking around the water-cooler is usually labelled gossip rather than learning. In reality, field research has shown that most conversations in these situations are about work issues and that a great deal of sharing and problem solving happens.

Another barrier to informal learning is the design of the work. Where work is structured so that workers see only a small component of the whole productive process, there is very limited opportunity for sharing understanding. Reflexite (United States manufacturer) reorganised its production lines to encourage people to understand the whole of the production process. It changed shift arrangements to allow for a 10-minute overlap, enabling employees to discuss work issues. It also integrated traditional office functions, such as the customer service department, into the physical layout of the plant, encouraging even more cross-communication between employees.

Some of these moves towards encouraging informal learning are also linked to recent 'knowledge management' initiatives. The aim is to capture the collective knowledge base of an organisation and share it more widely. Such initiatives highlight the need for employees to have the opportunity to share knowledge. The impact of technology (for example, the general requirement to use computers in many workplaces) only adds pressure to the need to share know-how.

For example, Honeywell Data Instruments uses teams extensively. A team-based structure demands that the teams have time to meet and talk about the work they do. Teams are encouraged to have informal meetings whenever necessary to resolve work issues. This means you will frequently see a group of workers standing around chatting. Rather than frowned upon, this is encouraged. For similar reasons, Xerox Business Services has redesigned its layout to create common areas where workers can meet informally. Conversation invariably turns to work issues; it is common for problems to be raised and resolved.

Other organisations focus on encouraging contact between new employees and experienced old hands. IBM teams up less experienced sales staff with those who have many years' experience. Boeing does something similar with its aircraft mechanics.

While these are not new ideas, few organisations take the process seriously enough to manage it actively. Many training staff think that their involvement in such matching processes is not the best use of their professional time. Evidence from the coalface suggests otherwise.

Managing informal training

In some cases, what is necessary is simply to take existing practice and formally recognise its importance. This can be done by giving a name to the informal learning process and actively encourage its use. This is what the US Army has done with its 'After Action Review' process.[1]

AARs were developed about ten years ago. Two versions are used: the 'hot wash', a review that takes place during the action; and the 'cold wash' which is done immediately after the action is completed. The pay-off of the process comes from the closeness of the review to the action. This immediacy ensures that the knowledge of the review team is fresh and current.

For example, the use of standard 80-pound packs of equipment carried by US peacekeeping troops in Haiti led to a serious dehydration problem for the soldiers in the humid Haitian climate. The AAR process was applied on the run and led to a re-examination of what peacekeepers really needed to carry. A lighter load was designed, and found to reduce exertion significantly, thereby eliminating the hydration problem. All this was achieved under battlefield conditions.

The AAR approach is a structured process guided by a trained facilitator (who may be the team leader) and follows a series of steps. The group focuses on a specific issue with the aim of reaching agreement on a specific 'next action' to be taken. In reviewing the action, the following questions are used:
1 What was the intent?
2 What happened?

3 What have we learned?
4 What do we do now?
5 Take action.
6 Tell others.

The facilitator (or team leader) has the job of promoting a 'focused, open, provocative, safe and reality-oriented exchange' among the group. This involves sticking to a number of principles such as being objective, balancing inquiry with advocacy, and ensuring a bias towards action to be taken. This is in direct contrast to a leader who determines the problem and proposes a solution—such an approach directly undermines the AAR process.

The pay-offs from the AAR process revolve around the following gains:

1 guiding the learning process by providing structure;
2 breaking down barriers such as hierarchy;
3 keeping the process of reflection close to the action;
4 recording what has been learned so others can benefit.

The power of the process comes from a useful combination of achieving immediate results (the next actions that arise from the process) while building an effective learning capability within the organisation that will deliver better results in the future. These dual benefits may possibly explain why some organisations have achieved major gains when other more traditional learning processes have failed to deliver.

The AAR process does demand a degree of rigour and discipline that some individuals and organisations would have difficulty in adhering to. Yet AAR does add an element that is not present with other techniques—the immediacy and urgency of finding future actions almost as the current action is being undertaken. It may well provide a solution where other techniques have not worked.

In most organisations, there are examples of informal learning activities that could be encouraged and promoted. It may take a little searching as much of it is usually hidden from managers. But once you find it, there is a great deal that can be done to celebrate its existence, value its worth and encourage its growth. And it is actually very inexpensive to do. That will definitely appeal to our captains of industry.

One of the risks in promoting informal training is that it may lead to declining interest in funding formal training. Formal training is still needed and the revival of interest in informal approaches should lead to complementary approaches rather than trade-offs. Informal training can never be a complete substitute for formal, classroom-based learning. But it can plug learning and development holes that are otherwise difficult to fill.

Guidelines

1 Check the purpose

All decisions about training should be capable of being justified.

If you are planning to arrange informal learning opportunities for an employee, make sure you are able to define why you are doing it. It's good self-discipline to write down the reason, preferably in terms of outcomes that will be achieved. If you have trouble explaining the reasons to yourself, chances are that the training is not appropriate.

2 Check the process

If the training has a valid purpose, check the learning processes to be used. The key question is: How will people learn in this informal training situation? The question has to be answered from the point of view of the learner, not the person doing the training.

Hopefully, you will get some answers that involve learning processes such as observation, skill practice sessions, discussion and personal reflection. Make a judgment whether the suggested processes seem appropriate to the content.

3 Check the outcomes

If the purpose and the processes seem okay, check whether outcomes have been set and whether the learning opportunity will be evaluated against those outcomes. Even professional trainers still have a great deal of trouble measuring the impact of the training.

Don't be too ambitious, but if you can push the evaluation beyond what the trainees thought of the training (Level 1 Evaluation) towards whether knowledge or skills have been acquired (Level 2 Evaluation), then you're doing very well. Occasionally, it is possible to test the impact of the training on the person's on-the-job performance (Level 3 Evaluation).

Almost never can you test whether the organisation has benefited from the training (Level 4 Evaluation).

For further exploration

Even though on-the-job training comprises by far the greatest proportion of all workplace training that actually occurs, it receives scant attention from the training industry. For example, the Australian National Training Authority publishes extensively about workplace training but has no material that is of any assistance to someone who just wants guidance on how to do on-the-job training.

Most of the available material relates to formal and structured training programs. These do happen on the job but typically involve an expert or even a specialist trainer. None of this has much relevance to managers trying to encourage one-on-one training on a just-in-time basis. This type of training is most often unstructured, unplanned and very informal. It is also extremely effective.

For some practical help try:

- R. Jacobs and M. Jones, *Structured on-the-job Training: Unleashing Employee Expertise in the Workplace,* Berrett-Koehler, San Francisco, 1995.
- B. Pike, L. Solem and D. Arch, *One-on-One Training: How to Effectively Train One Person at a Time,* Jossey-Bass, San Francisco, 1995.
- T. Hodges, *Linking Learning and Performance: A Practical Guide to Measuring Learning and on-the-job Application,* Butterworth-Heinemann, Boston, 2001.
- G. Sisson, *Hands-on Training: A Simple and Effective Method for on-the-job Training,* Berrett-Koehler, San Francisco, 2001.

Choosing the right direction

PROBLEM SOLVING 9

A manager's brain, or mind, is their best friend. In modern jargon, all managers are 'knowledge workers' by definition. Managers do their work by using their minds. Yet most think little about this organ.

It may help to think of the mind as a little machine that needs to be maintained in optimal condition. This means a bit of maintenance now and again, and maybe a major overhaul occasionally to bring it back to full capability—in other words, learning some new tricks. Without occasional upgrades, your mind may well find itself dropping off in performance as it falls into various bad (thinking) habits.

The human mind is a peculiar organ. It plays so many tricks on itself that you have to wonder whether we can trust any of the judgments it makes. Yet making judgments is a critical task of management. Managers spend more time on making decisions than they do on almost anything else. They are generally paid to get it right but we know that they often get it wrong.

Can you learn to think smarter and make better decisions at work?

Background

The costs of making wrong decisions can be and typically are significant to both individuals and businesses. If managers are to get better at making decisions, we first need to understand better how people think and how the decision-making process works.

One of the things that researchers have figured out over the years is that bad decision making may occur because the mind of the decision maker is sabotaging the thinking process. Part of the problem is that the mind is too busy to give its undivided attention to any one single decision. To expect such a degree of mindfulness is unrealistic in a day-to-day work situation. The mind is too busy to do that, so it uses short cuts.

Heuristics is the set of routine short cuts that the human brain uses to reduce complexity to acceptable levels. Heuristics helps us deal with the multitude of day-to-day demands placed on us. Yet it also creates biases in our thinking that can prevent us from making the best decisions. These routine short cuts are traps that warp our capacity to make the best possible decisions.

Thinking biases and traps

Researchers have started to describe and define heuristic traps.
For example, Hammond, Keeney and Raiffa[1] suggest the
following six common traps that affect our thinking.

The anchoring *trap*

When considering a decision, the mind gives disproportionate
weight to the first information it receives in relation to a
situation. Previous knowledge influences our current
assessment by becoming the *anchor* for further thought. It
creates a baseline from which the mind is reluctant to move
away.

In practice, those who understand its impact on our
thinking can exploit this trap. For example, the opening offer
by a seller will influence the buyer's expectations about what is
a reasonable price.

The *anchoring* trap can be managed by:
- viewing a problem from many different perspectives;
- thinking about issues before you discuss them with others;
- seeking input from many different people;
- not being anchored by others (such as those who give you
  advice);
- preparing a position in advance before you negotiate
  anything.

The status-quo *trap*

When considering courses of action, the mind prefers to leave
things as they are. Less change is better because it means there
is less to think about. Therefore, we look for reasons why the
no-change option is the best. This trap biases us towards
inaction and maintaining the *status quo*.

Unfortunately, many organisations reinforce this trap. For
example, a sin of commission (getting a decision wrong) is
often considered worse than a sin of omission (not having
done something). This means that managers may leave
decisions too late or not make any at all.

The *status-quo* trap can be managed by:
- reminding yourself of your ultimate objectives and relating
  your decisions to those objectives;
- never considering the status quo as the only option;
- considering whether you would choose the status quo if it
  were not the status quo;

- avoiding exaggeration of the costs of moving away from the status quo;
- evaluating options in terms of future benefits, not just current ones;
- avoiding falling back on the status quo option when it is difficult to choose between the other alternatives.

The sunk-cost trap

We like to justify our past choices, even when they are no longer relevant or even justifiable. Our past decisions are *sunk costs*—irrecoverable investments that should be treated as irrelevant to today. But typically this is not how we think of them. They continue to prey on our mind and affect our judgment about today.

An example of this trap is throwing good money after bad because you do not want to admit that you made a mistake. Bank managers will often approve further investments that chase a dubious initial investment decision. To avoid this trap, one particular bank requires a different bank manager to make subsequent investment decisions from the one who made the initial decision.

The *sunk-cost* effect can be managed by:
- seeking out the opinions of people who were not involved in the original decision;
- asking yourself why the earlier failure causes you distress;
- being aware of whether those who advise you have fallen into the trap;
- discouraging a mentality of fear-of-failure in yourself and others.

The confirming-evidence trap

This bias leads us to seek out information that supports our current or preferred point of view. It encourages us to ignore or not notice information that contradicts what we would like to be the case. It leads us to overvalue *confirming evidence* and devalue contradictory evidence.

Research has demonstrated that the same information given to people with two different points of view will be interpreted as supporting both contrary viewpoints. We tend to accept confirmatory data and not see contradictory data.

The *confirming-evidence* trap can be managed by:
- checking whether all evidence (for and against) is treated with equal rigour;

- becoming a devil's advocate and building the strongest possible case for the opposing position;
- examining your own motives as to why you want to do something;
- not using leading questions and avoiding the influence of 'yes-men'.

The framing *trap*

The way we *frame* questions will predispose us to interpret the answers in a certain way. We tend to be risk-averse if the question is posed in terms of gains but risk-tolerant when it is framed in terms of avoiding losses. Different reference points will bias us one way or the other.

The *framing effect* can be managed by:
- framing questions in alternative ways, looking for biases created by the frame itself;
- framing questions in deliberately neutral ways;
- questioning how things might seem different if another frame were used;
- questioning the frames used by others.

The estimating/forecasting *trap*

Managers do not get much feedback on the accuracy of their *forecasts* and *estimates* (unlike bookmakers, meteorologists and actuaries) and, as a result, most are not skilled at this activity. This leads to a group of traps to do with the accuracy of such processes. They include the *overconfidence* trap, the *prudence* trap and the *recallability* trap.

The *estimating/forecasting* trap and its subset traps can be managed by:
- considering the extreme ranges of what is possible and then working back to realistic estimates;
- stating your estimates honestly, and telling others that is what you are doing;
- avoiding impressions or hunches, and identifying 'hard data'.

Our brains rely on processes that sometimes hinder effective decision making. The first step to minimising the impact of this is to be aware of the tendency and to forearm yourself against its effect on your thinking.

Managers would do well to remember how tenuous and capricious their own thinking is likely to be. If that is too confronting, then at least remember how tenuous and capricious other people's thinking is likely to be. Act accordingly.

Solving problems

The need to make a decision, especially a difficult one, is usually caused by the presence of a *problem*. One way of thinking about problems is to consider them as situations that need changing or improving. If you are dissatisfied with the current state of affairs, then you are presented with a problem.

One solution could be to ignore the problem (a perfectly sensible strategy in many situations) by ignoring your dissatisfaction with the situation. In other words, instead of working on the problem you work on your own feelings about the situation; change your feelings and you no longer have a problem; therefore, no decision needs to be made. You learn to accept the situation and to live with the problem. (However, to do that is in fact making a decision—the decision not to deal with the problem—even if it often does not feel much like a decision.)

Most problems, however, cannot be solved by ignoring them. They need to be dealt with actively and positively, leading to the point where you make a decision on a course of action. Dealing actively with a problem can take many forms: look for the easiest course of action, randomly choose a course of action, ask another person what to do and so on. Unfortunately, many of these approaches are not very effective; they simply do not produce the best possible result.

There are many ways to dissect the problem-solving process. The following simple schema of four stages of problem solving may help.

1 Illumination—throwing light on the situation.
2 Exploration—finding out more about the situation.
3 Idea generation—thinking up ways of dealing with the situation.
4 Selection—deciding what to do about the situation.

You do not necessarily have to go through each stage with every problem you face, although such a rigorous approach will help with very complex problems. But at the very least you should think about what kind of solution you are looking for.

• Are you trying to gather all the facts about the situation so that you can make a better informed decision (*illumination*)?

- Are you trying to find better ways of understanding what you know about the situation (*exploration*)?
- Are you looking for entirely new ways of responding to the situation (*idea generation*)?
- Are you in need of help to choose the best response to the situation (*selection*)?

Making (not finding) solutions

Another factor to consider is the language we use in thinking. In general, our thinking is very much influenced by this language because language and thought are closely interwoven, almost inseparably so. The language we use, therefore, will influence our thinking and our approach to problem solving and decision making.

Our language is riddled with metaphors—descriptions of things that compare them to something else. For example, we often use expressions like 'looking for an answer' or 'finding a solution'. What is implied by such expressions is that solutions and answers are 'out there' to be found. It suggests that solutions are like objects to be discovered, objects that are lying around somewhere waiting for us to pick them up ready made.

The reality is that solutions generally have to be invented, created, manufactured or designed, all of which implies that solving problems is an active process of *making* rather than *finding* solutions.

The metaphor of *finding* absolves us from the responsibility to take an active part in coming up with a solution and making a decision. If that metaphor dominates your thinking, you may be inclined just to wait until you happen to find the answer you need. Your strategy will be to rely on luck.

If, on the other hand, you think in terms of *making* or creating a solution (rather than finding one), you are telling yourself that you have some work to do. Things don't make themselves. Neither do solutions. They require a bit of work and a bit of effort.

The language we use to describe our thinking offers two choices for dealing with the situations that we face in life and at work: wait for a lucky break and *find* a solution; or *make* your own solutions. You choose.

Guidelines

1 Think about thinking

Few people take the time to think about their typical way of dealing with situations. But a little reflection occasionally is a good thing. It sharpens the mind and for most managers their mind is their most valuable resource.

Think about your behavioural habits in decision making.

- What do you typically do?
- Are you the type to collect data first and then decide on a course of action?
- Do you sense what is the right way forward and then look for data to support that view?

Whichever way is your preference, *try it the other way round*, just for a change.

One way of protecting yourself against thinking traps is to become capable of thinking differently. Habits simplify life but they can also constrain you from making the best possible decisions.

2 Learn new tools

Decision making usually involves tools and techniques. We tend to practise the ones we prefer and become so proficient at them that they are almost internalised. We then use them unconsciously (or 'mindlessly'). But there are always more tools than you think.

Find a new way to make decisions or solve problems. Learn a new technique or practise using a new mental tool.

3 Ask others to explain their thinking

Most managers receive a regular flow of information and advice from others. Some of this is helpful for making decisions, but much of it is not. The thinking of others is likely to be as flawed (and may be more so) than your own. So learn to protect yourself against flawed advice by challenging the thinking of others.

To have greater confidence in the recommendations of others:

- Ask them to explain their decision-making process (many will interpret this as an invitation to explain the decision, but remind them that your question is not about the decision but how they arrived at it).
- Assess the quality of their process.

For further exploration

As is so often the case, an article in the *Harvard Business Review* means that a full book on the same topic is just around the corner. John Hammond and colleagues have produced the full monty on the subject of thinking traps with this book:

- J. Hammond, R. Keeney and H. Raiffa, *Smart Choices: A Practical Guide to Making Better Decisions,* Harvard Business School Press, Boston, 1998.

This covers the full gamut of the decision-making and problem-solving process, including problem definition, setting objectives, creating alternatives, considering consequences, making trade-offs, handling uncertainty, tolerating risks and coordinating decisions.

Their advice is based on research rather than just the opinion of the authors. This is what makes their work a little different from others who tend to provide good advice in the form of personal opinion. Hammond and colleagues provide the research evidence that backs up their opinions. If you need help with decision making, decide to buy this book!

DECISION MAKING **10**

Managers make decisions constantly. Most use trusted techniques and methods, to the point where they become the habitual way of making decisions. This is a strength and a weakness. It is a strength because it speeds up the decision process and you can become very good at it because you do it all the time. It is a weakness because habits close the mind to better ways of doing something, so better methods of making decisions tend to be excluded.

Generally, we do not bother to match the technique to the problem. A very structured and thorough technique such as root cause analysis may be applied where a much simpler technique would do. Sometimes, a simple technique such as cost benefit analysis is applied to a complex situation not well suited to it. Either way, you end up with problems that result from the decisions we make on how to make decisions.

Can we improve the way we make strategy decisions?

Background

Top management is often blamed for the failure to translate decisions into action, and action into outcomes. Although management incompetence (defined as 'not knowing how to make things happen') is one element of this problem, recent studies suggest that managers in many organisations actually do follow many of the standard prescriptions for how to make decisions and then achieve results.

Structured decision making can be characterised as follows:
- identifying management challenges, such as threats or opportunities;
- formulating the issue and considering alternatives;
- gathering useful data;
- analysing the issue;
- selecting the best alternative;
- resolving doubts about the choice.

Why things go wrong

In reality, many managers do follow most, if not all, of these steps in some way or other. Very few rely exclusively on intuition, and most do not prefer to make it up as they go along. In many cases, an action plan is formalised to the point

77

of knowing who will do what by when. But from this point on, much can go wrong and little may happen in the way of implementation. The problem is not the lack of a plan but the *lack of results that are in accordance with the plan*. This is often described as 'things going out of control'. This then leads to corrective action which can sometimes makes things worse.

This point may have been reached because of management incompetence. There are many decision-making traps the manager may have fallen into, including:

* trying to solve the wrong problem;
* overconfidence in understanding the problem;
* underresourcing the implementation process.

But detailed case-based research suggests that this happens far less frequently than is imagined. Usually, the decisions are about right and the managers are not especially incompetent in making them.

The finger might then be pointed at the manager's capacity to manage *implementation* of decisions. Peter Drucker suggested many years ago that it would be useful to build into decisions a process for a continuous feedback loop that checks whether the decision being implemented is still the correct one.[1] His advice has been largely ignored. Reviewing the implementation process is messy. It does not fit the 'can-do' image of an action-oriented manager determined to 'get scores on the board'. And yet such feedback mechanisms are in fact the most powerful tools we have for preventing what has been called *decision drift*.[2]

Many managers prefer the alternative strategy of blaming. The failure of a project is blamed on factors such as 'resistance to change' or 'unsupportive organisational culture'. The combination of 'leadership failure' and 'resistance to change' provides a satisfying explanation for project failures.

In many organisations, the process of making decisions is clearly not rational. Many factors impinge on the process, not all of them logical. Decisions may be made for reasons that are political, social, emotional, historical or highly personal. But the pretence has to be maintained that the decision was rationally made. This creates immediate stresses for the implementing manager: the causes of failure are being built into the decision from the moment it is made.

Managers deal with this type of situation all the time and manage it (consciously or unconsciously) by:

- going ahead and ignoring their personal fears that the project is flawed;
- doing nothing in order to see what happens;
- modifying the decision subtly to make it more likely to succeed.

These three strategies-in-practice are enough to explain the general tendency for decision drift in many organisations.

Much of this can be avoided by explicitly building a testing mechanism into our decisions. This can be as simple as a series of critical questions that check at various stages in the implementation cycle—not just at the time the decision was made—whether the decision is still correct. Questions may include:

- whether the problem still needs to be solved;
- whether the proposed solution is still the right one;
- whether the solution is achieving the intended benefits.

With this mental frame, the phenomenon of 'resistance to change' can be reinterpreted as a legitimate expression of caution, providing valuable feedback on the implementation process. It requires a different approach to the management/leadership role, one that tolerates ambiguity, respects complexity and is wary of certainty.

An approach to decision implementation that is based on fearing the worst and preparing for it becoming reality may well be the most sensible way to improve organisational decision making.

Bounded rationality

Strategic thinking and decision making are reasonably well understood concepts. But *strategic behaviour* (what managers do when they are involved in the strategy process) is less clear, even though such behaviour has an enormous impact on the strategy process. It is strategic behaviour that can make a group of decision makers agree on a strategic option that none of them supports individually, sometimes with disastrous consequences.[3]

The behaviour of a group is often driven by non-rational motivations such as an emotional commitment to a particular option or a desire to protect 'pet projects'. This interplay between rational thinking and non-rational reactions has been described as *bounded rationality*, in which a rational activity is limited by non-rational constraints. Much of managerial decision making is characterised by bounded rationality.

As a result, the strategic process in practice displays the following elements:
- It is only partly rational.
- The aim is often to avoid the worst rather than seek out the best options.
- It is rarely systematic.
- It looks like a stream of discontinuous activities.
- It generates strategy by small incremental steps rather than holistic jumps.
- It is often weakly implemented.

Research with a strategy team at British Telecom suggests key aspects of the strategy process that are often ignored:
- *quality of strategic thinking*—whether it is divergent (many possible outcomes) or convergent (one best solution);
- *shared mindsets*—the extent to which the participants understand the frames of reference that each is using;
- *achieving action*—the extreme difficulty in getting commitment to a specific action;
- *territorial barriers*—the organisational and personal commitments that intrude into the strategy process;
- *impact*—the extent to which the group can influence the rest of the organisation;
- *time expended*—constraints put on the process by limited time;
- *utility of outcomes*—the extent to which the process generates useful outcomes;
- *cognitive and emotional energy expended*—leading to frustrations about the process.[4]

Better decisions

The following model[5] provides practical and specific suggestions about managing strategic behaviour. The suggestions are grouped into the four stages of a strategy session.

1 Preparation
- Define the process as well as the content of the session, allowing at least 50 per cent of session time for this.
- Set expectations about the high-level strategic nature of the discussion to avoid getting bogged down in specifics.
- Define the role of the strategy group.
- Discuss how the views of other stakeholders not present will be represented.

2 Prioritisation
- Prune back the agenda to a few issues and display them at all times.
- Prioritise for importance.
- Avoid spending time on side issues.

3 Process
- Focus on one specific issue at a time.
- Build explicit 'mental maps' representing shared understanding.
- Make disagreements as explicit as possible.
- Monitor the level of complexity.
- Try to complete at least something (for example, agreement on relevant assumptions) before moving on.
- Define terms and concepts as you go along.
- Allow time for a review of outputs.

4 Meta-behaviour
- Define the role of the person facilitating the process.
- Move the discussion towards common ground rather than focusing on differences.
- Discontinue discussions that are going nowhere.
- When the discussion gets productive, let it run, even if other agenda items are pushed out.
- If the discussion gets too narrow, ask the group to reflect on the purpose of the session.
- If the discussion diverges too much, bring it back on track by summarising.
- Keep your own pet issues out of it.

This model draws attention to a neglected part of the strategy process that probably accounts for the majority of complaints about strategy setting—the behaviour of those who participate in the process.

The pretence that strategy setting is always rational must be accepted for the nonsense that it is so that we can start to make way for the reality of the situation; even the best management groups don't always get it right—after all, they're only human.

Guidelines

1 Making decisions
How do you make decisions in your organisation?

Most managers and most organisations rarely think about the matter. Most have preferred ways of making decisions that range from largely intuitive selection of choices to structured forms of decision making. Occasionally, a few people get excited and do a course on something like De Bono's 'Six Hats' but this soon wears off, leaving behind only the odd reference to someone wearing a black hat.

Try to raise the issue of how decisions are made.

Before making the next important decision, suggest that the group thinks briefly about the best way to make the decision. Do this a few more times until people get used to the idea that the first step of sound decision making is making a decision about how the decision should be made.

2 Learn about decision making

There are hundreds of different techniques for making decisions.

Learn some new techniques as part of your personal renewal process. Keep track of which ones you are learning and how useful they are in practice. Chances are you will find some better than others. This may be because they supplement what you already know how to do well.

Ask others about their decision-making techniques. Read some books on decision making.

Teach some other people how to make decisions differently.

3 Review your decision behaviour

Use the model explained above to analyse your own behaviour. What do you do well and what needs improvement? You may need to get some feedback from others just to keep yourself honest.

Find one or two behaviours that could make a difference to the quality and calibre of your decision making. Work on these by trying some different approaches.

Changing your own behaviour is never easy but only you can do it.

For further exploration

Tony Grundy is one of the best thinkers on the subject of strategic thinking. He is a consultant with extensive experience in helping management teams get their thinking right. Some useful starting points for his approach:

- T. Grundy and L. Brown, *Be Your Own Strategy Consultant: Demystifying Strategic Thinking,* International Thomson Business Press, London, 2001.
- T. Grundy, *Breakthrough Strategies for Growth,* Financial Times Prentice Hall, London, 1996.
- T. Grundy, *Strategic Learning in Action: How to Accelerate and Sustain Business Change,* McGraw-Hill, New York, 1994.
- H. Rubenstein and T. Grundy, *Breakthrough Inc: High-growth Strategies for Entrepreneurial Organizations,* Financial Times Prentice Hall, London, 1999.

PLANNING VERSUS STRATEGISING

11

Strategy is important. It is also much misunderstood. It tends to get mixed up with planning, which does neither activity much good. Both are important, even critical, for organisations but they are quite distinct activities. Confusing them only undermines them.

Of the two, strategising is the harder thing to do, mainly because it is a creative activity that can lead in many directions. Planning is more straightforward as it is analytical and rational. When passing judgment in retrospect, all we can say about a strategy is that it was either right or wrong in the circumstances; a plan, however, can be judged as good or bad purely on technical grounds.

So why is strategy so difficult? Because, unlike planning, it involves making choices that are not based on evidence alone. At some point in the strategy process, you take a leap into the unknown by saying: 'Let's do this and not that'. And that is a scary choice because it takes you into new territory. Even if the actual decision is confirmation of last year's strategy, it is still done in the knowledge that things may have changed out there. Strategy always involves a leap of faith.

How do we separate strategy from planning?

Background

When Henry Mintzberg announced the fall of strategic planning in the mid-1990s, some people weren't listening. Henry is an academic, but very much of the practical variety. He became well known and well respected for doing simple things that no one had thought of doing before. In the 1970s, when others argued about the role of management, Henry decided to spend some time walking behind a bunch of managers just to see what they actually did. And they did many things that management textbooks of the day did not mention, such as playing out ceremonial roles and handing out gold watches to retiring staff. Henry gave us the realistic view of management.[1]

So when Henry announced that strategic planning was dead, you would think the world of management would take notice.

But, despite a categorical demonstration in his book, *The Rise and Fall of Strategic Planning*,[2] that the process of strategic planning is inherently, unarguably and unavoidably contradictory, the world of day-to-day management took little notice. Strategic planners continued on their planning ways, strategic plans continued to be written, and executive teams continued to devote regular sessions to the strategic planning process. (If you listen carefully, somewhere in the background you can hear the sound of Henry banging his head against a brick wall.)

How can it be that a managerial activity such as strategic planning can be so soundly dismissed through meticulous argument and a wealth of practical evidence, and yet managers and organisations everywhere simply carry on regardless?

The fall of strategic planning

So, what happened to strategic planning in 1994? It is something of a travesty to reduce the iconoclastic prose of Professor Mintzberg to a single argument but such things are allowed in the age of the info-byte. Essentially, Mintzberg's argument is that *strategising and planning are two different and incompatible activities.*

- Planning is about *analysis*—it is a formal and structured process of creating a set of intentions to do something, usually resulting in a document called (not surprisingly) a plan.
- Strategy is about *synthesis*—it is a creative process in which options are considered and decisions are made but, ultimately, this is done by using human judgment rather than linear logic.

So, putting the two together does no more than create an oxymoron. In Mintzberg's words:

Analysis may precede and support synthesis, by defining the parts that can be combined into wholes. Analysis may follow and elaborate synthesis, by decomposing and formalising its consequences. But analysis cannot substitute for synthesis. No amount of elaboration will ever enable formal procedures to forecast discontinuities, to inform managers who are detached from their operations, to create novel strategies.[3]

In other words, the process of making a strategy decision does not involve drawing a nice straight line from gathering data to making a decision. The data will take you a certain distance but then you must jump into unknown territory. The data can inform your jump but it still remains a jump into the unknown. That's why analytical people hate making strategy decisions and pretend it is a linear process, and why creative people love doing it but can't explain how they do it.

At the core of the strategising process lies a creative act of synthesis that cannot ever be replaced by the accumulation and formalisation of data. While computers can be programmed to plan (as the 'if–then' capability of the simplest spreadsheet testifies), computers will never be able to strategise. Possibly the nearest computers can come to determining strategy is to select a strategy from among a range of known and existing strategies.

So the question is, why do managers continue to attempt to plan strategically when it is inherently pointless? It comes back to our need to impose order on chaos, to create a semblance of predictability in a managerial world that is anything but predictable. The very act of sitting down to plan strategically inspires a temporary feeling of control, of being in charge, of making things happen.

This irresistible urge to at least feel in control affects even the most mundane of managerial actions: how we work with others; how we report our achievements; how we portray our role in the organisation. Many managers, however, know that this sense of control is a figment of the imagination. This awareness presents two choices:

1 They can acknowledge that they don't really control the organisation and devise an alternative approach.
2 They can pretend that they do control the organisation and ignore all evidence to the contrary.

Those who choose the first learn eventually to deal with the real world of management, a world characterised by ambiguity, complexity and uncertainty; in response, they continue to grow from within. As to those who choose the second, stagnation is usually not noticed by those who stagnate.

The manager who does respond to the real complexities of the managerial world may wonder what can be done about the conundrum identified by Mintzberg. Just because *strategic planning* does not work, this does not mean that the separate activities of *strategising* and *planning* don't work.

If combining them is not a good idea, is it possible to get better at the two separate activities? We can, providing we question some of the accepted ways of doing things.

- Planning often fails because selling the plan is harder than the planning itself. This can be fixed through a more *participative* approach.
- Strategising involves making decisions, and *decision making* can be improved (see below, and also Chapter 10).

Better planning: the participative approach

When planners plan, they generally encounter many pitfalls, each of which drives the process inexorably towards failure. Mintzberg[4] lists the planning pitfalls as:

- lack of commitment;
- the impact of organisational politics;
- inability to cope with change;
- the pretence of control.

The first of these pitfalls (lack of commitment) can be overcome by more inclusive planning processes. Gaining commitment is only an issue if the planning model you follow is one that involves planners creating a plan, which they then have to 'sell' to others. Mintzberg argues quite convincingly that such an approach creates so many in-built barriers that the effort to gain the support of others usually outweighs the benefits of having a plan.

In other words, the commitment pitfall is a direct consequence of having planning as a specialised and exclusive activity. Lack of commitment might be minimised if the planning process becomes more inclusive—that is, from the very start it involves all those whose commitment is required to make the planning process productive. In extreme cases, where the commitment and support of the total organisation is required, it may even have to involve everyone.

The need to avoid the commitment pitfall may well explain why inclusive or participative approaches to planning are becoming more common. The idea of involving the many rather than the few in the planning process has emerged out of the frustrations that managers have experienced with the traditional 'specialised' approaches. And while the participative approach has its own risks and dangers, it does seem to address the fundamental issue of plans that are supported only by those few who design them.

Whatever the real or perceived advantages of participative planning, it has grown rapidly over the last ten years to the point where different schools of thought have emerged, typically formed around the different processes used in the planning activity. Involving lots of people in a planning activity is heavily dependent on some process or other to maintain order and achieve an outcome.

Many of these different approaches have emerged from the organisation development trends of the late 1980s, which in turn have their roots in earlier developments in community-based decision-making processes. For example, in Australia, by the late 1970s various techniques were emerging for bringing together large numbers of people to decide policies and plans for a 'community of interest'. One example of this occurred when all those who had a stake in the curriculum (the content of an educational program) for technical and further education were brought together. The techniques learned from staging a two-day meeting, involving 100+ people, to rapidly design a new curriculum still infuse the participative planning processes of today.

Other sources of inspiration were the traditional community gatherings in the United States ('town meetings') and the participative design elements of sociotechnical systems analysis, developed in the UK and Europe in the 1960s. All focused on the same fundamental principle: *people support what they help to create.*

Today, more and more organisations are realising that the uphill task of gaining support and commitment for a plan of action can be simplified by giving people the opportunity to have a say. The act of contributing to a discussion creates a psychological contract where, even if the final outcome is not your first preference, you are more likely to support it because of your involvement in the process.

The other three planning pitfalls may also be avoided by the participative approach. Organisational politics is much harder to play out on a stage where everyone is watching. Creating a consensus for change is much easier. And abandoning the pretence of control is made easier by adopting an inclusive approach to planning issues.

Out there in left field, the seers and visionaries predict the emergence of truly democratic organisations, 'communities-of-interest' in action, working together to achieve consensus around a common ground of purpose and values. I suspect that the good old profit motive may inhibit such developments just a little! But at least the participative approach to planning avoids some of the constraints on the planning process that Henry Mintzberg identified.

Better strategising: the decision-making process

Making decisions about strategy is never easy or straightforward. The assumption that it is a rational and linear process is not borne out either by research or by case study material. Sometimes, it helps to step out of the world of business into another arena to understand the reality.

This is exactly what Chung and McLarney[5] did with their detailed analysis of the Battle of Midway, where in June 1942 a small US fleet defeated a much larger Japanese naval force and, in effect, turned the Pacific war against the Japanese. The authors use the case study to explore strategic decision making, and the background to the battle is described in considerable and vivid detail.

The Battle of Midway case study shows that three elements of the strategy-setting process—*decision parameters*, *decision processes* and *decision implementation*—interact in ways that are highly dynamic and often not generally rational. Each of these three elements has been studied before in isolation but this framework brings them together into a dynamic structure that illustrates all the components in action and helps to explain why the Japanese side made the many errors of judgment that it did. The case study also provides an opportunity to contrast two different strategy decision approaches to the same well documented situation.

The authors provide an in-depth analysis of the decisions made in the battle, using the following conceptual framework.

1 Decision parameters
These include cognitive biases and the situational environment of the decision makers, and these in turn determine how the decision makers perceive information.
- *Bounded rationality*—the in-built constraints that all humans bring to the decision-making process, usually not recognised by them.
- *Limitations of strategic intelligence*—the assumption that we have available to us all the necessary information to make a sensible decision.

- *Reluctance to scan the environment*—the urge to limit the time spent on gathering more and up-to-date information.
- *Using mental short-cuts (heuristics)*—relying on past strategies because they were effective, and 'escalating commitment' where strategies continue to be used long after the situation has discredited them.

The above constraints tend to lead to a situation that the authors describe as *success breeds dogma*.

2 Decision process

This includes leadership style, organisational culture and structure, and how they influence the way in which information in interpreted.

- *Structure*—where decision making may range from tight control by a central group to delegated authority to make decisions. If the context is highly fluid, the first approach is very inefficient.
- *Leadership*—where decision-making styles range from involving a small group of 'commanders' to a more broadly based and participative approach. The second is more flexible.
- *Culture*—where the ingrained approach to decision making may range from simply obeying orders to active involvement in interpreting and implementing orders. The second works better in fluid situations.

3 Decision implementation

This is the convergence of the first two elements, and leads to actual decisions and their implementation.

The specific environment under which the first two elements are brought together needs to be understood by those who make the decisions. For example, in a highly volatile environment a different strategic response is needed from that required if the context is highly stable and well defined. It assumes a dynamic situation where the very application of strategy decision changes the environment to which it is applied. This contrasts with the static approach where the implementation of strategy is seen as a linear 'cause and effect' sequence.

In exploring the lessons from the case study, the authors contrast and compare the approaches brought to the battle situation by the two opposing sides. They conclude that there were dramatic differences in management styles, planning styles, strategy styles, tactics, communication, environmental scanning, execution and outcomes.

Some specific conclusions for practising managers include:

1 The crucial role of competitive intelligence cannot be overestimated.
2 Actions that led to previous success are a poor guide to future outcomes.
3 Given the turbulent business environment facing most organisations today, flexible approaches to strategy seem more appropriate than they might have been even one decade ago.
4 Strategy is a mental activity based on a reality that is constructed by our minds, and our minds can't always be trusted.

While a case study based on a World War II battle may seem remote to the pressing needs of today's business leaders, the lessons drawn are remarkably insightful. The formal frameworks of strategy developed by academics and researchers are brought to life by close observation of historical figures who made decisions that turned out to be crucial to the conduct of the war. If this study encourages more managers to contemplate just how they make the decisions that determine the future welfare of the organisations in their trust, they will find it well worth reading the original material in full.

Guidelines

1 Intelligence matters

Although data will not lead you automatically to the right strategy, there is no doubt that strategy should be grounded in reality. That is where competitive intelligence comes in.

While managers typically know lots about their own organisation, they often know less than they think about their competitors (or, for that matter, their customers and suppliers). This imbalance can skew the thinking of even the smartest managers, in that what is known seems to take on more importance than what is not known.

It is always the unknown that blows a seemingly good strategy out of the water. Internal pitfalls are far less likely to stuff up a strategy than external events.

Invest in competitive intelligence.

2 Flexibility matters

Despite the fact that the past is a rather poor guide to the present, the success of the past misleads us frequently. *Success breeds dogma.*

The alternative is to look quite deliberately for different ways of doing things. Prepare to do things differently, even if not yet.

Invent ways of responding to unexpected events so that at least you have a chance to survive if the worst-case scenario comes along (see Chapter 12).

Develop an internal capacity to change quickly. Map out what would need to happen if you suddenly had to change your strategy overnight.

Prepare!

3 Don't trust yourself

Because setting strategy is essentially a step into the unknown, be prepared to get it wrong.

Because strategy is a creative act rather than a reductionist one, don't trust your own thinking.

Involve others in the strategy process, especially those with a different approach from yours (diversity pays off in strategy sessions).

Beware of the familiar ways of doing things (see Chapter 10).

For further exploration

Henry Mintzberg is still the best guide to strategy and planning processes. Others provide specific tools that help (such as Michael Porter's Five Forces analysis, discussed in Chapter 18) but Henry takes the overview and provides his observations and conclusions in a most readable form.

- H. Minztberg, B. Ahlstrand and J. Lampel, *Strategy Safari: A Guided Tour Through the Wilds of Strategic Management,* Simon & Schuster, New York, 1998.
  A small taste:
- We are the blind people and strategy is our elephant.
- There is no formula for transforming any organisation, and that includes the very notion that the organisation needs transforming in the first place.
- Strategy formation is judgmental designing, intuitive visioning and emergent learning.

SCENARIO PLANNING **12**

The greatest danger for any business strategy is if the assumptions on which the strategy is based turn out to be incorrect.

Most strategies rely on assumptions (explicit or implicit) about the environment in which the organisation operates. It is every manager's nightmare to find a finely crafted strategy brought to its knees by a sudden change in external conditions. Many events can have this effect: newly emerging technology, newly emerging competitors, new ways of doing business, or simply a general change in business conditions.

Strategising tends to one of two approaches: rationalistic (finding the optimal strategy through a rational process of analysis) or emergent (evolving the best strategy over time through incremental changes). The major disadvantage of the rational approach is that it fails whenever the assumptions that sit behind the analysis turn out to be incorrect. This happens most frequently when unforeseen events occur. The major disadvantage of the emergent approach is that it is reactive, with strategy changing in response to events.

No one can stop unexpected changes, but we can prepare for them. No one can predict such events, but we can predict that unexpected things will happen. One technique for preparing a defence against the unexpected is *scenario planning*, which differs significantly from traditional strategic planning.

How can we plan and prepare for events unknown?

Background

Preparing for the unexpected and the unknown goes under many names, ranging from prayer to contingency planning. The latter seems more appropriate to the business context but the former also has its exponents in industry.

Contingency planning allows the organisation to prepare for eventualities that may never happen and to respond quickly and sensibly if they do. It may have a very narrow focus (what do we do if there is a major equipment failure?) to a very broad focus (what do we do if a new competitor enters our industry?). Contingency planning also varies in its time focus; it may range from the short term to the long term.

Short term contingency planning

Short-term responses to the unexpected (sometimes informally called 'Plan B') involve doing a kind of 'what if' analysis. In the financial arena, short-term contingency planning is made simple by the use of software such as spreadsheets (for example, Microsoft Excel). Spreadsheets have driven home to their users the idea that outcomes projected into the future always depend on making assumptions. Having programmed the assumptions into a spreadsheet, it is relatively simple to change them and then study the consequential outcomes.

If, for example, a profit plan for an organisation assumes that demand for their product will grow by 8 per cent in the coming year, and the inflation rate (as measured by the Consumer Price Index) will go up 1.8 per cent, then the plan will generate a certain level of results. Change either or both of those two assumptions, and the results will vary up or down accordingly. This enables the programmer to introduce a range of values for both the assumptions and then go fishing for the extreme results. Sometimes, these results are called best- and worst-case scenarios, with the programmer taking a guess at the mid-range as the most likely outcome and the most likely scenario.

This kind of short-term scenario analysis is made possible by the relative predictability of the range in which a given assumption will vary. For example, the inflation rate is likely to vary in the short term within a relatively small band. It may go as high as 3 per cent or as low as 0.5 per cent but a movement outside this range is highly unlikely in the short term. It takes a sustained move upward over a period of time to produce inflation of 5 per cent or 10 per cent. It does not generally happen in a one-year time frame.

As a result, our planning techniques are fairly good in the short term. We use recent data to predict the likely range of variance in our assumptions. This enables us to prepare for the possible outcomes, especially those of the worst kind.

The problems start when we begin to stretch the time frame. Data from last year or the current year is often a good guide for our assumptions about next year. But what if we want to look further ahead? What if we want to project the analysis five years out, or even further? That's when the reliability of our predictions declines rapidly. Beyond ten years, most organisations don't even bother projecting and predicting. The range in the variables becomes so great that the range of possible outcomes becomes impossibly large.

Long-range planning

Many events unfold over a longer time frame, not just one year. Some developments in industry or society at large happen over many years, if not many decades. The growth of globalisation, the emergence of green issues, female participation in the workforce, the rise in part-time work and many other developments took place over time. Only after these trends had started to affect the way we live and do business did they become obvious. Those who did 'predict' them typically also predicted many trends that did not emerge (or not yet at least!).

Further, some events come from so far out in left field that no one could have predicted them—the Great Depression, the Gulf War, the disappearance of communist economies, and the emergence of globally based terrorist organisations capable of blowing up parts of New York. Such discontinuous events hold a tremendous danger for organisations that have planned their futures around short-term events that vary only within a tight range of variance.

One response to such discontinuous events is *scenario planning*. It became well known because of its well documented role in enabling Royal Dutch/Shell to exploit the situation presented by the 1973 OPEC oil crisis. As oil prices rose to unbelievable heights, driven by an artificial oil shortage, Shell responded in accordance with a plan that had been devised many years before for just such a situation. Shell profited handsomely by taking decisive action while many of its competitors floundered; some went under altogether. Shell went from the least profitable global oil company to the most profitable.[1]

Scenario planning provides an alternative to traditional planning techniques by focusing on situations that may emerge in the future and preparing an appropriate response. It assumes that the business world is essentially unpredictable (as does the emergent-strategy approach) but that we can apply analytical techniques (as does the rational-strategy approach) to working out a plan for how to respond to situations that may emerge.

Approaches to scenario planning

There are at least two distinct approaches to the process of scenario planning.[2] The first version of scenario planning starts with a set of future states, usually descriptive stories about what the future might look like 10–15 years out. The task for the participants is to *explore the implications of those possible future states*. The purpose of the exercise is largely educational and designed to stimulate the thinking of the participants. It has a playful element to it that encourages thinking, insight, learning and growth.

The second approach starts with a policy or strategy or other set of circumstances, and embeds and extends these into a set of future states in order to *explore the potential consequences*. This opens up the possibility of making decisions now about whether to pursue those policies or strategies.

The first approach often does not deliver action outcomes (this is what we will do in the future) but rather educational outcomes (this is what we now know about the future). The second approach is much more analytical and questioning about specific detail. It seeks answers to particular questions (if we adopt this strategy, what might be the outcomes in the future?). The first strengthens overall capability; the second creates possible courses of action.

What is common to both approaches is the emphasis on *learning by doing*. You cannot hand scenario planning over to a group of experts and tell them to get back to you when they have a result. It has to be done by those who will work with the outcomes, as it is designed to inform their decision making.

Further, it is an art form rather than a science, as Peter Schwartz emphasises with the title of his book, *The Art of the Long View*.[3] Anyone who wants to do scenario planning must be prepared to learn how to participate in a process, not just apply cold analytical techniques. The process has rules and procedures but they are designed to ensure that participants have a worthwhile experience. It has been compared to learning how to dance: you do have to learn the rules but you can only do it by doing it, and you can only get better at it by practising.[4]

You don't need to have access to an expert process facilitator, but it probably helps. Any managers with the interest and inclination can skill themselves in the process to the point where they can run a scenario-planning session. Using a consultant will short-cut this need but comes at the cost of not developing in-house expertise. Shell's experts in scenario planning were all part of various in-house strategy advisory groups.

In reality, most organisations tend to prepare only a handful of scenarios, with each scenario describing a different set of future situations and events. They are essentially stories about the future and tend to be written in narrative form. Given that hard data (the preference of the rationalists) about the future is often difficult to obtain, stories allow a degree of detail that is not dependent on graphs and tables. Stories also have a stronger impact on the participants as they provide a richness of descriptive detail not matched by statistical detail.

Scenario planning is a long-range planning technique. Short-term thinking should be avoided in this process. The actual time frame varies from industry to industry and from organisation to organisation. Shell goes out as far as 25 years and, in one instance, as far as 65 years.

Managing the scenario planning process

Given that scenarios are always based on assumptions, part of the planning process involves challenging these assumptions.[5] Four separate premises form the basis for a scenario:
1 The future world will be similar to today but better.
2 The future world will be very much better than today.
3 The future world will be similar to today but worse.
4 The future world will be radically different from today.

In practice, most scenario-planning exercises are done on the basis of the first premise. This is largely because it is within the comfort zone of most managers. The process usually involves imagining an end-state and then working out the events that need to occur for that end-state to become reality. If those events then actually begin to occur, it provides a signal to the organisation that the imagined end-state may become reality.

The scenario-planning process revolves around the changing needs of customers or stakeholders. It is process-based and continuous (as opposed to the rationalist approach of 'one best way'). It follows a series of cycles in which the scenarios are developed, tested and improved (not unlike the Shewart cycle of Plan-Do-Study-Act). It focuses as much on the side benefits of organisational learning as it does on the actual outcomes.

Scenario planning has become legendary as a tool for protecting organisations against unexpected events. However, the tool has become somewhat warped over time as it is applied by business solely as a *protective device*. In some ways, using it in this way involves trying to turn it into an 'insurance tool' and is a bit like trying to read a crystal ball. Over time, as some of the scenarios are not realised, managers lose faith in the process. They forget that it is *not* a predictive device.

There are other pitfalls in the scenario-planning process. For example, it is not very useful without top management involvement (top management may well prefer to have a strategy 'presented' to them rather than be involved in its development). It may fail to generate new options due to lack of imagination. It is too long-term for some. And it often challenges managerial assumptions that may be deep-seated and impossible to question. In a sense, an organisation and its leaders need to be ready for scenario planning to obtain full value from it.

Scenario planning is treading a well worn path for management techniques, one that begins with rigorous discipline practised by the few and ends with a general and vague notion, applied occasionally and badly by the many. If an organisation wants to get better at dealing with the future, it needs to put in the hard yards. Tackling the future is not meant to be easy.

Guidelines

1 Learn about the process

Attacking the future can be a lot of fun.

If you are interested in tackling the process, try the starting points suggested in the article discussed in *For further exploration*.

Also see the Notes section for this chapter. In particular, Mercer[6] provides a brief step-by-step guide.

2 Apply the process

Keep in mind that the process is about learning.

As well as learning about your organisation and its future, learn about the process. What worked for you and what didn't? Why? What can you do differently next time?

These questions are different from the learning questions that need to be asked of the participants, so it is not advisable for you to act as a participant in a scenario-planning event that you are facilitating. Carrying out two roles at once (participant and facilitator) is very difficult for anyone.

3 Learn from the applications

Apply what you have learned by doing something different next time. There is plenty of scope within the process for experimentation.

It is not about getting the process 'right' according to the textbooks but about making it work. The test is whether it is working for you and your organisation (so think about your objectives in trying out the process) and that is the only test that matters.

Even if it does not 'work' for your management team or your organisation, that in itself will tell you something about your team or your organisation.

For further exploration

For those who want to read more, the *HBR* article below is an easily obtainable introduction:

- P. Wack, 'Scenarios: uncharted waters ahead', *Harvard Business Review*, 5(63), 1985, pp. 73–90.

For those who like to use the Internet, useful material on scenario planning is everywhere. There is some useful material in specialist online magazines aimed at particular professions. For example:

- For information technology managers:
  http://www.cioinsight.com/article/0,3658,apn=3&s=301&a
  =7142&app=1&ap=2,00.asp
- For finance managers:
  http://www.cfoeurope.com/200202h.html

Some of the material (as always with the Web) is seriously dodgy (such as the services that offer to knock up a scenario plan for you at a small fee!). Defamation laws prevent me from providing an example, but just put 'scenario planning' into the Google search engine and away you go.

Increasing competitive advantage

STRUCTURE AND PERFORMANCE

13

To many people, the only way to picture an organisation is to draw an organisational structure chart. That drawing often 'is' the organisation. And yet such charts are relatively recent developments. Organisations existed a long time before structure charts were dreamt up by organisational theorists.

Some are now questioning not just the structure chart but also the need for structure itself. The convergence of computing and communication technologies has opened up possibilities for doing business in ways that seem to be free of the need to organise people into 'organisational structures'. These new possibilities are attractive because they hold out the promise of more freedom to employees and fewer costs to the employer.

Can we do without organisational structure?

Background

The structure of organisations isn't what is used to be. Until recently, almost any organisational structure could be represented with neat, clean, straight lines on a piece of paper called the 'organisation chart'. The lines in the chart connect various jobs to indicate who reports to whom and who can issue instructions to whom.

Historically, the flat structure chart captures a concept of organisation that was the foundation of the two most enduring organisational structures we have seen in the past three thousand years or so: the Roman Catholic Church and its organisational (if not spiritual) predecessor, the army of the Holy Roman Empire. This chart has pedigree.

The development of the formal concept of organisational structure owes a great deal to the classic work of Max Weber (1884–1920) who gave us the first theories of bureaucracy (and the expression itself). Weber saw the organisation as a machine that could be finely tuned, with clear lines of accountability and precise descriptions of organisational units.

Today, the notion of organisational structure is more complex and more sophisticated. Bureaucracy and hierarchy are not fashionable words—we are more likely to speak of flat, matrix or distributed structures, containing elements such as profit/cost centres, business units or 'atoms'.

New and emerging options

One concept that is gaining currency is the notion of *virtual organisation*. This idea is so cutting-edge that it could be used as a blade. The problem is that it can also be devoid of meaning and is easily applied to every innovation from a network of commercial alliances to an Internet chat group.

What is the substance behind this fashionable notion, and what will be the impact on our concepts of organisational structure?

One important distinction often overlooked in the breathless discussion of 'virtual organisation' is whether the speaker means '*the* virtual organisation' (as in an entity) or 'virtual organisation' (as in a principle governing how various entities work together). The definite article makes the world of difference.

The first notion (*the* virtual organisation) is an organisation design option that differs from structures such as the hierarchical organisation, the lateral organisation, the matrix organisation or the team-based organisation. The most notable differences are that the virtual organisation may have no employees, no headquarters and only one small 'core' area of activity, with everything and everyone else outsourced.

There are virtually no virtual organisations. Most of the examples cited in the popular business press or the research literature are actually examples of the other meaning of virtual organisation, with the label simply misapplied.

Hale and Whitlam[1] define the virtual organisation as 'an organisation which is continually evolving, redefining and reinventing itself for practical business purposes'. This is not a very useful definition as most organisations would be happy to describe themselves as such. Which organisation has not at some time tweaked its structure, systems and processes, presumably motivated by the desire to improve its bottom line? Hale and Whitlam go on to explain that the essence of 'virtuality' is to deliver services through structures and processes that are fast, flat and flexible. While not many organisations achieve all three aspects, many would aspire to do so without seeking to be described as 'virtual'.

Most of the cited examples involve organisations that use information technology to do things that used to be done in other ways. But just because you order books from Amazon.com over the Internet does not mean that Amazon is a virtual organisation. Amazon has simply replaced a mail-order catalogue with something cheaper, faster and easier to access. Its core activity—selling books—is no different from that of my corner bookshop and its delivery mechanism (parcel express) is in my experience more expensive and slower.

IT, however, is an *enabler* of virtuality. There are many examples of small businesses that rely on IT in various ways and do resemble the virtual organisation. A typical example might be an entrepreneur creating a piece of software that is then sold over the Internet and downloaded directly into the computer of the purchaser. Such cases abound, but all share the characteristic that they are micro-businesses; it is rare to find an example with more than a handful of employees/owners/members. In fact, if such an organisation becomes successful and grows, it soon finds the need to impose the traditional trappings of organisation: command structure, internal policies, defined procedures, reporting systems and so on. Before long, we are back to the well known forms of organisational structure, albeit the employees may be wearing jeans and t-shirts to signal their virtual origins.

The second notion (virtual organisation without the 'the') is a way of bringing many people or entities together in a network or alliance where members work together cooperatively to achieve certain ends. The entities themselves may be very traditional organisations, but they interact in a way that is cooperative and mutually beneficial.

This second type of virtuality is more easily exemplified. The relationships are sometimes described in terms of a *network of interest* or an arrangement of alliances or a symbiotic system. All have in common a set of relationships that are contingent (participation is voluntary) and adaptive (arrangements are changed as circumstances demand); many are also temporary (existing for a fixed term of purpose).

One relatively common example of this approach is the movie-making business. Various specialists come together for a period and are coordinated to produce a product. They then go their separate ways on to the next project. But there are also many 'permanent' examples.

One of the most interesting case studies describes the reinvention of the textile industry in the Prato region of Italy, near Florence.[2] In the 1970s Massimo Menichetti inherited a large loss-making textile plant. He reinvented the business by breaking the plant up into functionally discrete areas, which he sold off to its employees. Menichetti retained only the marketing function with all activities independently operated by owner–workers. By the late 1980s, this approach had grown to include 15 000 independent businesses with an average of five employees. Another 20 000 people were employed in support service industries. This vast and complex network was connected by 'impannatores', who linked customers and suppliers in a complicated value-adding chain.

Developments in IT have speeded up the process of creating a solution for existing or merging customers but the fundamental ways of working remain the same. The hallmarks of the system are communication, cooperation, competition and coordination. Textile production in Prato has grown threefold and continues to expand, while in the rest of Europe it continues to decline.

There are other case studies.

- Puma, the German global sportswear company, retains in-house only the functions of strategy, marketing and network coordination.
- The PC display division of Finnish company Nokia turns over US$160 million, controlling 17 per cent of the US market with a total of five employees. In-house functions are brand control, marketing and finance, with everything else outsourced. Some of it (for example, manufacturing) is outsourced back to the parent company.
- Cavendish Management Resources brings together the business consulting and investment capabilities of over 150 free agents, who have built up an investment base of over 200 million pounds. It is effectively run by its founder and two administrative support staff.[3]

It seems there is a future for this kind of virtual organisation, one that is not dependent on hi-tech but rather on a successful blend of people and process management skills. It calls for a leadership skill set that is very different from the traditional organisational structure—the command-and-control personality need not apply.

Some of the other experiments now taking place may eventually bear fruit. Trying to run an organisation over the Internet or using video hook-ups is not easy and it will be many years before we can say whether it is even possible.

Those doing it now may claim success but it will take time to demonstrate whether it is a lasting way of doing business.

In the nineteenth century, Max Weber wrote about organisations that he saw around him, recording and describing their characteristics. Today, organisations are being set up with a 'look at us—aren't we clever' attitude. Even the dot-com crash that saw out the last century did not dent this confidence that organisations can be structured very differently from the traditional ways.

In any case, as more research emerges over time, it will become clearer what core competencies are needed for virtual organisation. In the meantime, *the* virtual organisation is still largely a figment of hi-tech, low-reality imagination.

Competitive advantage through structure

One reason for at least thinking about structure is that it is emerging as a potential competitive advantage. Those who are able to design and implement a structure that is driven by the needs of their business environment are likely to succeed where others may fail.

Organisational design is still emerging as a discipline but, over many years, researchers such as Nadler and Tushman[4] have brought considerable rigour to the process. In some ways they are unique, in that not many other researchers are able to combine disciplined academic research with the practical application they undertake as organisational consultants. In this emerging field, these two really do stand out.

Nadler and Tushman have noted a sea change over the last decade in how business is conducted. Information technology is finally making the impact on business that has been predicted for so long. Its impact on organisational structure is becoming apparent as we witness the emergence of new structures such as the virtual organisation, the network organisation, the global organisation and many other variants.

Organisation design aims to clarify the thinking that sits behind some of these changes. It is driven by clear principles:

1 The environment of an organisation drives its strategy.
2 The organisation's strategy determines its organisational 'architecture'.
3 There is a dynamic, not a static, relationship between strategy and structure.

4 The design of an organisation must balance the pressures for differentiation (pursuing different markets and developing new products) and integration (maintaining a cohesive and coherent organisation).

Today, the business environment is changing. Major changes include the globalisation of national economies, the impact of the Internet on business, the emergence of the information economy and the increasing fragmentation of consumer markets. These changes call for a strategic response from business.

New structural drivers

Nadler and Tushman identify a number of strategic imperatives that have come to the fore over the last decade that should inform thinking about structure for the next decade.

- *Increased strategic clock speed*—the need to respond ever more quickly to ever more changes in the operating environment, driven primarily by the adoption of new technologies.
- *Focused portfolios*—the emergence of strategic enterprises (in contrast with the conglomerate structures of the last twenty years) that bring a sharp focus on creating sustainable value, often using a narrow set of core competencies.
- *Abbreviated strategic life cycles*—the need to devise strategies that may last for only a year or less before they have to be recast and reinvented.
- *'Go-to-market' flexibility*—the ability to meet specific buyer needs in different markets whether by differentiation, pricing, service, customisation or speed of delivery.
- *Enhanced competitive innovation*—traditionally limited to products and processes, innovation is also needed in areas such as strategy development and organisation structure where it may provide a competitive edge.
- *Intra-enterprise cannibalism*—the need to invest in new products and distribution channels that may ultimately undermine existing revenue streams, and doing so in much shorter cycles.[5]

How organisations respond to these imperatives may well determine whether they will survive the next decade. The rate of decline and disappearance that is now obvious in the computer industry (remember former IT hardware giants such as Wang, DEC, Olivetti and, most recently, Compaq merging with Hewlett Packard) is spreading to other industries.

Nadler and Tushman suggest these responses.

- Increase the clock speed of your organisation.
- Design your organisation to be flexible.
- Promote a modular approach to organisation design, borrowing from templates to speed up the design process.
- Develop hybrid and novel distribution channels and review them constantly.
- Encourage diversity and innovation in R&D.
- Construct robust conflict-management processes to maintain stability.
- Develop organisational coherence through values, culture and shared goals.
- Use the 'executive team' concept to lead the organisation.[6]

In particular, they advocate the last two points as a way to survive what will be an increasingly turbulent environment. Whereas once the organisation was held together by formal structures (job descriptions, hierarchical structures, lines of command, etc.) and strong management control, those elements are now potential brakes on the emergence of more flexible ways of working together. In the words of Nadler and Tushman:

What is clear is that the organization of the future, in order to succeed, will become less dependent on the independent actions of disaggregated individuals. To succeed, organizations will have to develop a competency in the design and leadership of executive teams, a collective skill that will be just as important as the ability to design innovative strategies and organizational architectures.[7]

Structure may not be a sexy topic in management but it still has plenty of potential to provide competitive edge.

Guidelines

1 Review your structure

Many organisations still rely on a structure that was developed many years ago in circumstances that are no longer relevant, by people no longer in the organisation and for reasons no one can remember.

There are advantages in having an organisational structure that supports the strategies you are pursuing. At the opposite extreme, if the structure is a barrier to your strategic efforts, obviously it will hold back your organisation from achieving its objectives.

So, review your organisational structure on the basis of the principle that *structure follows strategy*. Work back from your strategy to determine what you want the organisation to be able to do. And then apply that logic to the structural and organisational elements. It's not rocket science and you don't need a consultant. You only need to be able to answer one question in the clearest possible terms:

Does the structure of my organisation support the achievement of our objectives?

If it doesn't, do something about it by making changes.

2 Examine your competitive advantage

While you may have discovered that some of your organisational arrangements (your structure) are less than helpful for achieving your organisational objectives, deciding what and how to change is not necessarily easy.

One way of deciding the most appropriate way to change is to do a bit of 'capability analysis'. Most organisations compete with others on the basis of being able to do something a bit better than their competitors. An organisation's competitive position may be based on being innovative or customer-focused or lowest-cost producer or many other things. This capability is sometimes called your 'competitive advantage'.

So, it is worth spending time to determine your competitive advantage (see also Chapter 14).

3 Choose the right structure

Once you understand your competitive advantage, work out what sort of structure will most support, enhance or enable that competitive advantage.

Example: If your competitive advantage is *customer focus* (that is, you already do or aim to provide superior customer service to your customers) then it makes sense to have an organisational structure that supports that strategy. This can be achieved by ensuring that staff who have contact with your customers are not burdened by excessive bureaucracy and layers of management when doing their jobs. In practical terms, this might mean that the first staff member to deal with a customer is able to help that customer with his or her entire needs. If, instead, the staff member must seek approval from further up the line for most decisions affecting the customer, then you have a structure that is not supportive of your strategy.

Alternatively, if your competitive advantage is *high-quality manufacturing*, you may well need several layers of management control to ensure that the final product is of exceptional quality. This demands a very different structure from the one required by a focus on responding quickly to customer needs.

Make your structure fit the strategic focus of your organisation.

For further exploration

The topic of organisation structure may sound a little boring to some but the very earliest efforts by management consultants back in the nineteenth century (such as Arthur D. Little) often focused on how to gain value from structure. Today, structure lags behind strategy as a source for competitive advantage but, for that very reason, it remains an area of organisational reform filled with high potential.

To explore these possibilities further, try the following books:
* S. Mohrman, J. Galbraith and E. Lawler, *Tomorrow's Organization*, Jossey-Bass, San Francisco, 1998.

This collection of articles covers the full gamut of what innovative organisations are doing with their structure. It includes such specialist areas as how to structure corporate boards, and how to create networked organisations, globally focused structures, learning-based organisations and a host of others.
* J. Galbraith, D. Downey and A. Kates, *Designing Dynamic Organizations*, AMACOM, New York, 2001.

This how-to guide is about designing and structuring an organisation from scratch. It assumes a 'greenfields' situation (that is, building an organisation from scratch) and provides a step-by-step process without too much technical mumbo-jumbo.
* D. Nadler and M. Tushman, *Competing by Design: The Power of Organizational Architecture*, OUP, Oxford, 1997.

In my view, these are the masters of the genre and this is by far their most accessible book to date. It provides the building blocks of the organisational design process using clear concepts based on the metaphor of designing a building.

THE INTERNAL RESOURCE ADVANTAGE   **14**

It is always dangerous when there is a dominant paradigm that grips thinking in an area of human endeavour. This is especially the case in management thinking. And in the area of strategic thinking, there is a paradigm so strong that many of its adherents cannot see room for any other way of approaching the subject.

Business strategy setting (the process of selecting what an organisation will focus on) is currently dominated by the ideas of Michael Porter, the Harvard Business School academic and consultant who has brought considerable discipline to strategic thinking. His contribution has been exceptional, but some challenges are now starting to emerge to his twenty-year-old paradigms.

It's early days, but it seems that data from the field no longer matches the assumptions made by Porter. The old paradigms are trembling.

Are there new ways of approaching strategy?

Background

Today, strategy is on every manager's lips. Everyone knows it is important in business to have your strategy right. Yet, it is a relatively recent steal from that other great field of conflict, the battleground. A hundred years ago or less, great writers on management such as Alfred P. Sloan (the man who created General Motors) could write on management without addressing the topic of strategy in any great detail.[1]

While others paved the way, Michael Porter can justly be credited with bringing the subject of strategy into vogue. In many ways, his name has become synonymous with the field of strategic management. Porter is a professor at Harvard University Business School and the author of sixteen books and over sixty articles, most of them on strategy. His key book, *Competitive Strategy: Techniques for Analyzing Industries and Competitors*,[2] was published in 1980 and the companion book, *Competitive Advantage: Creating and Sustaining Superior Performance*,[3] in 1985.

Although the finer points of strategy theory may seem remote from the competitive battleground of industry, this is another case where there is nothing as practical as a good theory. Management teams around the world are betting billions of dollars on whether they have the right formula for beating the competition. At stake is supremacy in the marketplace, and picking the right or wrong strategy can make or break the careers of even the most senior and respected figures in industry.

Today, the strategy-setting processes used by most companies are dominated by the writings of Michael Porter. No other researcher or academic has had such influence on how managers run their businesses. In particular, Porter's *Five Forces* model has become the standard way for management teams and their advisers to decide which markets to be in and what to offer the customers in those markets. The rigour and simplicity of the model account for much of its popularity, and it continues to be an effective tool for making strategic decisions.

The Five Forces model is a tool for analysing an organisation's industry structure. The model is based on the critical insight that a corporate strategy should meet the opportunities and threats that exist in the external environment. Porter identified five competitive forces that shape every industry and every market. These forces determine the intensity of competition and hence the profitability and attractiveness of an industry.

The objective of corporate strategy should be to deal with these competitive forces in a way that improves the position of the organisation. Five Forces analysis can help an organisation decide how to respond to particular characteristics of their industry.

The Five Forces are typically described as follows:

1 bargaining power of suppliers;
2 bargaining power of customers;
3 threat of new entrants;
4 threat of substitutes;
5 competitive rivalry between existing players.

Five Forces analysis can provide important and valuable information for various aspects of corporate planning, including:

- *statistical analysis* of an industry or a marketplace (for example, determining the attractiveness of an industry, assessing profitability levels and supporting decisions about entry into or exit from an industry or a market segment);

- *dynamic analysis* (for example, analysing the drivers for change in an industry by examining expected economic, social, demographic and technological changes);
- *options analysis* (for example, developing options to improve the competitive position of the organisation).

The Five Forces model is based on microeconomics. It takes into account factors such as supply and demand, complementary products and substitutes, the relationship between volume of production and cost of production, and market structures like monopoly, oligopoly or perfect competition.

As is the fate of all dominant theories, Porter's strategy framework is now being challenged. And the challenge is coming from industry research rather than strategy theory. The suggestion is that the assumptions on which Porter based his theories are not wholly in accordance with the real world.

Competitive advantage

Porter advises companies to identify their *competitive advantage*, a notion that is now part of management vocabulary. Competitive advantage allows companies to decide what it is that will enable them to survive and thrive in any given marketplace. The process he advocates for determining which advantage to pursue is largely based on a detailed analysis of what will work best in *a given industry*. Porter argues that an organisation must take into account the specifics of its industry when considering how to beat its competitors. He claims that some industries are inherently more profitable than others because of fundamental structural reasons. For example, in Australia there are some companies that thrive mainly because it is too difficult (often because of cost reasons) for overseas competitors to enter their industry. The simplest structural reason may well be a company's existing market dominance.

Porter's industry approach has been factored into many corporate planning sessions. As a result of this approach, many managers opted for low levels of performance because they were able to argue that they happened to be competing in an industry that was structurally low-profit.

The challenge to Porter and other industry-effect advocates is arising from economic data about how industries and organisations within them actually perform. Research over the last fifteen years has shown that the industry effect is much overstated. Detailed evidence from a range of industries suggests that internal organisational factors (such as market responsiveness, agility, speed-to-market capabilities or fast cycle-times) account for anything up to ten times the variations in performance than can be explained by industry factors.

Advantage from internal resources

The approach that is starting to replace Porter's theories is often known as the *resource-advantage theory* (alternative names are the *capability theory* and the *resource-based theory*).[4] The essence of the new approach to strategy is that each organisation should create sustainable competitive advantage by implementing a value-adding strategy that is *unique to that organisation*. This contrasts sharply with Porter's generic, industry-wide strategies.

Until the late 1980s strategic business thinking was dominated by the notion of *fit*. This involved a rational process of adapting the activities of an organisation to fit its competitive environment. The process typically involved the setting of objectives, the appraisal of strengths/weaknesses, the appraisal of opportunities and threats in the marketplace, and decision making about which products/services should be backed by investment choices.

Resource-advantage theory challenged the adaptation/fit approach by demonstrating that organisations that possessed certain skills and capabilities were able to outperform others who possessed different capabilities. That is, *internal* special capabilities were more important than *external* or industry factors, market opportunities or market forces. Further, despite open competition, some of these capabilities proved difficult for the competition to copy, and were possibly unique and not capable of duplication.

With the resource-based approach, the organisation bases its strategy on developing and maintaining those resources (or capabilities) of the organisation that can create a competitive edge (more about this later). Resources can be of three types:

1 physical resources—such as plant, location, or access to raw materials;
2 human resources—such as skills, knowledge or abilities;
3 organisational resources—such as culture, structure, procedures or systems.

For a resource or capability to be useful in creating a competitive edge, however, it must meet four criteria:

1 The resource must be *valuable*.
2 The resource must be *rare*.
3 There must be *no substitute* for the resource.
4 The resource must be difficult to *imitate*.

Examples of resources that meet these criteria are:

- the service culture in legendary retail organisations like Nordstrom's (it meets all four criteria);
- the incredible level of employee commitment in organisations like Southwest Airlines (other airlines copied Southwest's 'hub system' for aircraft routes but failed to copy how the employees make it all happen);
- the mass-customisation capabilities of Dell Computers (Dell eventually became vulnerable to attack from competitors because its capabilities did turn out to be imitable—but not before becoming an industry power-house).

In essence, the resource-based approach is that *the right combination of capabilities will ensure success regardless of industry conditions*. Richard Branson's Virgin Group is proving this over and over again as the company takes on tired old industries and revitalises them.

The most popular version of resource-advantage theory is that advocated by Gary Hamel and C. K. Prahalad,[5] although they focus on 'core competences' (such as organisational culture, employee skills base or leadership capability) which tends to exclude physical resources. Their version is in line with the current fashion for knowledge-based competition. However, many resource-advantage theorists argue that physical resources may well provide a more secure competitive edge than intangible capabilities. Either way, as stated earlier, the edge must be valuable, rare, non-substitutable and difficult to imitate.

The catch-cry of the resource-advantage advocates is that sustainable competitive advantage can be achieved by *competing from the inside out*. In other words, you start with some attribute of your company that you have or can acquire, and then you base your competitive strength on that by finding a market position or even a market that will value what you have to offer.

In Melbourne, for example, hire cars are taking over a substantial segment of the taxi industry simply because hire cars turn up at an agreed time and cabs will not/cannot make that commitment. Hire car companies offer their services at a slightly higher rate but, if you want to be picked up at a set time, it's worth it.

Challenges for management

So, in many organisations the search is now on for that unique set of characteristics that will make an organisation succeed whatever is happening around it. Unfortunately, the thinking tools to help management teams with this search are still in limited supply, possibly because it is a less technical process than applying Porter's standard Five Forces industry analysis.

One of the crucial questions is how to balance the competing forces of external conditions and internal resources. Porter's external factors still matter but now so do the internal factors. Having two sets of forces at work creates a more dynamic situation. Companies will have to create a balance and that is harder to do than blindly following the outcome of a Five Forces analysis.

There are few agreed prescriptions on how to do this and many different views on the best approach.

Despite this, in the last few years the resource-based approach has started to impact at boardroom level. In some cases, the change in emphasis in the strategy process is quite subtle; in other cases, it has led to high drama as pressure to define and refine internal competitive capabilities takes its toll.

The implications for managers are far-reaching. Responsibility for the success of an organisation is placed firmly in the hands of its management. Where the industry-based approach to strategy allows managers to attribute organisational failure to external factors, the resource-based approach places accountability almost completely with management. Management's strategic choices in deciding which resources to develop and deploy (effectively, picking which sustainable competitive advantage to pursue) will lead to either success or failure.

In the long term, the industry versus resources debate will settle down to a new paradigm, one that will infuse the thinking of the business schools and eventually that of industry.

Strategy is changing and, whenever change is afoot in areas as important as strategising, it usually pays for managers to keep a keen lookout. In this case, the challenge is to stay abreast of the issue, rather than make a specific commitment to action. Stay tuned for developments.

Guidelines

1 Check your capabilities

Regardless of whether or not you think Porter has the answer to everything when it comes to strategy, there are also advantages to considering the resource view (that is, that competitive advantage comes from within the organisation, and not from external conditions).

- Understand the internal characteristics of your organisation that give it advantage over others.
- Review how you create value for your customers compared with your competitors.
- Examine the barriers to others duplicating what you do (for example, if the capability rests entirely on the skills and knowledge of your staff, that resource could walk out the door to your competitors tomorrow).
- Can you control the full panoply of resources needed to deliver what the customer wants?

2 Develop your capabilities

It is likely that you will find some aspects of your overall capacity where you have advantage over your competitors.

- Identify those aspects and study them to fully understand their potential to do something that others can't do, or can't do as well.
- Be very realistic in this assessment; this is not the time for rose-coloured glasses. In fact, think worst-case scenario. But don't be discouraged—the mere fact that you are still out there in the competitive arena competing suggests that you are doing some things right, maybe 'righter' than others.

3 Identify possible unique capabilities

Maybe you will find some capabilities that are unique. Maybe you will find some that can be strengthened to the point where they are unique. These can form the basis for developing competitive advantage.

This could take time, but that is good because it will make it that much harder for others to copy you. For example, hiring skilled people can be easily copied by anyone. But having people work together in a cohesive way because of a culture that encourages that way of working can't be copied overnight by your competitors.

You will probably find that most capabilities with the potential to be of lasting strategic advantage are fairly ephemeral. Privileged access to external resources, to proprietary technology or to a market all tend to be equalised over time.

Having a strongly supportive organisational culture (for example, Microsoft) or exceptional leadership (for example, General Electric) or continuous improvement capabilities (for example, Toyota) are far less tangible but also far more powerful.

For further exploration

Paradigm shifts are always difficult to pick. Usually, no one can say for sure that the dominant paradigm has shifted until we have a historical perspective on the matter. It is a case of hindsight being the best viewpoint. But, occasionally, in the midst of the change, we can see the ground shifting away from one best way of doing something to multiple ways of doing it.

Until a few years ago, the only way to do strategising was to follow Porter's models. Today, other views are starting to penetrate the thinking of organisations. At the moment, possibly the most influential writer leading the charge away from Porter is Gary Hamel. This book had considerable impact:

- G. Hamel, *Competence Based Competition,* John Wiley & Co, New York, 1994.

More recently, Hamel has banged the drum for his version of the resource view in books such as:

- G. Hamel and C.K. Prahalad, *Competing for the Future*, Harvard Business School Press, Boston, 1996.
- G. Hamel, *Leading the Revolution,* Harvard Business School Press, Boston, 2000.

But however fast or slow the paradigm is shifting, Michael Porter's enormous influence on the subject of strategy continues. For a superb introduction to the subject, try:

- M. Porter, 'What is strategy?', *Harvard Business Review*, Nov–Dec 1996.

CULTURAL DIVERSITY   **15**

Many organisations claim that their people are their most
valuable resource. Yet few organisations behave as if they
actually believe that. If we were to judge from their actions, we
could only conclude that people are their most expendable
and contingent resource.

Those who really do believe in the value of their employees
are reaping some unexpected benefits. For example, for many
companies that are trying to compete in a global marketplace
the diversity of their workforce is becoming an asset. As a
country, Australia has a better multicultural approach than
many others. Australia's businesses, however, are yet to
maximise the benefits.

What are the real business benefits of diversity?

Background

With 'globalisation' the word on everyone's lips, the work of
Dutch academic researcher, Fons Trompenaars, and English
management consultant, Chris Hampden-Turner,[1] provides a
comprehensive and practical framework for understanding
cultural diversity, with a particular emphasis on the challenges
presented by managing cultural diversity for business success.

Cultural differences

The differences between cultures are explored through seven
dimensions of culture, each one a continuum. The first five are
about the relationships we have with others; the last two
concern how we relate to time and to our environment. The
continuum scales are:
1 universalism/particularism
2 individualism/communitarianism
3 neutral/emotional
4 specific/diffuse
5 achievement/ascription
6 sequential time/synchronic time
7 internal locus of control/external locus of control.

Some of the above may seem like techno-babble but the
distinctions do pick up on fundamental differences between
national cultures. For example, who in the Anglo (sequential
time) world has not made jokes about the meaning—or lack

thereof—of time in Latino (typically synchronic time) cultures? Or noticed the 'emotional' ways of doing things in many European countries (very obvious to people from Japan or Ethiopia, countries which have extremely 'neutral' cultures when it comes to emotion)? Or spoken of the importance of rewarding individual achievement (a low priority in highly communitarian cultures such as India and Mexico)?

Some national cultural patterns are quite surprising. For example, the achievement/ascription scale reflects how we accord status to other people: who you are versus what you have done. Only a handful of Northern European/North American countries are extremely achievement-focused (what you have done), whereas in the bulk of other countries around the globe achievement is tempered by a more relaxed view. Recent success is not everything, and past connections and relationships matter greatly (who you are).

When cultural differences meet—as they must in global business—the potential for misunderstanding and conflict is extremely high. Such conflict can be at the very least a barrier to successful business and at worst completely destructive.

Another issue to be considered is the impact (if any) of national cultures on organisational culture. In a multicultural society such as Australia, the culture of a particular enterprise is usually an amalgam of the national cultures of the employees, overlaid by the Australian national culture. This creates dynamics that are far more intense than might be the case in a more homogeneous society. It is common to see a Melbourne-based factory with Anglo-Celtic senior managers, older Italian or Greek supervisors and a shop-floor melting pot of Asian, Slavic, Arabic and South American workers. It makes the concept of organisational culture somewhat fluid!

The benefits of diversity

Diversity implies the inclusion of all groups at all levels in an organisation. In addition to the moral and ethical reasons for adopting and encouraging diversity, economic and strategic benefits accrue for an organisation able to integrate diversity into its cultural objectives. In addition, the ethnic demographic in many countries affects not only the employee body, but also the customer base.

Diversity adds value because it provides the organisation with a wide range of competencies. It bestows benefits that are cumulative over time. In some ways, it can be likened to a 'virtuous circle'. As an organisation becomes known as a good place to work (and diversity adds to that reputation), it attracts high-calibre people from diverse backgrounds who, in turn, help to make the organisation more successful. This enhances its reputation even further and so the circle is perpetuated.

Despite equal opportunity legislation and affirmative action policies, a commitment to diversity has not been universally embraced in the business world. Some companies conform in principle, but find that delivery falters.

Managing diversity

Successful management of diversity requires attention to policies, education and action. But does this happen in practice?

Gilbert and Ivancevich[2] conducted a three-year study of two companies, both part of major conglomerates in the United States. Their findings (released in 2000) provide a case study of how to (and how not to) use diversity to the advantage of the organisation. Although the two examples represent top-level companies, the findings are equally applicable to smaller firms.

In the first company (termed 'the Multicultural Organisation'), diversity was a dominant feature of planning and management sought to build on that approach. The second (called 'the Plural Organisation') experienced difficulty in maintaining early initiatives and hoped to improve on its record.

The authors established five crucial features influencing the success or otherwise of diversity initiatives:
1 CEO initiation and support
2 human resource initiatives
3 organisational communication
4 corporate philosophy
5 establishment of measures of success.

So how did the two companies compare in their support and implementation of diversity initiatives?

Role of the CEO
- *The Multicultural Organisation.* The CEO was committed to the philosophy of diversity and its long-term benefits, and assumed an educative role.
- *The Plural Organisation.* The CEO, though aiming at global recognition, did not have a perception of the *value* of

diversity. He attributed the company's low performance to issues of pay and competition, and did not recognise the negative effects of racial conflict and gender bias. Minority workers, particularly women, were not attracted to the company and were underrepresented at management level.

Role of the HR department
- *The Multicultural Organisation.* The HR department implemented a number of inclusionary policies. The CEO promoted a plan for the year 2001, with emphasis on hiring 50 per cent women and non-whites as new recruits, and aiming to promote the same two groupings to one-third of supervisory positions. In order to pursue recruiting opportunities, the company forged strong links with college campuses that espoused diversity. Attendance at career fairs and ethnic-based professional conferences was also targeted for recruiting purposes. The company instituted 'family-friendly' workplaces, including leave variants, flex-time, job sharing, telecommuting and childcare, as well as promoting religious tolerance.

  Management elevated the status of diversity issues by designating a vice-president to be responsible for overseeing practices, conducting an annual conference and preparing educational material.
- *The Plural Organisation.* The organisation showed no such enthusiasm, lacking any comparable HRM involvement across the corporation.

Communication about diversity
- *The Multicultural Organisation.* Communication was assisted by the appointment in several of the plants of employee equality councils. Suggestions were considered for keeping the subject of equality before the entire workforce, as were complaints or negative comments. A continuous two-way flow of information across the company, and specific promotions to celebrate ethnicity and difference, were vital to the scheme.
- *The Plural Organisation.* Racial tensions built up and were not dealt with effectively. Efforts to promote communication were inconsistent and not necessarily followed through. Workers were not kept informed of findings of such initiatives as surveys and expected no significant changes.

Corporate philosophy

- *The Multicultural Organisation.* A corporate-wide philosophy was adopted and became a common cause to which all employees were accountable. Workers were encouraged to see the competitive edge of diversity.
- *The Plural Organisation.* Each plant was autonomous, reducing the strength of policy making and risking inconsistencies in practice. Plants that did endeavour to implement a policy of diversity did not receive funding support for promotion and education.

Measures of success

- *The Multicultural Organisation.* It focused on the value of human capital and sought to be an employer of choice, known for good management. Managerial accountability was taken as far as linking a percentage of remuneration to successful interaction with diverse individuals.
- *The Plural Organisation.* Diversity was used as a PR tool, rather than a core element of competitive advantage.

Management at the Plural Organisation did not openly disparage diversity, but the absence of any pro-diversity message had a similar impact. By comparison, the CEO and executive team of the Multicultural Organisation actively endorsed diversity. The philosophy of 'everyone being different' as opposed to 'a few people looking different' was a major contributor to successful management.

As to the ultimate pay-off for the Multicultural Organisation, yes, it is more profitable. But this study focused on two different ways of handling the diversity issue rather than proving the pay-off point. (For more details of the economic benefits of multicultural organisations, see Hampden-Turner and Trompenaars.[3])

On a broader scale, it is interesting to note that data from the Fortune 500 firms in 1999/2000 indicates that, although three-quarters have some form of inclusion policy, in many of those firms education for diversity was not taken seriously. Only a small proportion reported CEO involvement, with a much larger percentage showing that the support was minimal.[4] This has clear consequences for management of diversity.

As for Australia, it remains in the forefront of creating a peaceful multicultural society. Our migration programs continue to drive a wide-ranging ethnic diversity without raising much controversy. The issue for business is how to take advantage of this situation. And that issue does not always make it into the executive boardroom. The following questions sum up the issue for management.

- How can effective management of diversity contribute to your organisation's performance?
- What actions are needed to achieve or increase diversity?
- What educational programs or initiatives will be needed to support and reinforce the process?
- What will be the benefits of diversity to your organisation, and how can they be measured?

Guidelines

1 Explain the value

Explain to all stakeholders that a commitment to diversity implies an acceptance of difference in all people associated with the organisation.

Diversity adds to the range of capabilities that an organisation is able to draw on. For example, a culturally diverse organisation is much more capable of operating in a global marketplace with its attendant needs for language and other cultural skills. If you need to deal with suppliers and customers overseas and you can do so in their language and customs, then you are ahead of the competition.

2 Include people

Implement an 'inclusive policy' backed up by leadership initiatives, education and reinforcement. Inclusion means that people are made to feel that they can contribute even if they do not fit the stereotypical image of the Australian manager: white, male, old and Anglo-Celtic. Leaders tend to look for people like themselves because they fit their idea of competence. (The researchers call this tendency 'homosocial' selection—that is, picking people like us because they fit our image of successful people.)

Find ways to include diversity into other corporate initiatives.

3 Realise the value

Promote the fact that diversity is a contributor to organisational performance. To do that effectively, you need to know what you've got in the way of culturally diverse resources.

Most Australian organisations have people with a multitude of language and other cultural skills yet they seem unaware of this resource. Do a survey to find out; look for projects that will enable you to include people for their special capabilities; find ways of drawing out the skills that people have. It is a fact of life that, when migrants move to a new country, they typically find employment at a lower level than they are qualified for in their country of origin. (Proficiency in English or lack of portability of formal qualifications holds them back.)

Find out who you've got buried away in the back rooms of your organisation and help get them back up to professional scratch.

For further exploration

Diversity tends to be treated as an issue for human resource management professionals (that is, the Personnel Department) rather than something that line managers have to worry about. If your idea of diversity management amounts to more than just adhering to legislative requirements, then try:

- F. Trompenaars and C. Hampden-Turner, *Riding the Waves of Culture*, McGraw-Hill, New York, 1998.

This book makes the topic more accessible to business and management people than most others.

The other great writer and researcher in this field is Geert Hofstede. His best known work is possibly:

- G. Hofstede, *Cultures and Organizations*, McGraw-Hill, New York, 1996.

Hofstede provides a slightly different framework for describing culture but also gives sound advice on how to manage and take advantage of cultural diversity. There is something of a longstanding feud between Trompenaars (the former student) and Hofstede (the former master) which infuses their debates with an interesting emotional tinge. There is actually more in common between their respective approaches than they like to admit.

- C. Hampden-Turner and F. Trompenaars, *Building Cross Cultural Competence: How to Create Wealth from Conflicting Values*, Yale University Press, New Haven, 2000.

This book tackles the diversity issue from the point of view of how to build and develop the managerial competencies that allow organisations to take advantage of the diversity in their organisations and beyond.

ORGANISATIONAL CULTURE 16

Organisational culture has become the handy all-round excuse for a host of ills in our organisations. Whenever a manager tries to explain why something isn't working, there is a tendency to reach for the explanation that the culture in the place is just not right. Ask that same manager to define or describe what is mean by culture, however, and the conversation soon dries up.

Although it is true that culture explains the reality of an organisation, the concept is by no means simple, and working with culture is a whole lot more complex and difficult than doing a restructure or recruiting people. Changing the culture requires a degree of effort that is beyond most organisations. Even worse, there is still so much debate about what organisational culture actually is, that from a practical management viewpoint it is most perplexing.

Is it possible to do anything meaningful about organisational culture?

Background

In industry, the phrase 'organisational culture' has become a mantra. In academia, the model building and theory constructing carries on apace. In between, we have the consultants, devising ever more ingenious applications.

It is probably the case that management's real interest in the concept of organisational culture derives from its failure to mould organisations and people to its will. The traditional mechanisms of job description, structure chart and lines-of-authority have recently not delivered the kind of pliant but effective organisation that management is seeking. The problem is that the discretionary component of most people's jobs is increasing.

Management wants to engineer employee commitment without giving up control. Fiddling with organisational culture appeals to the engineering mindset and provides a chimera of hope: that it is possible to create commitment without ceding any power. Unfortunately, experience is starting to show that it is only a chimera.

Nevertheless, we should celebrate the fact that industry is at least and at last taking an interest in a model of organisation that is not mechanistic. If 'scientific management' gave us the corporation as a machine, at least the advocates of organisational culture have given us a more complex view of the entities in which most of us spend our working lives.

The concept of organisational culture

Developments in Britain (sociotechnical systems thinking from the Tavistock Institute) and the United States (the human relations school from the National Training Laboratory) in the 1950s drew our attention to the *human* side of the organisation, thereby describing a facet that Fred Taylor had not so much ignored as tried to engineer away.

This view of the organisation received a major boost in the 1970s, when anthropologists started to take an interest in the modern organisation and organisational theorists started to take an interest in what the anthropologists were saying. The language used was that of anthropology—that is, the organisation was seen as a *culture*. Culture was defined as 'a construct describing the total body of belief, behaviour, knowledge, sanctions, values, and goals that make up the way of life of a people'.[1]

The year 1982 saw the publication of the books *In Search of Excellence*[2] and *Corporate Culture*[3] which contributed to both the academic and popular transformation of culture in organisations to *organisational culture*. The former book linked excellence to a strong and unifying organisational culture, based on a shared vision. *Corporate Culture* added substance to the growing debate and helped to popularise the concept. From that point on, culture was 'in' and vision was the way to get to it. An earlier and simplistic description of organisational culture—'the way we do things around here'—was quickly rediscovered and widely disseminated.[4]

Various attempts have been made to integrate competing models into a holistic approach[5] and today there is a variety of approaches to 'operationalising' the concept of organisational culture. From the point of view of managing the development of an organisation, two notions stand out as showing some promise: the distinct concepts of *types* and *levels* of organisational culture.

Cultural type and cultural levels

One way of coming to grips with diversity is to group whatever phenomena we are examining into groups or types.

For example, the grand diversity of human behaviour is much better understood when we group people on the basis of some perceived similarities. So the psychologists provide us with 'personality types'. They have developed instruments that make it easy to categorise people into one type or other—for example, the Myers-Briggs Type Indicator which is much used in industry to match people to jobs.[6] And so it is with organisational culture.

Types of culture

Researchers have used the notion of *cultural type* in an attempt to give us categories that make it a bit easier to understand what sort of culture we are dealing with.

One application of this idea is that of *national cultural types*. This field of research is a lively and dynamic one, providing much amusement for the observer—for example, the incessant sniping between the old master Hofstede and the former student Trompenaars[7] as to which of their models is more effective in capturing the impact of national culture on organisational culture. Both actually propose similar models of cultural type that allow us to understand better the differences between nationalities (see also Chapter 15). The two theorists spend much of their time consulting to multinational corporations that are trying to cope with all the different nationalities represented in their organisations.

Another approach to cultural type is to try to categorise the diversity found *within* organisations. Most people have a sense that the organisations they know about are different and yet similar in many ways. The most accessible and useful examples of this approach are the models proposed by Roger Harrison[8] and Charles Handy.[9] The work of both is well applied in industry, providing similar models that help to explain that organisations embody elements of four distinct organisational types. Using Handy's language, the types are:

1 **Power culture**. This type of culture values central control, which is typically exercised by appointing loyal individuals who are subservient to the centre and who will work to maintain the power structure. Power is exercised on the basis of personal influence rather than on the basis of procedures or logical reasons. Effectiveness is judged on results achieved in shoring up the centre of the organisation.

2 **Role culture**. Often referred to as a bureaucracy, this culture works by logic and rationality. Its pillars are functions and specialisations. Departmental functions are delineated and power comes from role—for example, finance is powerful because of what it does. The work of the organisation is controlled by formal procedures and role descriptions. There are well defined systems such as committees and procedure manuals. Efficiency comes from the rational allocation of work and conscientious performance of defined responsibilities.

3 **Task culture**. This culture is like a net of small teams and cells. It represents the 'small team' approach to organisations: the network organisation. So the large organisation consists of lots of little ones that make their contribution. Power and influence are distributed to the interstices of the net. The emphasis is on results and getting things done. People are brought together and given decision-making power to get on with the task, and are allocated resources as needed. The main focus and working relationships are founded on capability rather than status.

4 **Person culture**. The individual is the central point. If there is a structure it exists only to serve the individuals within it. If a group of individuals decide to band together, the group lasts only as long as it gets something done for the individuals involved. This culture may be the only acceptable organisation to particular groups, such as consultants or lawyers, where individuals basically work on their own but find some central back-up useful. Power is by consent, influence is shared and the power base, if needed, is usually the expertise of individuals.

The idea of cultural type, however, does not explain the full story of organisational culture. Type theories are limited by the fact that they are rather one-dimensional. The measurement tools that back them up tend to put organisations into one pigeonhole or another, rather than provide a whole and complete picture.

It is somewhat similar to people being pigeonholed by the Myers-Briggs Type Indicator into a box with a four-letter description attached to it such as INTJ. Some people are very annoyed by the idea that they could be so simply and easily categorised. Organisational culture might, if it could speak, make the same complaint and say that it is more complex than just this or that type.

This complexity led some researchers to an entirely different idea for coming to grips with culture.

Levels of culture

The real challenge in all this is how to operationalise some of these concepts. In other words, what can managers actually do with these notions? One of the better attempts to do this treats organisational culture as something that has *levels*.

The notion of levels is associated mostly with Edgar Schein.[10] However, his framework has been developed and enhanced by, among others, the Bath Consulting Group[11] over a long period of time. It is an elegantly practical way of dealing with the complexity of the issue of culture.

The *levels* framework portrays organisational culture as having five distinct levels:

- Level 1—**Artifacts** (for example, policy statements, vision statements, dress codes, building layout).
- Level 2—**Behaviour** (for example, what people do, what is rewarded, how mistakes are dealt with).
- Level 3—**Mindset** (for example, how the organisation sees the world, the paradigms that drive it).
- Level 4—**Values** (for example, the shared beliefs of the organisation, what is held to be important).
- Level 5—**Motivational roots** (for example, the deepest sense of meaning that the organisation provides for its members).

The levels can be used to understand what it is you are trying to do. This understanding can drive the actions you take as a manager while also accepting the limits of those actions.

Unfortunately, many managers work on the superficial first level. For example, in discussing cultural change, they focus on artifacts (Level 1), but struggle with behaviour (Level 2) and never even dream of the rest. This may well explain the failure of vision-driven change programs!

Operating only on Level 1 exposes managers to the oft-heard charge that they rarely do themselves what they expect from others. For example: the vision statement says that the organisation encourages innovation, yet every mistake arising out of experimentation is punished; the mission statement says that the customer is king, yet any deviation from procedure to satisfy a customer is severely dealt with.

Managing culture for advantage

Turning an understanding of culture into a practical management tool is another matter. The notion of culture has strong explanatory power, but that does not make it into a handy tool for gaining benefits. It does allow managers to link some of their actions to an ultimate objective—that is, creating a certain kind of culture. We have few tools that will assist managers in this task (but see *For further exploration* for some suggestions).

Culture as a brand

One interesting approach that leverages off the notion of culture is to consider the image that the organisation projects to its own employees (and potential employees).

Employees are playing an increasingly critical part in realising an organisation's objectives, so the organisation's ability to attract, retain and mobilise its people is vital. It follows, then, that the company's culture is an important factor in meeting employees' needs. To ensure that the culture supports the organisation's goals, the culture must be identified, guided and carefully managed, otherwise it may develop characteristics that work to counter what the organisation is trying to achieve.

A way to achieve this is to manage culture by using the marketing concepts of *brand* and *touch points*.[12]

- An organisation's culture can be viewed as a *brand* because it affects the operation of an organisation in the same way that a consumer product brand image affects the thinking and purchasing behaviour of consumers.
- The *touch points* of an organisation are all the ways that consumers come into contact with (or touch) the brand (for example, packaging, product quality or customer service). The goal in marketing is to ensure that each touch point communicates a consistent and positive message, which then contributes to a strong brand image.

Almost everything that people do or produce can be a *cultural touch point*, because culture is embodied through *actions*. For this approach to be successful, however, both management and employees must be aware of how people, both internal and external, come into contact with a company's culture, and ensure that a consistent message is portrayed via each touch point. In other words, it must be managed accordingly. If touch points are left unmanaged, the result will be mixed messages that can result in a weakening of the organisation's culture. Examples include the elements of corporate life listed below. Each drives employees' behaviour, either towards one extreme or towards its opposite. This may be through cooperation or competition, individualism or collectiveness, formality or informality. All such behaviour collectively drives culture.

- **Compensation programs**. Is teamwork or competition among employees to be rewarded?
- **Office layout**. Is it to be conducive to teamwork and collaboration or to individual work?
- **Communication**. Is it formal and closed or comfortable with informal channels?
- **Policies**. Both the choice of policies and the way in which they are presented should be considered.
- **Perquisites**. Perks should reflect the desired culture. For example, are family benefits emphasised, or are rewards for individuals encouraged?

It may help if we look at culture as if it were the personality of the organisation. Setting the tone for behaviour and interactions within a company, it deeply influences how employees work together to identify and execute strategies. Organisations can manage their culture through various touch points, and these can be used to reinforce or modify the culture in a way that supports both the organisation and its goals.

Case study—Jellyvision Inc.
A case study of the use of touch points is the US company, Jellyvision Inc.[13] (interactive media experiences). Jellyvision has put a great deal of effort into managing its culture through touch points, particularly the less obvious ones, such as the way it communicates with its employees, rewards them and confers titles.

The result is a strong culture, broadly categorised by collaboration, teamwork, trust, creativity and open communication. This has served the company well in attracting, retaining and focusing employees, and influences all company dealings.

Jellyvision has a unique organisational flow chart, which incorporates a circus theme! It depicts a cluster of hand-drawn figures organised into levels through balancing on trapezes and tightropes, while performing appropriate acts. For example, the producing/coordination position is held by a figure juggling several items. The chart illustrates every aspect of the company's culture—for example, trust and collaboration are depicted by the fact that if one person is removed the whole structure will collapse.

This small example demonstrates that communicating what is important in an organisation needs more than a vision statement in the foyer. To create meaning, it may be necessary to do something exceptional if only because exceptional things attract interest and attention. If your organisation wants a culture that truly values its customers, find a way of proving this to your employees by some unforgettable means. Or don't bother at all.

The manager's role

Changing organisational culture is difficult and some researchers argue that it is impossible. But managers *can* affect the culture of their organisation. Indeed, a manager's behaviour constantly shores up the culture of a workplace (or otherwise—but such managers usually don't last long!).

1 The *current culture* must be examined to determine the extent to which it supports business objectives. This is easier for companies with a strong and distinct culture. Some of the clues that help to understand a company's culture have been outlined (see the discussion of touch points above). Important information can also be gained by asking the opinions of employees.

2 The *ideal culture* must be examined. This should be a reflection of the long-term vision, mission and strategy of the company. It is then possible to identify the types of behaviour necessary for the company to reach its objectives.

The jury is out on whether the concept of organisational culture is actually useful or not. It helps with understanding but does not really offer many options for managerial action. Meanwhile, an organisation's culture will evolve whether it is actively managed or not. Given its apparent importance to organisational success, it seems sensible to do what we can within our limited understanding of this rather shady concept.

Guidelines

1 Use culture as a lever

Consider culture as one more lever that can be used by managers to gain business results. Culture is harder to work with than organisational structure, for example, but it has far greater potential to shape the organisation and align it with the strategic intent being pursued.

Culture is more resistant to change, but that only means that if you can align it more effectively with strategy then you have a powerful instrument on your side. Further, it is an organisational element that others will have great difficulty in copying.

So, creating a preferred culture can be more worthwhile as an investment of management time than most other levers available to management.

2 Culture can be managed

Although it takes a bit more thought than an organisational restructure (anyone can draw lines and boxes), culture can be changed.

First, it involves understanding the notion itself.

Then create a picture of both the existing and the preferred culture. The preferred culture should derive from the needs of the strategy of the organisation.

Then, use all available mechanisms to drive change towards the preferred culture:

- recruitment
- training
- managerial behaviour
- communication
- all other systems and processes.

It requires effort but the pay-off is far better than a new org chart will ever deliver.

3 Manage the brand

Use the notion of *culture as brand* to review what your organisational culture looks like. It is likely that some people in your organisation are experienced in using brand to shape opinion and beliefs (try the marketing department).

Marketing concepts and tools are well researched and proven. Use them to create the kind of brand that you want for the organisation.

Manage your *internal brand image* as you would the external brands that you promote to your customers.

For further exploration

Despite a general fascination on the part of managers with the notion of organisational culture, operationalising the concept has proved rather elusive. The academics are still building theories, and the consultants don't advertise in detail what they can do for you (but I can guarantee it won't be cheap!).

One approach that is both sound and practical is provided by the group of researchers, academics and consultants associated with Professor Robert Quinn. This group has no qualms about putting its methods into the public domain and the most practical of their books so far is:

- K. Cameron and R. Quinn, *Diagnosing and Changing Organizational Culture*, Addison Wesley, Reading, 1999.

The book is a practical manager's dream (and possibly a consultant's nightmare) in that it provides a step-by-step process for understanding, measuring and changing the culture of an organisation. Every tool is provided and explained. Even the theoretical discussions are approachable and comprehensive.

As a further step, you might want to consider Quinn's highly personal approach to painting the dilemmas of management. I know of no other writer who so powerfully captures the impossibilities of the job and all its accompanying trials and tribulations:

- R. Quinn, *Beyond Rational Management*, Jossey-Bass, San Francisco, 1988.
- R. Quinn, *Deep Change*, Jossey-Bass, San Francisco, 1996.

RENEWAL AND INNOVATION **17**

Renewal is not a hot topic for management. It tends to be placed on the back burner because too many other and more pressing issues take priority. And, in effect, that means that for many organisations the topic is never addressed. You can check on this by asking any manager you know (or yourself) when was the last time the most senior managers in the organisation thought about how the organisation could reinvent itself for changing circumstances.

Part of the problem is that renewal, as a topic, sounds a bit academic. It certainly isn't as tough-sounding as talking about competitive advantage, strategic decision making or restructuring. Another part of the problem is that many managers don't know where to start when thinking about the issue of renewal. For example, they may have a vague feeling that things are speeding up in the marketplace, and that action is needed by the organisation just to keep up. But an actual starting point for renewal and growth escapes them.

How do you encourage organisational renewal?

Background

For many companies, the new and pressing realities are global competition, emerging technologies, ever increasing customer demands and the need to create greater shareholder value. Organisational changes introduced to meet these challenges all share one common element: the loosening of organisational boundaries.

Organisational boundaries

Organisations have found success in renewal in many different ways. Motorola, for example, reduced product development cycles by replacing traditional functional approaches with cross-functional teams of professionals. GE flattened its hierarchy to four or five levels. SmithKline Beecham used teleconferencing to involve 100 people worldwide in designing its new structure.

All are examples of changes being made to the *boundaries* of the organisation:

- internal vertical boundaries (hierarchy);
- internal horizontal boundaries (linkages between functions);

- external boundaries (customer–supplier relationships);
- geographical boundaries (global cooperation).

Make no mistake: boundaries are needed, not least to define the organisation. The nature and utility of those boundaries is the issue.

Case study—Retail Financial Services (GE)

Retail Financial Services (RFS), a subsidiary of GE Capital, supplies private label credit cards to industry. In ten years, it transformed itself from a dying enterprise into a global dynamo.

In 1982, when RFS was failing financially, GE tried to sell the business but was unable to find a buyer. A new management team was installed with instructions not to lose money. The new team quickly identified that past thinking had focused on the end-users: card-carrying customers. The new team realised that the real customers were the stores that issued the cards. This led to the realisation that speed of processing new card applications was the critical success factor for gaining and retaining business.

The *external boundary* of slow processing was fully appreciated when the CEO 'walked' an application through the full process. It took several weeks and dozens of employees, each executing their little piece of the process.

Company resources for improving the process were limited but the CEO did obtain some GE Capital systems resources to work on a solution. Once the new systems were in place, functional groups involved in processing a card application were brought together and given the challenge of reducing the two-week processing period to two days. This very precise and specific goal energised the workforce and within months the issue time was down to two days.

Now that the processes were organised around meeting customer needs, the next matter to be addressed was the *vertical boundary* created by expensive management control systems. The traditional management hierarchy was replaced by regional business centres staffed with cross-functional teams, thus generating considerable savings. More savings were realised when the centres were established as self-managing teams. As well as cost savings, this led to better customer service and increased job satisfaction.

The abolition of hierarchy did not happen without a number of difficult problems. Resistance was encountered from many, and turnover of staff and managers was substantial. Managers in particular had problems adjusting to the new way of working. Almost all the former authority of the managers went directly to the teams. Many managers could not adjust to the role change this brought.

RFS was now positioned to expand and it did so with great success, moving into markets in the UK, Austria and Sweden in the space of a few years. Today, each business centre in each country operates independently but as part of a global enterprise. The final boundary of *geography* is being conquered through information and communication technology.[1]

Boundary-busting renewal

Boundary-busting requires considerable effort and takes time. Here are five key principles to keep in mind:[2]

1 The goal is not to become boundary-*less*. The goal is to institutionalise the improvements (for example, speed of processing or innovation) that lead to sustainable corporate success.

2 Success at creating the improvements requires the involvement of many in solving problems. A few people working alone cannot do it. And once the successes start, be prepared for what can be achieved.

3 A short-term goal is better than a long-term aspiration. Find one key element for change that everyone can focus on (for example, speed of response), one that is highly visible to all and where success will be obvious to all. In one sense, a short-term goal motivates in the same way that a crisis or emergency motivates people: they just get on with it because they have to.

4 Resistance is normal and is to be expected. Not everyone will reach the point where they are willing or able to change. Complaints, 'catastrophising' and turnover are par for the course. Change won't happen overnight. But if sufficient people are turned on to the possibilities, it can become an unstoppable process.

5 The boundary-busting process can become infectious with each success breeding other possibilities for more success. Boundaries constrain people, often for reasons that were relevant in the past but are no longer today. The 'de-boundaried' organisation is a reality for some companies today and a goal for many others.

Renewal through creativity and innovation

One of the best sources of new ideas for doing things better is the workforce of the organisation.

A recent British survey, however, suggests that one in four employees think that they are not listened to when they make improvement suggestions.[3] About the same proportion claim that they are never asked by their boss for their ideas. Many companies appear to have corporate structures that actively stifle creativity.

More than 40 per cent of those polled in the survey nominated obstacles that stopped them from contributing ideas. The biggest barrier was 'no one listens', followed by lack of motivation, a belief that ideas would not be taken seriously, fear of making a mistake, and a feeling that contributors would be seen as trouble makers. The most depressing response was 'new ideas are not relevant to my job'.

There are various ways to tackle this situation:

- Appoint a director of 'change, creativity and growth'.
- Include idea generation in company vision/mission statements.
- Get managers to walk-the-talk on creativity.
- Build idea generation into employee review processes.
- Conduct an annual creativity audit.
- Create awards for ideas contributed.
- Give people time and space to be creative.
- Encourage teams to brainstorm creative solutions to problems.
- Set up cross-functional teams to encourage different points of view.
- Train staff in creative thinking techniques.
- Make sure all ideas are accepted in a positive way.

While creativity is frequently viewed with suspicion, such an attitude says a great deal about a company and may send the wrong message. For example, what does an inability to listen to your employees say about your company's ability to listen to your customers? If bosses turn a deaf ear to the people closest to them, what chance does the customer have of being heard?

Many industries are dependent on creative ideas and companies like 3M have shown that creativity can be a direct contributor to commercial success. One area where it is crucial rather than a luxury to have employee contributions is new product development.

Continuous product innovation
Traditional approaches to new-product development are giving
way to faster methods, such as continuous product innovation
(CPI). While in its early stages of development, CPI offers
opportunities for speeding up the innovation cycle
substantially and enables organisations to assess their innovative
capabilities.[4]
The ability to innovate faster than competitors is emerging
as a significant competitive advantage. The project-by-project
approach to developing new product is now giving way to
approaches that enable continuous product development.
Innovation thus becomes a continuous and cross-functional
process of improvement. This demands a new set of
management tools and techniques.

This new approach to product development emerged from
the perceived shortcomings of traditional approaches as well as
from emerging changes in industry. For example, the software
industry has pioneered the idea of putting partially completed
product into the marketplace and encouraging customers to
assist in the final development of the product.

CPI extends the traditional cycle of product development
by including not only product design, development and
launch, but also other phases of the product life cycle such as
improvements in manufacturing, customisation and product
upgrades. It also changes the perspective from 'single product'
to that of 'family of products'. Innovation, therefore, may be
relevant not just to product development but also to product
enhancement and product extension.

Clearly, this involves a degree of cross-functional
coordination not normally required within organisations. It
demands integrated systems and the management of cross-
disciplinary processes. This in turn changes the role of
management from functional control to cross-functional
coordination.

Five classes of variables impact on the CPI process:
1 *innovation performance* (for example, level of idea generation,
  effectiveness in implementation, and consolidation);
2 *behaviours* (including encouragement of experimentation,
  resources being made available, knowledge sharing, etc.);
3 *managerial levers* (for example, product strategies, innovation
  process definition, organisational mechanisms and HR
  policies);

4 *capabilities* (for example, knowledge generation, learning alignment, knowledge transfer, knowledge consolidation);

5 *contingencies* (external ones such as the operating environment and internal ones such as company characteristics).

The model is hierarchical and suggests that each class of variables is driven by the class below it. Performance is driven by behaviour, which is controlled by managerial levers, and so on.

While CPI is only one of many new approaches to speeding up innovation, it does hold the potential to be an assessment tool in an area of corporate capability not easily captured or depicted. It is still under development and not yet fully operationalised, but the model seems to capture information about innovative capability that is otherwise difficult to obtain.

Each of the examples above demonstrates that organisational renewal is possible, is happening and is paying off. Maybe your competitors are doing some of it right now.

Guidelines

1 The state of flux

One of the earliest recorded observations by a philosopher in the Western tradition was made by Heraclitus who observed that 'everything is in a state of flux'. In business, that means any organisation that stands still is falling behind.

The answer is to structure into the organisation mechanisms that will drive your renewal processes. The principle of entropy suggests that, if you don't structure it in, it will never happen. In other words, if renewal relies entirely on the good intentions of managers to do something about it, then it will never happen.

Work on your renewal strategy.

2 Making renewal happen

There are many sources for renewal in any organisation. For example, renewal can come from new people, which may explain why the tenure of senior executives is getting shorter all the time.

Renewal can also come from systems and processes that are part of how the organisation functions. These tend to be more reliable as a source of ideas about how to renew the vitality of the organisation. Such systems and processes may range from simple mechanisms such as employee suggestion schemes to much more complicated and technical mechanisms like Total Quality Management or its latest incarnation, Six Sigma.

Review your options for renewal:
- What does the organisation already do well?
- Can you do more of it?
- What stops renewal in your organisation?
- Can you remove those barriers?
- What else can you do?

3 Personal renewal

It's not only organisations that are in need of renewal. You are as well.

Personal renewal follows a similar path to organisational renewal. You tend not to get around to it. There are many barriers. There's no system that forces you to do it, so it doesn't happen.

Stephen Covey talks about this under the heading of 'sharpening your saw'. Traditionally, we call it personal development or professional growth. Make room for it.

It's usually about finding the time to learn new stuff and unlearn some old stuff. Knowledge and skills are the key elements. Sometimes values come into it (what matters to you?).

Find time for personal renewal or it won't happen and, just like the organisation that stands still, you will be overtaken.

For further exploration

If you need guidance on how to make your organisation start thinking about the need for renewal, David Hurst's seditious book is a good place to start:
- D. Hurst, *Crisis & Renewal: Meeting the Challenge of Organizational Change*, Harvard Business School Press, Boston, 2002.

Hurst advocates committing acts of 'ethical anarchy' to make organisations sit up and take notice of what is happening around them. Creating a crisis may be the only way to precipitate change.

While this sounds very dramatic (if not treacherous!), the reality is that all organisations create their own crises anyway, simply because of the pressure to grow and develop. Cycles of growth, development, expansion and ultimately decline are the destiny of all organisations. Hurst offers some sound advice on how to roll with the punches and take advantage of the opportunities that arise in order to keep your organisation vital.

For an Australian perspective on corporate innovation and renewal, try the first book in the AIM Management Today series:

- Carolyn Barker (ed.), *Innovation and Imagination at Work*, McGraw-Hill, Sydney, 2001.

This collection of articles explores the factors that drive innovation in Australian organisations, including creativity, imagination and leadership. The premise is that innovation is not about R&D or technology, but about people doing things smarter, faster and better.

Structure and design

ENDURING ORGANISATIONAL STRUCTURES **18**

Not many organisations have been around for very long. Enterprises are dynamic structures operating in turbulent environments. Longevity is not usually part of the scene. Many of the 'excellent' organisations reviewed in the book *In Search of Excellence* [1] have disappeared since its publication in 1982. Mergers and acquisitions, bankruptcy and collapse take their toll over time. When writing the book *Built to Last*, [2] Collins and Porras found eighteen companies that had lasted for fifty years. If they had gone back another fifty years, it would have been a very short list indeed. All this makes the very long perspective a difficult one to sustain.

But some forms of organisation have lasted for more than a thousand years. What makes these structures last and can we learn anything them?

What will be the enduring organisational structures in this millennium?

Background

The arrival of a new millennium has a fascination about it that is neither logical nor easy to explain. The portentousness of the event exercises the mind and seems inevitably to invite a comparison between the present and a thousand years ago. From the standpoint of organisational studies, it invites a consideration of how organisations have fared over that time frame.

Millennial structures

Only a few organisations that existed in 1000 AD still exist today. Religious organisations stand out as the survivors—the Catholic Church springs most readily to the Western mind but let's not forget Jewish and Islamic religious organisations, Buddhism and a host of others. Between the beginning of our calendar about two thousand years ago and the year 1000, each of these religions spawned long-lasting organisational structures of varying size and scope.

The church

The Catholic Church is possibly the most structured of these religions. Borrowing heavily from its organisational predecessor (the Roman army), it is still cited frequently today as an outstanding example of a lean organisation. With few layers in its formal structure (Pope, Cardinal, Archbishop, Bishop, Priest, Laity), it manages a membership of millions. Even today there are few, if any, organisations that manage such a feat with even one thousandth of that membership. This is all the more astonishing because the Church has lasted about 1500 years so far (though the first 500 years were a bit scrappy from an organisational point of view).

Whereas I can recall no modern business organisation that has kept the same structure for more than fifty years, the Catholic hierarchy is still safely in place after 1500 years. Neither globalisation (yes, the Church has been at that for about 2000 years longer than anyone else) nor spin-off ventures (okay, they may not have been voluntary but breakaways such as the Protestants have been successful in their own right) nor strategy differences (some of those Vatican Councils over the years were fiery affairs) has fundamentally changed the way the organisation functions.

No doubt some of this has to do with the centralised structure of the organisation. Control is exercised from the centre in the tradition of the iron hand in the velvet glove. Opposition is weeded out quick smart and the handing over of central control from one generation of top managers to another is tightly managed. Succession planning is based on competence, not on connections or blood lines. Stacking the top management team with favourites is the closest the current leader gets to influencing the organisation after shuffling off this mortal coil.

Centralisation of control, however, will work only if there is a *shared set of core values* that binds a membership together. And that is where the Catholic Church has been exceptional. While there are regular debates over policy matters and longstanding policies are occasionally changed (for example, Papal infallibility is a recent phenomenon, introduced in the nineteenth century), the core Christian values are maintained. In fact, the shortest route out of the organisation is to question these values. Breaching protocol is forgiven; breaking the faith is not.

In the year 1000, when the Church had grown strong enough to pursue its globalisation strategy, there were few other formal organisations around. Even fewer have survived to the year 2000. The monarchy, for example, despite being as powerful as the Church back then, has had its day as an organising principle; the state itself has survived as a concept but is structured so differently that comparisons are almost meaningless; and though the warring tribes of Europe are still at war, it is now a populist activity rather than one run by princes.

However, the state did spawn that other great Roman inheritance, the military machine. The organisation of a fighting force virtually gave birth to the practice of management and to the study of organisation, both in a practical sense and linguistically. It was only a small step from handling the horses (*manidiare*, which gave rise to the expression 'managing') to handling people. The Roman army (or armies, to be precise) lasted only a few hundred years and gave us organising principles rather than a lasting structure.

The artisans
What was well established by the year 1000 was the manner of employment for skilled artisans and, to some extent, this has endured. While the trade may have changed from stonemason to computer programmer, the way organisations use these skilled people has not changed much. They are still itinerants who know their value to the organisation and charge accordingly. They move to where the work is and move on when it is done.

As in the past, skilled artisans live comfortably today but rarely own an enterprise themselves. If they do start a venture and it becomes successful, they will usually realise that only professional managers can sustain and grow the business. Those who don't realise this need typically fail and go back to being an artisan. They are bound by their special secret languages and readily form societies to promote a cause. The Free Masons of yesterday are the Linux developers of today. From opposing the Catholic hierarchy, they have gone to opposing the Microsoft juggernaut.

The artisans represent the antithesis of organisation. They resent and even oppose being formalised, structured and processed. Their organisation is anti-organisation or, in today's language, *the virtual organisation* (see Chapter 13). As the stonemasons created the most impressive monuments of their day—the churches—so the programmers have created the most impressive edifice of today—the Internet. And, like their predecessors, they are appalled at the use to which their invention is being put. They can no longer control their creation and many revile its commercial applications.

The stonemasons may have worked with their hands but their value came from the knowledge component inherent in that manual work—the know-how applied by a self-directed worker. The ability to design and build something as magnificent as Notre Dame in Paris was a triumphant combination of knowledge and applied skill. If they were not exclusively knowledge workers, knowledge comprised a big slice of their job. And the know-how was as treasured then as it is by today's system builders.

The scholars

Pure know-how was also the province of the universities and, by a stretch of a few decades, we can include them in our list of millennial organisations. Scholars coming together to form a learning community borrowed something from the tradition of the Church (it sponsored many of the earliest universities) and from the tradition of the travelling artisan (the teachers were often itinerants peddling expertise).

Universities have changed little over time. Today, they may reside in office towers but their self-organising principles are much the same. In fact, many pride themselves on retaining the processes, the policies, the structures and even the language and other symbols of medieval times. For evidence of this, simply observe any graduation ceremony: the gowns and caps, the seals, language and typefaces on the degrees awarded, the ritual behaviours such as the doffing of the caps, the titles bestowed and the archaic language used in the conferring ceremonies.

The power of the scholars may be somewhat diminished, but the debates of today about what matters within a university would not be foreign to the students of one thousand years ago.

Like the Church, learning communities share some core values, although they are less codified and less spiritual. Like the artisans, the scholars survive on the usefulness of their ideas and concepts, although the emphasis is on pure knowledge as much as it is on application.

Not much else has survived the thousand years from an organisational perspective. We are left with the enduring strength of a central organisational structure based on:
1 shared values;
2 the enduring practicality of skill-based employment;
3 the long shelf life of learning communities that share knowledge.

As today's organisations struggle to reinvent themselves in order to survive the rigours of global competition and local sustainability, their efforts are dwarfed by the achievements of the Church, the artisans and the scholars.

Inevitably, however, new forms of organisation will emerge. In fact, we can see some of these forms today in their early stages of development:
• the virtual organisation;
• the network organisation;
• the temporary organisation;
• the knowledge-based organisation.

No doubt many others are yet to come. Behind each we may well recognise one or more of the organisational principles that have outlasted the last millennium.

Hot groups—the next millennial structure?

Some researchers suggest that the fundamental structural unit of future organisations will be the small group.[3] They argue that survival in an increasingly competitive environment demands speed, flexibility and creativity, yet large organisations are notoriously bad at these things. Small groups that are firing on all cylinders, known as *hot groups*, are very good at these things.

Hot groups are a concept distinct from teams or groups. A team may be a hot group, but many are not. Hot groups:
• require a plural state of mind, one where there is a shared obsession with achieving a result;
• share characteristics such as single-mindedness, an urgent drive to succeed and dedication.

Examples of hot groups include:
• the group of programmers working with Bill Gates to develop/adapt the first PC operating system;
• the cast and crew of the TV series *Hill Street Blues*;

- President Kennedy's Cuban missile crisis management unit.
  While these groups are very diverse, they share many similar characteristics.
- Members feel they are engaged in an important task.
- The task absorbs the group members almost to the exclusion of everything else.
- Interpersonal relationships take second place to other issues such as the excitement generated by undertaking the task.
- The experience is usually short-lived.

Even though a group of people may form a hot group for a particular task, that doesn't mean that the same group of people will function as a hot group if reformed at a later time (for example, the *Hill Street Blues* group had trouble recapturing the earlier feelings when many of them started to work on another TV series). Further, a group that has failed earlier may fire up and become a hot group for a different task (for example, many of those who worked successfully with President Kennedy on the missile crisis were the same people who had failed miserably in the Bay of Pigs fiasco).

In trying to explain the power of the hot group, we need to move beyond the traditional explanations of human motivation found in Psychology I textbooks. An alternative explanation is the idea of *flow*, as developed by Mihaly Csikszentmihalyi (the surname is pronounced 'chick-sent-me-high' for those who casually want to drop the name), which describes the human sense of moving forward to accomplish things that are worth accomplishing (see Chapter 25). Hot groups are a peak experience of this phenomenon.

As the chaotic and competitive environment of hi-tech industries spreads to other industries, through processes such as globalisation and hyper-competition, the idea of capitalising on the benefits of a hot-group style of operation is becoming attractive even to traditional organisations.

The normal operational functioning of organisations, however, is diametrically opposed to that of hot groups. Where organisations prefer regularity, predictability, control and certainty, hot groups thrive on their opposites.[4] So, in many cases, hot groups only survive in large and traditional organisations because certain conditions are in place. For example:
- The organisation does not formally know that the hot group exists (if it did become aware of it, it would kill it).

- A crisis is in progress and the seditious presence of the group is tolerated for that reason.
- Someone high up in the organisation both supports and protects the group.
- The organisation's core values provide a supportive surrounding for the group.

Managing hot groups

Hot groups are unlikely to work in all situations. By definition, they are project-focused entities. Their very nature seems to be driven by the finite and discrete nature of the tasks they tackle. In all organisations, there will always be those tasks that are routine and predictable.

Further, it takes management effort (possibly the most undervalued resource in any organisation) to set up and drive a hot group. Not every manager has the skills to do the job. Not every manager has the emotional resilience to go with the ups and downs of team growth and development. Not every manager has the risk tolerance to rely on such an ephemeral structure.

Despite this, it is worth considering the potential of hot groups as an organisational structure because we are unlikely to see the return of the 'good old (quiet) days'. Group-based ways of working are taking over the corporate world and large organisations are unlikely suddenly to become nimble and light-footed. Hot groups are one way to harness the high levels of energy that come from individuals working together successfully.

So how can leaders cultivate an environment in which hot groups can thrive? Ways include:
- Nurture the hot groups but don't try to run them.
- Find the right people to join instead of training the less right.
- Minimise controls.
- Judge the group on progress, not on individual contribution.
- Put the group under pressure to deliver.

The organisation of the future is more likely to rely on such mechanisms as shared values, complementary skills, shared focus on knowledge and learning, and dynamic group structures than on the traditional structures that can be drawn on a chart using little boxes with job titles.

The best of today's organisations already focus on the hidden potential that lies between the boxes.

Guidelines

1 Think 'group'

Deploy the group response whenever you can. Instead of allocating special projects or tasks to one person, try to involve two or three people.

Using groups is a bit like being a gardener. You can prepare the ground, fertilise it, plant the seed in the right place and keep it watered, but you can't make it grow. It will generally grow if the right conditions are provided, but not always. If it doesn't, it is not your fault.

If you did not provide the right conditions, then you should blame yourself.

2 Capture energy

Find the people who want to contribute. High-energy people attract other high-energy people.

Look for the volunteers in your organisation, not the 'prisoners of the system'. A 'hot' state of mind comes from the people themselves, not from any mandate of management.

Experiment with how you can bring people together to work on stuff. Combine people and recombine them.

3 Un-organise

Manage such groups with a minimum of bureaucracy and hierarchy. Keep the paperwork away from them.

Give the groups freedom to experiment within whatever bounds you deem necessary to protect them, you and the organisation.

Keep it simple. Keep it short.

For further exploration

If the longevity of your organisation is of interest to you, a great read is:

- J. Collins and J. Porras, *Built to Last*, Century, London, 1995.

Once again, the simple formula of gathering data in the field serves these authors well. By examining eighteen exceptional companies (including General Electric, 3M, Hewlett-Packard and Proctor & Gamble) and comparing each with its closest but less successful competitor, the authors provide real insight into what makes some companies great and others just also-rans. The 1998 paperback edition includes a new 'how-to' section that provides detailed practical guidance.

The number of books on teams and teamwork continues to grow at an alarming rate. Can there really be that much to say about teams? Maybe it's better to concentrate on the 'how-to' side. In which case, try:

- K. Fisher, S. Rayner and W. Belgard, *Tips for Teams: A Ready Reference for solving Common Team Problems,* McGraw-Hill, New York, 1994.

WORK DESIGN **19**

Managers design work. Many managers do not think of themselves as 'work designers' but that is what they are whenever they decide which duties go with which job, or choose which jobs to bundle together into a work unit. The design will impact directly and significantly on the efficiency and effectiveness of the work unit.

There are two competing philosophies about how to design work. One approach is based on the idea that *jobs are just simple collections of tasks* that can be analysed and reorganised for maximum efficiency. The other approach is based on the idea that *the job can't be separated from the person doing the job*, and that the person and the job comprise a 'whole system'.

These two approaches require different management techniques and generate different outcomes. Each is rooted in a different paradigm, with the first drawing on *engineering* thinking and the second on *social science* thinking. Each has its own tradition and both are beset by research problems, largely because the research has followed the conclusions rather than the other way round. Each approach has its strong advocates and 'true believers'.

The engineering approach is probably still the dominant one in industry, although which one will triumph in the long run is impossible to say.

How should we design work?

Background

If the hallmark of a profession is a common body of accepted practice and wisdom, then we have some way to go with the practice of management.

In the past, management has paraded itself as a science (witness the various university departments still glorying in the likes of 'Department of Management Sciences'). However, there is so little in the field of management studies that is universally accepted by its researchers, teachers and practitioners that the phrase 'practising manager' is justifiably ambiguous.

One characteristic of a non-professional body of practice is the ready acceptance of myths. When medicine was practised by barbers, widespread but unfounded beliefs about what made people ill ranged from the bizarre to the dangerous. This was especially worrying for patients when the chief tool of the trade was a razor!

Management is similarly beset by unfounded beliefs that have grown to mythical proportions over the years. Some have reached the point where it is all but impossible for the reality to be acceptable. The gap between the myth and reality is such that to abandon the myth is simply too difficult.

If we could only reduce the tasks of management to the easy application of a few core principles, then work and life would be easier. For managers, the hunger for mechanistic answers with simple applications is never far below the surface of a job that is filled with the uncertainties, complexities and ambiguities of working with people. What is known as the *Hawthorne Effect* is an example of our abiding desire for simplicity in the practice of management and work design.

Wrong lessons from Hawthorne

Managers exposed to even a modicum of management training are likely to be aware of the impact of changing working conditions in order to improve performance. The Hawthorne Effect suggests that the actual change is immaterial.

The Hawthorne Effect arose from a series of seven research studies undertaken by Australian Elton Mayo, a professor at Harvard Business School, and a group of colleagues at the Hawthorne plant of the Western Electric Company in Chicago between 1924 and 1932.

The researchers studied the effect of changing the working conditions of a group of women who assembled electrical relays. They were looking for connections between working conditions and productivity. When the amount of illumination in the women's work area was increased in the first three studies, productivity went up; when Mayo subsequently turned the illumination down, productivity went up again. And so the Hawthorne Effect was born: change the environment (no matter how) and you change the level of productivity. This 'principle' is still influencing the actions of some managers today.

But what is it based on? Unfortunately, Mayo never wrote up his famous study. The only report we have of the study is a 12-paragraph story in a local newspaper at the time, along with an internal Western Electric memorandum that has since been lost. What we know is that the research involved five women workers. What is usually forgotten is that other changes were made to working conditions apart from the lights going on and off. First, the women's pay structure was changed at the beginning of the research so that their pay became directly linked to their group performance (as their performance went up, so did their pay). Second, the women were given direct and immediate feedback on their performance (this had not happened before). No wonder performance increased—I doubt the women even noticed that Elton Mayo and his colleagues were fiddling with the lights in the background somewhere!

The story of the Hawthorne Effect was debunked more than 25 years ago,[1] but nevertheless its influence remains undiminished in some management circles. Although it is true that working conditions can be either motivating or demotivating, unfortunately the link between performance and environment is not as simplistic as the Hawthorne Effect would have us believe.

The Hawthorne experiments point to a larger issue for management. Although this particular experiment was flawed, there is no doubt that there is a general connection between productivity and the structure of work. This may well explain why there has been so much interest in what was really a marginal piece of research. The connection between work design and work output is of clear interest to managers. That there is such a link is not only obvious but has been demonstrated many times over by those who have designed and redesigned work. Two thinkers stand out in the field of work design, bequeathing us two radically different approaches.

Engineering versus social science

In a sense, the challenge of management can be caricatured as a choice between two approaches to work design, one simple and one complex: it could be called *the choice of the two Freds*.

The engineering approach
On the one hand, there is the attractive simplicity of Fred Taylor (1856–1915), the father of Scientific Management, whose approach was fundamentally reductionist. This Fred advocated carving the job into its smallest performable components, and manipulating these elements to remove waste and optimise job output. This created a level of control for

managers and engineers that they had only dreamt of before. Designing jobs in this way led to dramatic improvements in productivity, and this was an issue of national and international significance. Taylor was called before the US Senate to explain his theories; as a result, business and government worked together to spread the gospel according to Taylor.

The approach gave rise to the image of the 'time-and-motion' engineer in a dustcoat, carrying a clipboard and stopwatch as he observes the workers in action. Each action was recorded along with the time taken; the data gathered was then used to prescribe the best way to do the job in the shortest possible time. The only problem was that the workers often did not like the idea much, as it so often led to speeding up the job or constraining how it could be done. Even worse, the redesigned jobs often lacked the social interaction of the old jobs. As a result of worker (and union) resistance, on many occasions the changes made through work redesign led to a loss of productivity, not a gain.

In its heyday, Engineering Fred's approach delivered dramatic results as waste and inefficiency were eliminated from many jobs. The techniques are still used today although probably more subtly. For example, workers today might be taught the basic principles of data collection and invited to do their own analysis and improvement. The emphasis is more likely to be on doing the job 'smarter', removing hazardous steps or building quality assurance into the process.

The social science approach

On the other hand, there is the rich complexity of Fred Emery (1925–97), the pioneering Australian researcher who demonstrated that human performance depends on a rich and complex tapestry of interactions between people (social) and their (technical) working environment.

This Fred tells us that to fiddle with one component of the sociotechnical equation may bring change, but not necessarily the desired change. In other words, you can't separate the job from the person doing that job, and you can't separate that combination from a particular setting. You must treat the entirety of the situation, seeing it as part of a whole 'sociotechnical system'.

This approach advocates that the only way we can strive for desired change is to take a 'whole-system' approach. Only by considering workers, work and technology as a whole system can you create truly productive and satisfying workplaces.

Much of Emery's thinking came from his personal experience of seeing the introduction of expensive new technologies that were supposed to deliver productivity gains. When they often failed to do so, Emery went looking for the reasons. These usually involved the fact that the new technologies treated human operators as cogs in a mechanical system rather than as a thinking part of a whole system.

Some interesting things happen when your perspective changes from the reductionist, Taylorist approach to the whole-system approach.

1 Those who change the system become part of the system— this is the *there is no such thing as an independent and objective observer* principle.
2 Those who do the work know the work and can make the work actually work, or not—this is the *discretionary effort* principle.
3 Change any part of the system and the result is a different system—this is the *whole-system* principle.
4 The system is at all times dynamic and readjusts itself to circumstances that are planned or unplanned—this is the *dynamic system* principle.

But which Fred?

As we practise management, we make our own choices as to which Fred is the one for us. Those choices are probably influenced by the models in our minds of what makes people tick, or at least the strategies we believe work in the workplace to encourage people to tick. They may even relate back to our own personal values and personalities.

The contrast between the two Freds may not be as stark as it is sometimes made out to be. Taylor believed strongly that his methods would improve the lives of working people and make jobs safer, more interesting and easier to perform. And Emery's approach still requires that data is collected, analysed and then used as the basis for redesign, even if the workers themselves do much of this.

Occasionally, the two alternatives do force themselves back into notice as two opposing contenders. The recent invention of the call centre is one situation in which the two work-design options are clearly visible. Bringing together lots of telephone operators (often on behalf of many different organisations) in one location, to offer a 24-hour service to customers, has created what its critics describe as a 'battery-hen' situation. Every operator's every move is monitored and measured. Work layout, call procedures, and minimum and maximum times for calls are all strictly controlled for maximum efficiency. But job turnover is so high that selection and training costs for new staff go through the roof. All this may well affect the overall performance of many such centres to the point where they offer little benefit.

The two Freds would no doubt analyse the call-centre situation quite differently and prescribe different solutions. But, for now, Taylor still seems to be the preferred choice of management.

Work design flexibility and productivity

Regardless of which work-design approach we take, many organisations aspire to the key work-design principles of creating and enhancing flexibility. This desire is based on the perception that the operating environment for most businesses is so dynamic and turbulent that the idea of coming up with 'one best' design for a job is plain silly.

The goal is to create jobs that can change with the changing conditions of the marketplace. A major driver of this is the speed at which we now all do business. And this demands a degree of responsiveness that cannot be delivered by a bureaucracy. Hence, the new objective in work design is flexibility.

The most obvious route to flexibility is multiskilling—that is, training the workforce to be able to do more than just a narrow range of tasks (this is also very much part of the Emery approach to work design).

Although the origins of multiskilling lie in the manufacturing industry, service organisations have also reaped significant gains from this approach. Furthermore, it delivers benefits to the employees as much as it does to the employer.

Employees in organisations that encourage workforce flexibility cite a wide range of reasons for their support of the process:
• better variety in their work;
• greater control over their environment;
• improved employability;
• opportunities for higher pay.

It is sometimes difficult for managers to quantify the gains from workforce flexibility. There are, however, a growing number of organisations that have been able to do so. For example, Motorola claims a reduction of 77 per cent in defects in the production of cellular telephones as a direct result of a workforce flexibility system based on 'pay-for-skills' principles.[2]

A study by the US Center for Productivity and Quality examined the impact of workplace changes on a variety of performance indicators. Organisational performance increased overall by 30–40 per cent with multiskilling and reduced job categories most highly correlated with these gains. A study of 86 electronics manufacturers analysed cycle-times and their link to workforce flexibility. It concluded that fastest cycle-times were obtained in workplaces where *work and skills were integrated* rather than in those where just the work flow was redesigned and improved by experts.[3]

Three other examples establish the link between workplace flexibility and bottom-line value:

1 Ralcorp (US retailer and cereal manufacturer) reduced total plant costs and significantly improved overall plant productivity.
2 BHP Copper increased productivity by 20 per cent with no increase in costs and major improvements in safety.
3 Qualex (US film processing) improved workforce management in a seasonal business with tight margins.

Each of these three companies set out systematically to achieve the gains of flexibility, overcoming the obstacles traditionally put forward (for example, time, costs, a unionised workforce). But how did they do it? Essentially, it was a challenge of leadership and people management. In addressing these challenges, the three companies followed the five principles discussed below.[4]

1 Involve employees

Following many grievances from its employees, BHP Copper undertook a work-redesign process involving every employee in their tank-house unit. The changes that were made came directly from involving the employees in an eight-step improvement process; everyone was deeply involved in problem identification and resolution.

Ralcorp involved its employees in more than just the production work; employees selected new employees, trained those employees and were responsible for problem resolution.

2 Organise around work processes

Employees need to know the whole of the work process to understand how best to make their contribution. An understanding of what comes before they do their part of the manufacturing process and what comes after has a direct and immediate impact on indicators such as quality and speed. Ralcorp created one single classification for all employees, training its people in all the skills utilised in the plant. The start-up operation provided the opportunity to involve all employees in all parts of the operation.

Qualex battled high turnover and huge seasonal fluctuations (which caused major quality problems) by training a core group of employees to do all tasks. These permanent employees focused on the more complex tasks, leaving other tasks for less highly skilled temporary staff. The workforce is now stable, more productive, more skilled and more secure in its permanent status.

3 Provide training

The training provided should go beyond technical skills. All three companies train their employees extensively in business skills as well as in skills such as problem solving and dispute resolution. This investment in training pays off by gains in self-management and rapid problem solving.

4 Share information

Employees need to understand the wider context of the organisation. Management needs to share as much information as possible. As organisations face more difficulties, this need only increases. When times are tough, the need to share detailed information about company performance becomes critical.

Ralcorp required all employees to attend two-hour plant-wide briefings every four to six weeks. Everyone had access to corporate information through Lotus Notes. Teams met at least once a month for an hour. All team members attended continuous improvement meetings twice a month.

Says David Kibbe, Ralcorp Vice-President, Manufacturing:

We kept up a steady diet of meetings to reinforce what needed to be done, the ultimate vision for the entire undertaking, that it was okay for employees to make mistakes, and that employees had authority to manage and change their work environment if it would help the plant attain its goals.[5]

5 Build supporting systems

If an operation is to become focused on its people, the supporting systems need to be adapted to this way of working. Such systems include recruitment, performance management, rewards, training, and many others. The old systems, designed for a traditional low-involvement way of doing business, are unlikely to suit the new ways.

Ralcorp uses a peer-review process to improve systems continually. It emphasises employee ownership of those systems.

BHP Copper developed a 'pay-for-skills' system together with its unions and employees; the system determines pay levels and is driven by access to training and development. It enables extensive job rotation.

All three companies shared a philosophy that employees needed to be involved in the process of involving employees. They followed a structured and planned process. They overcame traditional prejudices such as the belief that such approaches were not possible in a unionised environment. Their approaches were different but all shared the outcomes of a highly flexible and highly productive workforce, and showed it can be done.

How to go about doing work design continues to interest managers and organisations, mainly because it is a way of creating competitive advantage. If you can get it right, a competitive advantage based on the flexibility of people can be hard to copy by your competitors.

Any company can buy a new piece of technology and compete with you. But if you can get your people and work methods to the point where they deliver unique benefits that others cannot match, it will take your competitors a long time to imitate your work design.

Guidelines

1 Redesign the work

The way work is done in organisations is often driven by imperatives that were valid many years ago but have become less relevant over time.

The design of work and jobs needs to be revisited at regular intervals to validate that the design is still optimal. Involving employees in this process generates significant side benefits. Involving only experts tends to have the opposite effect of alienating those who do the work from that work. Review how jobs and work are reviewed in your organisation. Are you following 'best practice'?

2 Create flexibility

Use the list of five principles that worked for Ralcorp, BHP Copper and Qualex to rethink your organisation's approach to creating workplace flexibility.

Most organisations become arteriosclerotic over time, just like the human body. Only regular reviews and improvements can stop it grinding to a halt altogether.

Each year the bar for organisational performance is set a little higher. In this sort of competitive environment, standing still is not an option.

3 Upskill yourself

Learn more about the impact of work design on issues such as organisational performance. For managers, this is not an issue that will go away. It is not somebody else's responsibility to structure the workplace; it is the responsibility of management.

And don't just move the boxes in the organisation chart. That is not work redesign.

For further exploration

There is a little bit of a tendency to leave work design up to the specialists, whether this means internal specialists such as human resource managers or external specialists such as consultants. I'm not sure this is actually necessary. With a little bit of reading, some experimenting in the workplace and a whole lot of talking with those who do the work, work design and redesign can be done by any competent manager.

Some practical books that will help include:
- F. Frei, *Work Design for the Competent Organization*, Quorum Books, Westport, 1993.
- T. Horgen, D. Schon, W. Porter and M. Joroff, *Excellence by Design: Transforming Workplace and Work Practice*, John Wiley & Sons, New York, 1998.

- P. Smith, *Creating Workplaces where People can Think*, Jossey-Bass, San Francisco, 1994.

  For a more general discussion of how the design of work impacts on workplace productivity, try:

- M. Weisbord, *Productive Workplaces*, Jossey-Bass, San Francisco, 1987.

SELF-MANAGING WORK TEAMS **20**

At times, it must feel to some managers that they are a threatened species. Waves of downsizing at the end of the last century decimated their ranks. The notion of middle management became anathema. Information technology further added to their reductions in number. Careers disappeared, especially in generalist fields of management. At the same time, new forms of organisation appeared that seemed to suggest that management was surplus to requirements.

For a generation brought up on the notion that a move into management was a move towards security, long-term employment and career prospects, this had a devastating impact. Highly skilled managers at the peak of their working careers suddenly saw only the alternatives of early retirement or a mowing franchise.

Taking the logic of all this to its extreme, is it possible to abolish the management function? Is it conceivable that we could create a corporate structure in which management has no place?

Can we do without management?

Background

In the last twenty years, the management function has been threatened on a number of fronts. Individually, none of these presents a mortal threat to management. Collectively, it is possible to construct—at least conceptually—a corporate entity in which the function of management has all but disappeared. The question is, just how big or small is the management that is left?

The decline of management

Possibly the first serious threat to management came in the 1980s when the downsizing fad, in conjunction with the short-lived business process re-engineering craze, removed several layers of management from most organisations. Until then, the idea of multi-layered management structures was the norm. Most people employed in organisations in the 1970s will remember a multitude of levels in organisation charts of mind-boggling complexity. As a 16-year-old working in a manufacturing company of about 1500 people, I recall being on the bottom of a management pile that comprised thirteen layers. I reported to a leading hand who had never met the manager of our division who was five levels above him.

Stripping layers of management out of such overly bureaucratic and unwieldy structures was a long overdue task. Recommending such changes made consulting companies very rich. Middle management became a threatened species, and while there has been some 'relayering' in recent times, we are unlikely to see the old days of leading hands, foremen, assistant supervisors, supervisors, senior supervisors and assistant managers return.

Reducing the size of management was possible partly because the actual size of organisations was also being reduced. My old factory now employs about 400 people and yet produces more product than it did twenty-five years ago. Improvements in production equipment, information technology, work processes, employee skill levels and the design of work all contributed to a need for fewer staff.

Nevertheless, in terms of proportion, more management positions disappeared than frontline employee positions. Consequently, the span of control has widened significantly for those managers who remain. Today, it is not uncommon to see a lean management structure based on only two or three levels of management (team leaders and manager) involving 100–200 employees. It would not be unusual for this to have only 8–12 team leaders. Such a lean structure is positively anorexic compared to the typical operation in the 1970s.

So downsizing has given us two elements that account for the disappearance of management: greater spans of control and fewer layers in the management structure.

Teams that manage themselves

During the same period (mid-1970s onwards), the introduction of *employee self-management* provided another threat to the career future of managers. Growing out of the Work Design/Redesign movement spawned in the UK and Scandinavia in the 1950s, employee self-management created the possibility of even leaner management structures. The technology was now available to combine the social and technical aspects of work to the point where the idea of supervision was eliminated. Many tried this approach but almost as many failed. Those who succeeded did so through a rigorous process of redesigning the work, which in part included designing out supervision.

This period saw the introduction of the *self-managed work team* (SMWT). This special type of work team initially grew out of the work-redesign process and was a means of creating a workplace without multiple layers of supervision. The idea was to build self-supervision into the team structure by clearly defining boundaries and accountabilities for natural chunks of work. It contrasted with the artificiality of work in highly bureaucratic and multi-layered organisations. By encouraging team accountability for a bundle of tasks that involved creating a whole product or delivering a whole service, it became possible to dispense with the managerial functions of coordination and communication. Self-managing teams led to flat organisational structures.

Fuelled partly by a variety of books[1] that praised the concept, SMWTs took off as a management fad. Many organisations tried the concept as a stand-alone idea, without doing the hard yakka of redesigning the workplace to accommodate this new way of organising people. In some cases, it was merely announced and used as an excuse to fire supervisors.

By the late 1980s some factories had a plant manager and 8–10 SMWTs, with each team comprising 6–10 employees. These SMWTs were substantially leaderless although a strong sense of shared leadership prevailed within the teams. The position of team leader evolved into a series of separate and distinct leadership functions that rotated around the members of the team. It is not too far-fetched to describe these plants as having only one layer of management involving one manager. In a plant of 100 people, this is the ultimate lean-management structure.

Organisations built on the principles and practice of self-managing teams can successfully achieve this level of leanness, and there are sufficient instances to prove this. The discipline required to evolve to this point, however, is beyond most organisations. For a start, reorganising an enterprise around team self-management requires *time*—something in the order of five to seven years. Many managers are unable to think in such a time frame, partly because their organisations won't allow them this luxury. Further, it demands a type of management to which some managers cannot adapt, a style that relies on *trusting* the teams to do the right thing.

But, where is the evidence that SMWTs will actually work?

Case study—Motorola

An important example is Motorola.[2] This company achieved significant productivity improvements in short-cycle manufacturing processes by restructuring the configuration and management of its workforce. SMWTs reduced manufacturing cycle-times and improved business performance by removing the obstructions and deficiencies in both the organisational design and the manufacturing processes.

After the discovery that a disruption to a manufacturing project was exacerbated by the addition of staff to the assembly program, Motorola management decided that the problems they were experiencing in their short-cycle manufacturing process necessitated a restructuring of the workplace. Self-managed teams were progressively given responsibility for achieving productivity improvements, and workers were encouraged to decide for themselves how to design and implement changes to operating procedures.

Motorola had everything to gain from the new structure. The manufacturing program was not operating efficiently or economically. The workforce was structured into a traditional hierarchy, with a project leader overseeing a production task leader, who in turn oversaw three group leaders, who were each responsible for the operation of a section of the manufacturing process. The three sections operated separately and individual assemblers built only one type of product.

Typically, the review of weekly operations took from two to five days. Productivity reports were not available until one week later, and it often took another week to institute corrective action. A further two weeks would then pass before the results of the changes could be assessed. Although assemblers made suggestions to group leaders, the production task leader made all decisions relating to changes to the production line.

Motorola management was prepared to give the experiment every opportunity to succeed. Five years was allowed for a gradual introduction of the changes. The product was well established and required few changes to the manufacturing process, and there were extensive records of how the process had been performing in regards to cost, quality and scheduling.

The self-managing teams were formed with the primary goal of achieving measurable reductions in the short-cycle manufacturing process. The section manager in charge of the project believed that team unity would be enhanced through job sharing and the setting of specific targets. Job enlargement and enrichment were seen as necessary precursors to developing a unified team spirit. Productivity was expected to improve as employees gained greater job satisfaction.

The layers of supervision within the section were gradually removed as teams took over the decision-making process. Self-management was achieved within four years. Teams now carried out the activities of the production task leader, the group leaders, the materials manager, the quality engineer and the test engineer. The teams had a project leader and product quality specialists, but all other positions were given a common title. This enabled team members to perform cross-functional tasks.

The results of the restructuring were impressive. Although three weeks are required for the fixed testing procedures of the product, the system cycle-time was reduced from twenty-two weeks to five. Quality improvements led to a reduction in defects from 750 per million opportunities to 22 defects per million. Reductions in labour requirements facilitated significant reductions in the cost of manufacturing the product. The factory space required to operate the project was reduced by more than half, and the contract was completed well ahead of schedule.

The reasons for this spectacular result cannot be attributed solely to improvements in job satisfaction. The self-managed teams were characterised by the frequency, quality and speed of their improvements to operating systems. Daily team meetings meant that changes to operating systems could be made within twenty-four hours. After each change was made, further obstructions were identified, facilitating a process of continuous improvement.

The section manager identified three reasons why teams operated more efficiently than the traditional command and control structure:

1 improvements to the transfer of information regarding project performance;
2 daily analysis of project performance;
3 the close involvement of individual employees in the decision-making process.

All employees were able to contribute to improvements in quality. As team members became multiskilled, they became more committed to improving the quality of the entire manufacturing process. Small delays in the manufacturing process that would not have been seen by the production task leader were now analysed and improved. The traditional structure typically required twice the number of steps and much more time to complete the installation of a select component.

The Motorola case study illustrates that self-managing teams can enhance business performance. But it requires a degree of persistence and hard work not much relished by many organisations. To make a successful transition to team-based organisation, the key principles seem to be:

- Design the change and have a detailed plan.
- Give it time (five to seven years is about right).
- Treat it as a business decision, driven by business imperatives (not because 'teams are a good thing').
- Follow a disciplined implementation process (don't make it up as you go along).

Managing the self-managed

The challenge of self-management is actually greater for managers than it is for the teams. The teams usually see self-management as a sensible step, providing management is able to paint a picture of what life will be like in the team-based organisation. The question is whether we can paint a picture for managers as well. Where no such picture exists, it is inevitable that managers will see team self-management as a lessening of their role and standing in the organisation.

What is at issue here is how managers see their contribution to the organisation. If they have a mindset that sees that contribution in terms of providing authority and ensuring control, then the whole idea of self-management at shop–floor level is interpreted as a threat. If the mindset is directed more towards encouraging and developing the capabilities of others, team self-management becomes an opportunity.

It may well be the case that moving towards team self-management is about *changing the behaviour of the managers* rather than that of the managed. Managers may not see it this way. You can expect some to speak in terms of shop–floor employees not being ready for self-management (why aren't they?), saying that the risks are too great (what has management *not* put in place to create this risk?) and that the 'culture' of the organisation is not supportive (who made the culture what it is?). Such examples tell us more about the managers than they do about the teams.

The end of management?

The concept of self-management extends beyond SMWTs and is not dependent on them. The most common descriptions of it feature the idea of *empowerment*—that is, that employees can be given a greater level of discretionary power than is usually envisaged (see Chapter 4). The notion is very attractive to senior management (who typically remain unaffected by it in practice) and loathed by middle management (who are expected to make it work). For many middle managers, the combination of downsizing and empowerment is a lethal combination, leading to either early retirement or higher stress levels.

Some of this is made more manageable by the emergence of smarter ways of defining and describing jobs (for example, changing from 'duty statements' to 'accountability statements').

We have become better at structuring jobs so that they require less direct supervision. The use of role descriptions, organisation value statements, and even 'mission and purpose' statements makes it possible to explain a job to an employee and then let her get on with it.

What is making an even greater impact today is the use of technical infrastructure in the workplace. The astounding capabilities of information technology, in particular, make it possible to supervise employees at a great distance. With its use, it becomes possible for a manager to have only virtual contact with an employee, managing through results rather than through process.

This leads to the question of why such people should be employees at all. The outsourcing craze continues unabated and will probably continue to speed up. There is no function left that cannot be or has not been outsourced. Even core functions like strategy setting and human resource management have been handed over to outside suppliers. Even management itself in the form of consultants and management companies has been handed over. Nothing is sacred when it comes to what is core and what is not.

Where will it end: greater spans of control, fewer layers of management, high levels of self-management and fewer corporate functions? Each is a threat to the manager's career path. Put them together and they become a threat to management itself.

Maybe it will end only when each organisation has just one manager, spanning many staff organised into self-managing teams (or, alternatively, highly empowered individuals) and focusing on a few core functions, while relying on external suppliers for the rest.

Whether there is a limit to all this is anybody's guess. The trend, though, is one-directional and no one is calling for more managerial control and less self-management and self-reliance. The resistance may well come from the staff, who may consider self-management a hidden strategy for extracting more work from fewer people. Either way, only those who actually undertake the self-management journey are likely to discover its limits.

Guidelines

1 Empowering employees

Empower employees through teams to gain improvements in productivity and workforce morale.

- Teams have the advantage of allowing you to structure the extent and degree of autonomy.
- Teams provide a support framework within which the notion of self-management becomes a realistic goal rather than a wishful thought.

This requires some planning, and self-managing teams do still need to be managed. It takes an investment to get to a reasonable degree of autonomy but, once there, the pay-off is real and significant.

2 Monitor improvements

Analyse business performance daily to improve continuous improvement programs.

The reason for implementing teams is to get a business result and teams should be monitored on that basis. (Don't even start with teams if you are doing it for the sake of 'doing teams'.)

Everything has to be linked back to business goals. Write down the specific goals you have for implementing teams. If you find that difficult to do, read and think further about the whole idea.

Moving towards a team-based way of operating is not easy; it requires dedication and effort. Don't start until you know what you are doing and why.

3 Organise for success

Organise the workforce to maximise business performance rather than accept the status quo.

The whole point of having a layer (or layers) of management is to have people who will organise and reorganise for success. Managers have responsibility for improving organisational performance, and that means you have to be able to take the long view of things.

While most managers spend most of the time in day-to-day problem-solving mode, you somehow have to get above all that to work on the organisation itself.

For further exploration

Self-management is not a topic that is addressed directly by many books or other resources. Instead, you need to look at particular applications. For self-managing work teams, try:
- J. Katzenbach and D. Smith, *The Wisdom of Teams,* Harvard School Press, Boston, 1993.
- J. Zenger, E. Musslewhite, K. Hurson and C. Perrin, *Leading Teams: Mastering the New Role*, Irwin, New York, 1994.
- J. Orsburn and L. Moran, *The New Self-Directed Work Teams*, McGraw-Hill, New York, 1999.
- R. Wellins, W. Byham and J. Wilson, *Empowered Work Teams*, Jossey-Bass, San Francisco, 1993.
  For empowerment in a more general form, try:
- K. Blanchard, J. Carlos and A. Randolph, *The Three Keys to Empowerment*, Berrett-Koehler, San Francisco, 1996.
  For outsourcing, try:
- D. Oates, *Outsourcing and the Virtual Organization: The Incredible Shrinking Company*, Century Business, London, 1998.

CONSULTANTS 21

Management consultants have become a standard element of the business landscape. Many organisations have become dependent on the external advice of consultants as a key part of their decision making in areas such as strategy and finance. This is a dramatic change from even twenty years ago when we hired managers to make the decisions now often made by consultants. But this change remains largely undiscussed.

Today, managers expect to be able to access and use the services of consultants for a wide range of purposes. While this may help to spread ideas faster from one organisation to another, it also comes at a cost to many organisations.

Are consultants worth it?

Background

Open a conversation about consulting and it is almost inevitable that someone will tell you a joke about consultants.

Joke # 1:   Question: What's the difference between a management consultant and a used-car salesman? Answer: The used-car salesman knows when he is lying.
Joke # 2:   A consultant is like a man who knows a hundred ways to make love to a woman but doesn't know any women.
Joke # 3:   A consultant is somebody who borrows your watch and then uses it to charge you for telling you what time it is.
Joke # 4:   A consultant is a disease in search of a patient.

The jokes are not entirely inaccurate in highlighting both the role of consultants and why they have become such an all pervasive phenomenon in the last few decades. Consultants peddle solutions and they have thrived only because managers perceive that they are in need of solutions.

Growth industry of the twentieth century

Although some have suggested that management consulting is the second oldest profession in the world (and not dissimilar to the oldest), it is in fact very much a phenomenon of the last 150 years. But only in the last twenty years or so has it become a truly phenomenal growth industry.

In 1980 there were about 18 000 management consultants worldwide, earning a total of about $US2 billion per year. The largest consultancy (Booz Allen Hamilton) turned over roughly $US150 million per annum. By the late 1990s the industry was worth more than $US62 billion globally, with about 140 000 consultants involved. There are now more than thirty firms employing over 1000 consultants, compared with only five firms in 1980. That's a growth rate of more than 20 per cent per annum, something that most other industries can only aspire to in their wildest dreams. *Consultants News*, the leading industry journal,[1] predicts that the current growth rate of 13 per cent per annum will continue for the foreseeable future. Further, the available 'consulting talent' continues to lag behind demand.

The industry is very much an American home-grown development. Arthur D. Little started the first consulting firm in 1886. Today, of the fifty largest consulting groups in the world, only four are non-US.[2] The industry's recent rapid growth has led to a situation in the United States where, for every two executives with the authority to hire consultants, there is one external consultant. This ratio of 2:1 compares with a ratio of 10:1 in 1980.

The first wave of groundbreakers (mid-nineteenth to early twentieth century) comprised Arthur Little, Frederick Taylor and Henry Gannt, the founders of the tradition, who worked largely as loners, building theory and practice rather than building up bank accounts.

The second wave (1910–60) was driven by the founders of firms that we still know today: Edwin Booz, James McKinsey and, in Europe, Lyndon Urwick. Following World War II, this wave peaked with the formation of a host of second-tier firms such as CRESAP, Hay Associates and Tower Perrins.

The third wave (still growing today and taking on tsunami-like qualities) was driven by a number of developments. First, Bruce Henderson left Arthur D. Little in 1963 to establish the Boston Consulting Group. Almost single-handedly, he operationalised the strategy process and invented strategy consulting. Eventually, this led to a host of imitators (Bain & Co, LEK Partnership, Monitor Company) but BCG still holds a treasured position in the strategy consulting game.

Possibly more portentously, major accounting firms began to create management advisory groups late last century that augmented their accounting practices. Today, the consulting arms of Andersen, PricewaterhouseCoopers, Deloite & Touche,

KPMG, and Ernst & Young rival or overshadow their accounting parents in size and revenue stream. A very recent development has been for accounting firms to spin off their consulting arms into separate organisations.

A number of reasons have been cited for the spin-offs including conflicts of interest and the fact that some consulting arms have become bigger than their parents. The most acrimonious separation was between Arthur Andersen and Andersen Consulting, which now glories under the name of Accenture. Accenture is thriving at a time when its former parent accounting group is struggling for survival.

Then, in the 1960s, the universities moved into the consulting game, establishing centres that combined academic research with professional advice: Stanford Research Institute, Cambridge Research Institute and the Management Analysis Center were some of the earliest. Today, it seems that every university has its own consulting arm.

What does it mean for management?

The sheer growth of the industry has changed the landscape of management. Management consulting is as much a part of management practice as staff management and operations management. It has become a management process in its own right.

It has been observed that innovation in management practice is now driven almost exclusively by consultants.[3] Virtually every initiative in management practice in the last twenty years has come out of the consulting industry rather than out of management practice—whether it is a long-lasting and proven tool such as the Boston Consulting Group's Market Strategy Matrix (dogs, stars and cash cows) or a short-lived fad such as business process re-engineering (CSC Index).

Strangely, you will not read much about the development of consultancy in the professional literature of management practice. The intrusion of management consulting into the fabric of the management process remains largely undiscussed and underresearched. For example, why has the management consulting industry developed in this way? Why do we now readily turn to consultants for inspiration and guidance? Why do managers so easily give up their ownership of idea generation to outsiders? Why has it happened more in some places (United States) and less in others (Japan)? And why has it happened so intensely in the last few years as opposed to the previous 100 years?

It seems extraordinary that a complete and globalised industry can emerge and grow to the size that management consulting has without much awareness of its history, or any real appreciation of its current impact, and no idea whatsoever of its future. Hopefully, the research will happen and we will learn more about this phenomenal industry of the twentieth century.

Future concerns

In the meantime, the industry keeps evolving. Two of the latest trends are for consultants to lead the way in founding IT start-up companies and for consulting groups to invest in their clients' businesses. While the first is the subject of considerable amusement, given the enormous failure rate of the not-much-lamented hi-tech stock market boom, the second is more insidious.

When a consulting company invests in the business of the client, the relationship suddenly becomes very different. The advisory role changes to one of vested interest. Such developments raise a raft of questions about the nature of large consulting companies. As they transform themselves from their traditional role as expert adviser into a myriad of other roles (owners, directors, stalkers, etc.), they face many new situations and relationships. Some of these involve or could eventually involve conflicts of interest. How will they handle the potential for conflict of interest? Are they even thinking about such issues? Do they care?

For those who use the services of consultants, these developments also raise a number of questions. Can you truly expect honest advice from your consultants if there is a hidden agenda that involves driving the client into bankruptcy in order to acquire its assets? How can clients manage consultants imposed on them by part owners? At what point does the fiduciary duty of directors get overridden by the strategic intentions of those directors? And, finally, can you ever trust a consultant again?

Guidelines

1 Learn to manage consultants

Consultants can be useful if they are managed properly. Problems arise most typically when consultants have not been given a framework in which to do their work. Provide a framework by:

- always preparing a brief that describes the work to be done by the consultant;
- stipulating both outcomes and processes, along with all the usual stuff about timelines and commercial arrangements;
- making sure the response to the brief indicates exactly who will do what (this is to avoid the 'rainmaker syndrome' where the big-hitting consultants do the selling and inexperienced ones do the work);
- doing formal and periodic reviews of progress.

2 Learn to evaluate consultants

Hard as it is to believe, most consultancy work is not evaluated. It is not up to the consultant to ensure that an evaluation is carried out. It is a clear managerial responsibility. If possible, tell the consultant up front that there will be an evaluation and what form it will take (detail it in the brief). Then do it!

Evaluation criteria should refer back to the original brief. These can be as simple as:

- Were the outcomes required by the brief achieved?
- Were the outcomes achieved in the way that was agreed?
- Was the project completed within the agreed time frame and budget?

3 Learn to do without consultants

Why are you using consultants anyway? If you can't state a clear reason (such as lack of expertise within the organisation, or the need to be able to blame someone else if a project goes pear-shaped) then find another way.

- Set the project up as a learning opportunity for an ambitious career-minded staff member.
- Use internal service providers.
- Do it yourself by delegating other routine tasks.

Consultants are best considered as a last (and maybe desperate!) resort.

For further exploration

Still the most entertaining and thorough book on the subject of consulting is:

- J. Micklethwait and A. Wooldridge, *The Witch Doctors: What the Management Gurus are saying, why it matters, and how to make Sense of it,* Heinemann, London, 1996.

This book, by two journalists from the *Economist*, focuses primarily on the ideas peddled by consultants, but in the process it provides a host of stories and anecdotes about what goes right and what goes wrong when you use consultants. It is fairly scathing about the consulting industry but grudgingly admits its role in industry as a propagator of ideas.

If, on the other hand, you are considering becoming a consultant (and none of your good friends has had the sense to talk you out of it), you might find value in what many would argue is the industry classic:

- P. Block, *Flawless Consulting: A Guide to getting your Expertise used,* Jossey-Bass, San Fransisco, 1991.

Block provides practical and ethical advice on getting the job done in a way that serves the interests of both client and consultant.

If you are running a consulting organisation, then chances are that you will have read:

- D. Maister, *Managing the Professional Services Firm,* The Free Press, New York, 1993.

This book provides a thorough guide on how to structure, manage and develop a consulting organisation—or any professional service firm. It also reveals to managers how consulting organisations really work, and they may well find that knowledge helpful.

Working with people

CHANGE MANAGEMENT   **22**

Many people in many organisations have now been touched by the management fad called 'change management'. The ever increasing pressure to become and stay competitive has meant major change in most organisations. Most managers now believe that such changes have to be managed and that this requires specialist knowledge of 'change-management techniques'.

Many managers cry out for assistance, support and better techniques for handling change situations. What is not often discussed, however, is the amount of management time that is involved in change management. Any formal change program can easily drain scarce management resources to the point where nothing else gets done.

Another problem is that there is very little specialist knowledge to be found out there. Many claims are made about such knowledge but most of it is a mish-mash of postulation, assumption, presuppositions and just plain bad theory.

Is there any substance in change management?

Background

Change management was a key obsession of management in the last century. It is hard to be precise about when the concern with the pace of change in organisations reached the point where managers felt they needed the help of consultants. But by the late 1980s, the perceived need had developed to the point where consultants weren't enough, and then training programs emerged, and finally psychologists got involved. And so the change-management industry emerged.

It was supposed to help

Interest has died down a little in the last few years but it is unlikely that organisations and managers have entirely rid themselves of this obsession. The questions remains: Why was change management taken up with such gusto and why didn't it deliver any worthwhile results? After all, many fads have made worthwhile contributions (for example, teams, quality management, strategic planning) before evolving into just one more technique in the toolkit of management.

Change management is different because it appears to have made no discernible contribution to anything. In fact, it is hard to think of another fad that came so quickly, cost so much and disappeared so rapidly. (Only business process re-engineering springs to mind as a possible contender.)

One possible answer is that the solutions offered by change management did not match the actual needs of the moment. In other words, there was a real need and an issue that had to be addressed by management (the rapidly increasing pace of change in organisations) but the response by management to that issue (change management) was inappropriate, ineffective or both.

Most management activities involve people and therefore most management fads relate somehow to people. Organisational change, however, is *quintessentially* about people. Change management, by definition, is about managing the impact of change on people in such a way as to minimise pain, whether to the organisation, its managers or its employees. (One way of categorising change-management programs is to determine which of these three the program aims to help.)

The human factor is one of a number of elements to be considered when implementing quality management or structural change. Change management, however, is about people first and foremost. There is nothing else to talk about— it starts and finishes with people.

If a change-management program is about people, it is logical that the program must make assumptions about people, how they think, behave and react. So it is useful to examine what the program claims to know about human nature and how these assumptions will be implemented.

Human nature and change

A cursory examination of some typical programs suggests that most make no *explicit* claims about their subject. Most have some rudimentary model of how change impacts on people, but universally such models are based on unstated assumptions about what people are like. For example, possibly the most common model for understanding and explaining the impact of change is the one borrowed from the work of Elisabeth Kübler-Ross, who worked extensively with dying people.[1]

This example is interesting, not just because of what it tells us about change management but because it demonstrates a principle of how management fads work. Typically, fads are borrowed from disciplines other than management. Cultural change is borrowed from anthropology; neurolinguistic programming from discredited linguistic theory; strategy is borrowed from the battlefield; management styles of behaviour from psychology; and so on. Management itself rarely generates new ideas.

Despite its sombre origins, change-management propagators love the Kübler-Ross model. Kübler-Ross is famous for working with dying patients when the medical establishments simply did not want to deal with them. She established that people facing death go through predictable stages in their emotional reaction to the fact that they are dying. These stages are categorised as denial, anger, bargaining, depression and acceptance.

When casting about for a suitable model to depict the stages people go through during organisational change, this model seemed ideal to the propagators of change management. It needed only a few small word changes: 'depression' becomes 'confusion' and 'acceptance' becomes 'renewal'. The latter change is important because the propagators had to handle the incontrovertible fact that no one actually dies as a result of organisational change, and senior management (those who sign the cheques) insist that we have a happy ending. 'Bargaining' is often dropped because somehow it doesn't quite fit.

It can provide a good deal of personal amusement to ask those who deliver change-management programs based on the Kübler-Ross model for evidence that people subject to organisational change actually go through these stages. At best, you will get anecdotal assertions that the model is 'true', that 'everyone' knows that the model is valid and that simple observation holds it self-evident. The reason for such evasive responses is that the research evidence does not exist. There is no worthwhile research evidence that demonstrates the relevance of this model to organisational change. And so the process of dying provides an illegitimate legacy for organisational change.

All of this is not to say that theorists (and please remember the aphorism that 'there is nothing as useful as a good theory') are not active in trying to understand the connection between human nature and the workplace. To take one example—Carol Steiner is one of a handful of thinkers to analyse in depth the assumptions of the human individual upon which change-management programs are based. She is a philosopher who works with organisations. Usually, companies only call on the services of philosophers when wishing to explore ethical obligations. Steiner, instead, works on the issue of how people in organisations think.

Steiner's approach[2] (based on the work of German philosopher Martin Heidegger) emphasises that most of the behaviour in organisations is based on adherence to organisational demands for *conformity*. These demands extend to the way people think, and attempts to think in non-conformist ways are stifled. The all pervasive influence of conformity has negative consequences for the organisation (especially with regard to innovation and creativity, flexibility and responsiveness, knowledge management and empowerment).

Steiner attacks the rationalist perspective (our dominant intellectual paradigm) which treats the human experience as fully 'knowable' (in other words, the assumption that what happens to us as human and sentient beings is always capable of being understood by those to whom it is happening). Her approach explains some behaviour in organisations that does not fit easily with the rationalist explanations of how people behave (for example, when managers do one thing and say they are doing another). It also provides a validation for those managers who regularly (but without admitting it) rely on their gut reaction, intuition and feelings to make critical decisions.

Steiner argues that most approaches to change management are based on a view of human nature that restricts the individuality of the people who work in organisations. Such approaches tend to consider people in organisations as things to be manipulated for their own good and for the greater (organisational) good. The consequence of this type of thinking is that we reduce people's humanity by treating them as pawns in an organisational game. Once people realise or sense that this is how the organisation thinks of them, any notion of commitment, let alone loyalty, goes out the window.

Steiner's work encourages a more thinking approach to organisational issues and, for that matter, to all human experience. And if that means we start to see through the emptiness and meaninglessness of activities such as change-management programs, then it is timely advice.

Coping with change

So how do you help yourself and others cope with change? I know of no simple formula, but the following principles[3] have served various organisations well over the years as they struggled to come to terms with never ending change. These principles assume that we are dealing with people who are capable of understanding organisational imperatives for change—in other words, adults.

1 The *centrality* principle. Change processes must be based on the fundamental strategic issues of the organisation. In other words, either do it for a very good reason, or don't do it at all. And 'very good reason' here means that it is a critical part of the strategic (that is survival and growth) direction of the organisation.

2 The *fix the pain* principle. Change strategies will be more powerful if they deliver solutions to the strongly felt needs of the people of the organisation, particularly the opinion leaders. Be prepared to articulate how the proposed change will improve things for the people who will be affected by it. Focus on how their circumstances will be better after the change.

3 The *stakeholder* principle. Change planning must be sensitive to the needs and aspirations of key internal and external demand groups who have power and/or influence over organisational performance. Diverse and sometimes competing demands will be made by those who have a stake in the organisation and you need to understand these demands and work with them as drivers for change.

4 The *light on the hill* principle. Change planning will be more effective if it is based on a future vision of greater excellence rather than limited to current problems or immediate opportunities. New policies, values and required behaviour must be formulated and articulated clearly. People are always more willing to take a risk (and going along with change is always risky) if they understand that there is some greater purpose (however it is explained) that is served by the change.

5 The *total systems* principle. The success of the change processes will be optimised if you address their impact on all key dimensions of organisational functioning and ensure *congruence of change elements*. Most change consists of lots of

bits and pieces of small change; they must all fit together into a rational whole (to avoid falling into an irrational hole) and this requires careful coordination of all the elements that comprise the change.

6   The *leadership modelling* principle. Strategies for change with a long transition period require strong, visible, consistent and distinctly different leadership behaviour. There must be a clear demonstration of commitment at the top. You cannot delegate the driving of change initiatives to someone lower down in the hierarchy; if you're not leading, it will not be credible.

7   The *managing expectations* principle. Change planning requires the full, open and consistent communication of motivations, plans, methods and successes in bringing about change, and must provide for feedback from the people impacted so that unwarranted positive and negative expectations can be effectively managed. Any change initiative will raise expectations (realistic or otherwise) and you need a mechanism to deal with them. Typically, this means lots of communication and then yet more communication.

8   The *involvement* principle. Change success is strengthened by the genuine inclusion and involvement of maximum numbers of people impacted by the plans to facilitate the development of widespread ownership and commitment. People support what they help to develop. Their involvement will strengthen understanding of and commitment to the process.

9   The *critical mass* principle. Change strategies should aim at multiple entry points in the relatively healthy parts of the organisation, develop networks of supportive people and selectively build up irresistible momentum rather than wasting energy on resistant forces or attempting too much too quickly. You need to find and energise those who support the change in order to develop momentum.

10 The *critical path* principle. Change planning requires the development of a logical sequence of progressive change activities based on purposeful change goals over a realistic time frame. People need to see that stuff is happening, so structure progressive steps that advertise that the change is occurring.

11 The *inevitable resistance* principle. Change is inherently 'conflictful' so planning must encompass a clear, early

understanding of the forms and sources of resistance to the changes contemplated and provide effective forums for dissenters to express disagreement. This will enable the effective management of unconstructive conflict.

12 The *change champion* principle. Change planning must be supported by a nucleus of highly committed, well informed change agents who facilitate the process and are willing to draw on necessary internal and external expertise to maximise chances of success. It's often a full-time job and may need dedicated (in both senses of the word) staff.

13 The *there's no such thing as a free lunch* principle. Change on a large scale costs time, money and personal effort and is often painful and stressful; these risks and costs must be assessed. Be realistic about how long it will take, what it will cost, and what it will deliver.

Using principles such as these puts people back into the organisational change equation. This approach stops managers from treating people in organisations that are going through change as if they were simpletons to be protected from bad news. If change management is really about people, let's start treating people as people, and not as children.

Guidelines

1 Tell people

Someone once said that people do not fear change—they just fear the unknown that comes with change. You can therefore make the change process a lot easier for people if you tell them as much as possible about it. And where you don't know what's going to happen, admit that and promise to tell them as soon as you do know. People will trust you about change if you're honest. No one these days expects managers to know everything about what is going to happen.

Tell them what you can, admit the bits you don't know and 'keep them in the loop'.

2 Involve people

If you do have some control over the change process, involve as many people as is practical. People support what they help to create, and by involving the many rather than the few you maximise easy acceptance of change.

Within most organisational change, there is a degree of discretion as to how it is executed. Involve, consult, ask for advice, and you will probably be surprised at how much more smoothly things go.

3 Monitor impact

During change, check constantly with your people regarding how the changes are impacting on them.

The act of checking and asking how people are going indicates that you care and are concerned. This will be appreciated and will be repaid generously when you need to rely on their goodwill in the future.

You will also discover things that you did not know were happening. Managers only ever see a small part of what is actually happening in their organisation. Much is hidden from the eyes of management.

Talking to your people allows you to tap into what is really going on.

For further exploration

Despite the vast number of books on the subject of change in organisations, much of the information is of little use to the practising manager. Consultants pounced on the subject with great gusto, but the most obvious impact of this was simply to cause managers to worry about how to do stuff they had been doing for many years without the help of outside experts.

Of course, some writers have added value to the topic by providing ideas for managing change. A good range of ideas is presented in:

- G. Huber and W. Glick (eds), *Organizational Change and Redesign: Ideas and Insights for Improving Performance*, Oxford University Press, Oxford, 1995.

Many of the experts in specific fields of organisational change management are represented: Kim Cameron on organisational redesign; Andrew Van De Ven on innovation; John Slocum on organisational alliances; Richard Daft on communicating organisational change; and many others. The book provides an excellent historical overview of the literature on organisational change as an appendix.

Another worthwhile collection is:

- D. Hambrick, D. Nadler and N. Tushman (eds), *Navigating Change: How CEOs, Top Teams and Boards Steer Transformation*, Harvard Business School Press, Boston, 1998.

This book contains the contributions of many well known executives such as Paul Allaire of Xerox, James Houghton of Corning and Robert Baumann of Aerospace. Other contributions come from eminent academics in the field such as Kets de Vries from INSEAD, Chris Bartlett from Harvard, Sumantra Ghoshal from the London Business School and Kathleen Eisenhardt from Stanford.

Finally, John Kotter's contribution to any management topic is always likely to be of a high calibre.

- J. Kotter, *Leading Change*, Harvard Business School Press, Boston, 1996.

This book is no exception and is an outstanding contribution to the field. His focus lies mainly with the role of leadership in driving change and has been described as inspirational by various commentators. It is well written and provides excellent guidance to senior managers.

MANAGEMENT AND METAPHORS

23

Sometimes we forget that the activities of management are largely executed by means of *language*. If, as some say, management is about getting things done through other people, then language is the medium used to manage those interactions. The intent of one person is expressed in language that hopefully conveys that intent to another. The fact that managers and their direct reports so often misunderstand each other highlights the fact that language is a creative medium, involving a creative act of expression and a creative act of interpretation. No wonder it goes wrong so often!

It is worthwhile to think about how the linguistic mechanism actually affects (interferes with?) the process of management. After all, if we could understand this a little better, maybe we could also get a little better at using language in the workplace.

One aspect that brings both opportunity and challenge is the use of *metaphoric language* to inspire and explain what is going on in organisations. In particular, we seem to turn to metaphors when we need to describe complicated concepts such as organisational culture and organisational change. Ordinary language just does not do the trick in these situations.

But using metaphors comes at a price. Not everyone will interpret the meanings of metaphors in the same way.

What is the role of metaphor in the workplace?

Background

'The road ahead is long and hard; but if we all work together as a team, stay true to our vision, then we will make it.' So speaks the Managing Director as he outlines his plans for the company's future to the assembled employees.

To convey the difficulties that lie ahead for the company, he resorts increasingly to descriptive language: battles to be fought, mountains to be climbed, dangers to be averted, victories to be achieved.

Of course, he doesn't actually think the company is a vehicle travelling on a road or an army unit on the battlefield.

The non-literal descriptions in his speech (metaphors) are just a rhetorical device. As most spruikers know, figurative expressions bring something powerful to the task of communicating vital points. And metaphor is the most powerful and compelling device of them all. Managers use metaphors constantly. Metaphors are everywhere in organisational life. We use them to describe the purpose of the organisation (the big picture), how the organisation will operate (like a family, like a finely tuned machine, like a flock of birds), the role of the leader (conducting an orchestra, steering the boat) and why the organisation must change (to defeat the enemy, to win the battle, to capture the spoils).

Using metaphors to make sense of work

One reason for the prevalence of metaphors in organisations is that they capture the big idea better than literal descriptions. A metaphor like 'the information superhighway' contains a dozen different ideas in one simple phrase. This makes the phrase so much more powerful than if it had been a long list of how we will combine various IT and communication applications into a comprehensive service for consumers.

Another reason for the prevalence of metaphors is that they can capture a vague concept in a way that makes it seemingly more understandable to an audience. For example, back in the 1940s, one of the first social scientists, Kurt Lewin, used the language of the natural world to describe the process of how organisations change (unfreeze, change, refreeze) to bring sense to something rather vague and obscure.[1]

Ultimately, sense-making and sense-giving are probably what underpin the use of metaphor in organisational settings. The risk, however, is that the metaphor will be treated as the reality: if you think of an organisation as a machine, the leaders may want to play mechanic, tinkering with the parts; if you think of it as an organic entity, the leaders may prefer to think of themselves as gardeners (or genetic engineers or farmers or viral agents!).

Treating metaphors as reality is often described as 'confusing the map with the territory'. Famously, eighteenth-century Italian researchers considered thunder to be much like a cannon exploding and proceeded to study the cannon in great depth for many years. They learnt much about cannons but little about the weather.

Writers on management have been using the analogies offered by a good metaphor for many years. At various times, the organisation has been described as a machine, an organism, a political system, a neural network, an orchestra, a jazz band, clouds, soap bubbles and termites. (By the way, the first and last in that list are by the same author—Gareth Morgan—in publications separated by thirteen years, which I guess shows some progress away from mechanistic models.[2])

Formal studies have looked at how metaphors are used in decision making, leadership, change management, organisation development, training, strategy, policy, computers and production management. These studies tried to understand how organisations function. Since metaphors are the building blocks of the mental maps that guide management thinking, the research hopes to unearth useful lessons that can be applied by others.[3]

This, of course, makes it inevitable that there are consultants who specialise in how to make the best use of metaphors. This may or may not be a good thing. Many people will have heard the metaphorical description of consultants as 'diseases in search of patients' or 'hammers in search of nails'.

The impact of metaphors

One of the research findings is that metaphors can hide dissent—or, rather, they provide apparent consensus. While everyone in an organisation may agree that there is a rocky road to be travelled, what remains unsaid is who will be travelling first class and who will be pushing the carriages. This may lead to disappointment!

Nevertheless, a good metaphor can galvanise people into action by creating a compelling and shared view of the world, even ennobling the role of employees. When Steve Jobs described Apple as 'the force for freedom', Apple employees immediately knew the vital importance of their work in saving the world from IBM PCs. Netscape employees do something similar by reputedly describing Microsoft as the 'Death Star' with Bill Gates in the role of Darth Vader.

Metaphors can shake up the accepted wisdom and force people to think differently, even creatively. If the future of IT is the information superhighway, who will control the toll booths, sell the petrol, maintain the edges, clear up the road kill, patrol the speed limits, service those who have broken down? Indeed, who will be the road kill?

Whether all the newfound knowledge about the role of metaphor is actually beneficial remains to be seen. In one recent project, involving major changes that would affect almost everyone in a very large organisation, an 'internal change agent' was heard to remark that his job was 'to make the turkeys look forward to Christmas'. Now there's a metaphor!

Metaphors and cultural change

One aspect of organisational life that is particularly susceptible to metaphoric description is organisational culture. Culture has been described, in its simplest terms, as 'the way we do things around here' (though this possibly hides more than it explains, see Chapter 16). Part of the need to describe organisational culture is that it is a common target for change projects, and to change something you need to be able to identify it first.

Cultural change projects often resort to metaphoric language. For example, there is a mechanical view of culture change, which sees an organisation as a static unit requiring a shake-up delivered by an outside force. In the long run, this process is generally not of lasting value. Alternatively, cultural change may be seen as something constantly evolving from forces generated within the group of individuals who make up the workforce. These two metaphorical descriptions (mechanical versus evolutionary) imply different views about how things work inside the organisation.

One example of how metaphorical language can affect our thinking, and therefore the actions we take, is explained by Richard Seel, a consultant who works in the area of organisational change. Seel uses the metaphor of a *flower* to illustrate the relationships between various aspects of an organisation's culture.[4] At the centre of the flower is the paradigm—the shared ideas and values that form the unifying basis of an organisation and originate in the communication process. Influenced by the paradigm are the surrounding *petals*—structures, systems, routines and processes—which Seel calls the manifestations of culture. The traditional approach to change concentrates on the practical (the petals) and very often the positive effects are not lasting. The paradigm (the centre of the flower) is what filters perceptions and influences reactions and should, therefore, be the starting point for change.

Complexity arises from the complex interactions between the members of the organisation's community, which are themselves complex units. When the connection between individuals is established and allowed to flourish, significant changes are possible. Once again, Seel uses an image to explain, this time *grains of sand*, to indicate that the impact of even small changes can be large: adding one tiny grain to a pile of sand may cause a complete collapse.

Seel favours yet another metaphor to explain his tenet that the agent of change has a central task as facilitator: *the midwife*. The facilitator role is currently limited by a detached, external view of intervention, where a clinical assessment is formed and a solution delivered. Even when getting closer to the action, the facilitator is still operating outside the system. Seel argues that the agent must work within the organisation, aiming to ensure preparation is so effective that the facilitator can withdraw when the group is able to support its own process of change.

Seel cites a personal case history of a model for change, likening it this time to a benign virus. He describes a workshop he conducted which aimed to 'sensitise people to the power of culture and paradigms . . . to encourage them to discover a compelling vision of a future culture which would motivate them to behave differently'.[5] Again, communication was the focal point—'middle-out' rather than 'top-down or bottom-up'. The connections were encouraged across the board, at the level of day-to-day issues of importance. The risk of resistance was acknowledged—the organisation's 'immune system' counteracting the infection of new ideas—and a warning given of the potential for power play. Senior management is in a strong position to counteract negative attitudes and can make the difference between success and failure.

Meaningful changes to organisational culture can be implemented when the process is effectively managed from within, and when all those involved are encouraged to participate—'using the midwife metaphor . . . worked with rather than worked on'. This is a challenge, both for management who are looking for the right approach and for those who will initiate the inquiry and evaluation.

An organisation's culture is a blend of many factors, both the visible and invisible, and subject at any time to a shift in emphasis or focus. When its potential to be a positive force is recognised and utilised, it can become more vital, an asset rather than a liability.

In areas such as culture, it may well be that metaphoric language, despite all its drawbacks, is the only means we have to talk about something so ephemeral.

Guidelines

1 Watch your language

It is very easy for a person's thinking to be swayed by the language used to express it to others. Such language can be powerfully motivating but it can also hide the reality of the situation.

Metaphors are attractive because they capture something of the situation in just a few words. However, if the reality is complex (as it usually is in organisational matters), those same metaphors may fall short of the mark in adequately capturing what is happening.

2 Watch other people's language

It is also easy to be swayed by other people's rhetoric when describing organisational issues. Your thinking will be influenced by the words used by others to describe what is going on.

In critical situations, try to look beyond the rhetoric to the reality that is being described. Develop your own take on the situation, using your own descriptions of what is happening.

Language is often used to mislead and this is not confined to corporate brochures or advertising campaigns. It is just as prevalent in the workplace.

Remember that organisational issues are always complex and can rarely be captured adequately by a single metaphor.

3 Reduce complexity

There are some situations in which metaphors are very useful and practical. Mostly, such situations involve the need to explain complex things in simple language. For example, in manufacturing, the need to operate with the minimum resources in order to be competitive is often described as 'lean' manufacturing. The need to be very flexible and very

responsive to customer needs may be described as 'agility'.
Both these metaphors communicate a great deal in just one
word. To that extent they are useful in reducing a complex
topic to just one word. This can help to communicate
something that is new and not well understood by others.

For further exploration

The idea of applying creative thinking to the way we manage
organisations is still a bit novel so there is not that much
material out there to act as a guide. The outstanding
contribution is probably from Gareth Morgan:

• G. Morgan, *Imaginization: New Mindsets for Seeing, Organizing
  and Managing*, Berrett-Koehler, San Francisco, 1997.

Morgan is well respected as an author, academic and
consultant, and has worked for some of the world's largest
organisations. So when he decides to combine 'imagination'
with 'organization', it might pay to take note. The book is an
interesting mix of playfulness and business awareness. This
results in such things as 'Strategic Termites', 'Spider Plants',
'Boiling Dry' and 'Futureblock'. To assess the usefulness of
these ideas, you will have to read the book.

DISCUSSING THE UNDISCUSSABLE

24

There is much that we are not allowed to talk about in our organisations. Special codes of silence mean that a whole range of issues that ought to be discussed are not. People know what can be discussed and what cannot. But, not being able to talk about some things seriously inhibits our capacity (individually and collectively) to learn.

Chris Argyris is Professor of Education and Organizational Behaviour in the Graduate Schools of Education and Business at Harvard University. He has been researching and theorising about learning and what inhibits it since the 1950s. Some 150 or so articles and books later, he is still trying to make us understand our limitations when it comes to getting smarter at what we do.

Some of his ideas are powerful but not always easy to grasp. Others are immediately obvious as soon as he has explained them. One of these is the concept of undiscussability. It may seem at first sight a rather obscure topic but, as soon as you start to think about what makes organisations tick, it becomes obvious that any organisation that cannot discuss its own inner workings is unlikely ever to become a high-performing organisation.

How do we discuss the undiscussable things that hold organisations back from success?

Background

Chris Argyris is not a fashionable guru. While the Harvard professor has provided us with many of the critical concepts we use to understand how organisations function, the unforgiving complexity of his work has made his research inaccessible to most practitioners.

Not for Argyris the snappy simplicity that turns deep insights into an unforgettable acronym, a technique that appears to underpin the process of management fad creation. You cannot apply Argyris's thinking in one minute, nor does it reduce easily to seven or so principles.

Argyris and organisational behaviour

Argyris is the pioneer of organisational learning, exploring the behaviours that make an organisation smarter than its competitors. His work predates the more faddish 'learning organisation' of Senge[1] and others by several decades. He gave us the 'theory-in-use' and 'theory-in-action' contrast that helps explain why managers do different things from what they think they do. When managers explain why they do the things they do (their 'theory-in-use') it is often the case that this does not match up with the actions actually taken by those managers (their 'theory-in-action').

Argyris gave us the concepts of 'single loop' and 'double loop' learning, explaining why so many of us deal with problems without learning from them, and thus are unable to prevent the same problems arising again. 'Single loop' learning allows us to respond to a problem and fix it; 'double loop' learning enables us to ask why the problem occurred in the first place. If you can only do the first and not the second then you are likely to be fixing a lot of the same problems over and over again.

Argyris also made major contributions to the research methods we use in trying to understand the management process. His rigorous research methods demonstrated a third way between the sterile extremes of statistical analysis on the one hand (the scourge of many Psych I students) and the vagaries of anecdotal description on the other hand (the scourge of anyone trying to overcome subjectivity). While some of the results of his research have entered the language of management, the meticulous research that generated those results is rarely copied.

Almost perversely, Argyris shrouds his work in theoretical complexity, seeming to prefer the arcane when the transparent would do. Nevertheless, how many academic researchers can lay claim to a website detailing their every piece of research, which is lovingly maintained by devotees?[2]

Beyond the daunting complexity of his work (and who is to say that research in organisational behaviour should result in less complexity than disciplines such as quantum mechanics or theoretical linguistics?), there is another feature of his work that holds it back from greater understanding and use by practising managers. And that is the lack of 'operationalisation' of his theoretical concepts.

As an 'action researcher', Argyris obviously uses specific techniques while wearing his consultant's hat. He even describes some of his data-gathering and 'training' techniques in some of his writing. But there is no substantive body of process technique that you can point to that would answer the question 'What do I do to make my organisation smarter?'

Or the material is so embedded in academic publications that access is effectively denied to the practitioner. Even his occasional foray into the pages of the *Harvard Business Review* is little more than a teasing trailer for the tools and techniques that seem so tantalisingly effective in delivering results to his research subjects. One recent book has a temptingly popular title but inside you will find the same theoretical density that prevails in all his other work.[3]

It is as if a lifetime of understanding and wisdom about how organisations function is waiting to be popularised. If Steven Covey made his millions by means of the single bright idea of reading 1000 texts on the meaning of leadership and distilling their essence into seven habits, then what populist possibilities lie in the Argyris archives?

Undiscussable issues

One of Argyris's more practical but underexploited concepts is the idea that *there are matters in all organisations that are simply undiscussable*. Further, the undiscussability of these matters is also undiscussable.

Even at a glance, this goes a long way towards explaining why sometimes the people in organisations cannot see the wood for the trees, and continually do things that are known to lead to failure. If a detour from a pathway that is known to lead to failure involves wandering into undiscussable territory, then we can predict that the organisation will press on with the well known paths to proven failure. Such organisations cannot learn.

This anti-learning mechanism is explained by what Argyris terms, in his typically user-unfriendly language, 'primary inhibitory loops'. He describes these as 'self-reinforcing patterns of action strategies and anti-learning consequences'.[4] My translation of this is that managers, in trying to solve problems, tend to resort to tactics that prevent them from speaking about situations truthfully. (See below for some reasons for this.) This leads them into a 'loop' of avoiding the real problem of the situation, which is followed by a failure to learn anything about that problem, which is followed by more conversations that avoid the real problem. After a bit of this, those involved in the process all agree that they are wasting their time but don't understand why this is the case. Everyone leaves the discussion feeling dissatisfied but not knowing why nothing was achieved.

Managers are trapped in these loops for various reasons (Argyris calls them 'conditions for error') such as vagueness, ambiguity, untestability, scattered information, information withheld, undiscussability, uncertainty, inconsistency and incompatibility. The 'undiscussability' error is common knowledge to most people working in organisations. Most people know the matters that cannot be raised openly in discussion in their organisation, and if such matters are raised they are likely to be ignored. Such matters are clearly known to all, but mentioned by none.

One of the consequences of this pattern of individual behaviour, driven by the mutually reinforcing interplay between primary inhibitory loops and conditions for errors, is a secondary pattern that Argyris calls 'secondary inhibitory loops'. These loops exist at the group level and are somewhat like norms that reflect and reinforce the anti-learning behaviour of the individuals. For example, if enough people in an organisation repeatedly avoid talking about the fact that the computer staff and the line managers cannot communicate, the organisation as a whole will create a pattern of behaviour that avoids dealing with this issue. It will become the norm not to discuss the fact that there is a complete lack of cooperation and understanding between the two functions. The breakdown between the two has become 'undiscussable'.

The powerful feedback mechanism of anti-learning norms reinforcing individual anti-learning behaviour explains why collective learning, even in organisations populated by very smart people, is still extremely difficult. In fact, Argyris went out of his way to conduct much of his research in what were considered smart organisations, including one of the most respected international consulting organisations, where an MBA is the minimum entry ticket.[5] He showed over and over again that these very smart people could not learn from their mistakes, individually or collectively. (This may explain why consultants are never wrong!) If such very clever people can't get it right, what hope for the rest of us?

These anti-learning mechanisms explain how a combination of failure and the inability to learn from that failure rapidly leads to distrust, suspicion and cynicism. When the true reasons for organisational failure to learn cannot be discussed, alternative explanations will breed like a computer virus. These in turn progressively obscure the true reasons for failure until those reasons become undiscoverable.

Subversive defence routines

The loops are part of a phenomenon Argyris calls 'organisational defense routines':

These are actions and policies, enacted within an organisational setting, that are intended to protect individuals from experiencing embarrassment or threat, while at the same time preventing individuals, or the organisation as a whole, from identifying the causes of embarrassment or threat in order to correct the relevant problem.[6]

These routines are entirely logical and rule-driven. Essentially, the logic comprises four rules:

1 Craft messages that contain inconsistencies.
2 Act as if the messages are not inconsistent.
3 Make the ambiguity and inconsistency in the message undiscussable.
4 Make the undiscussability of the undiscussable also undiscussable.[7]

A simple but common example of how the rules apply is when a CEO announces a new initiative, such as encouraging employees to be innovative, empowered or customer-focused. Most employees go along with the new initiatives despite knowing that the CEO does not mean it—those who act on the new initiative (do something different, use their own judgment, refund an unhappy customer) risk getting into trouble. Some do get into trouble and are dealt with. The whole process is known to be a charade but no one talks about it in that way. The failure of the CEO's initiative is attributed to other reasons, such as lack of commitment by employees. The initiative is soon forgotten. The organisation has gained nothing and learnt nothing.

The four rules have a clear capacity to predict behaviours and outcomes in organisations. That alone makes them a rarity in the field of organisational research.

The rules also explain why change is so difficult in organisations. They point to how change can be made more effective by challenging the cycle of defensive routines that inhibit learning. In a sense, it means that organisations and individuals have to learn how to learn.

Argyris observes that:

> We believe that our analysis helps to explain the characteristic life cycle of such organisational fixes as TQM, Flat Organisation, Reengineering, and Management Empowerment. In each such instance, a prescription for organisational reform appears on the horizon, supported by plausible-sounding theory and stories of successful implementation by early adopters. Often at the core of the reform there lies a significant insight, for example that managers should be freed up to take on greater responsibility and make greater use of local knowledge, or organisational processes should be rethought in the light of possibilities opened up by advanced information technology. Usually, however, the prescription is converted by its advocates, and the consultants who undertake its dissemination, into a readily understandable package of procedures. Not infrequently, the package is accompanied by an ideology that takes on quasi-religious overtones.
>
> Organisation managers, thirsty for solutions to the persistent predicaments in which they find themselves and impatient with calls to wrestle with the complexity of the predicaments or with their own possible collusion in reinforcing them, latch onto the package. A bandwagon effect ensues as managers adopt the package because managers around them are adopting it. Then over time, as experience with the reform builds up and as good intentions are subverted by organisational defensive routines . . . a literature of disillusionment begins to appear. The normal cynicism begins to reassert itself. Lower-level managers begin to mutter that those at the top never really meant it, and top-level managers express their frustration at the intractable resistance to change exhibited by those below them. People begin to say, 'We tried that!' and a readiness for the next reform package begins to take shape.[8]

Argyris's explanations of what happens in organisations are very powerful. His prescriptions for what to do about some of the less desirable things that happen are complex. We can only hope that someone will build a practical bridge for us that connects the two.

Guidelines

1 Put on a new hat

One way of avoiding some of the worst effects of the anti-learning mechanisms that Argyris describes is to have someone (you?) move away from the traditional role of manager to another role, that of facilitator.

Facilitators are there to keep an eye on the *process* rather than the content of a group session. Their job is to ensure that the group is using the right tools for the job they are doing and check on how the group goes about achieving its outcomes.

Although it is helpful to have trained and/or experienced facilitators perform this role, everyone can do it at some level. For example, the most basic facilitation technique is to ask such questions as 'Why are we doing this in this way?' and 'What are we trying to do here?' or even 'What is happening now?'.

The important thing is to have someone dedicated to the role, since it is very difficult to contribute to the content of a group's session and try to facilitate the process at the same time. By giving the job of facilitation to a particular person for a particular session, you ensure that the process is attended to properly. In this way, if a group starts to adopt courses of action that seem counterproductive, the facilitator can draw attention to this. All of which helps to raise awareness of *how* things are done, in addition to *what* is done.

There is nothing as sobering as having a facilitator draw attention to the fact that the group is waffling, spinning its wheels or avoiding the real issue.

2 Make people aware

As a manager, you can draw attention to one or more of the ideas of Argyris. You don't need to name them or do a formal presentation on them but you can raise them in various casual ways.

For example, many people find the notion of *undiscussability* quite interesting and intriguing. You could open a group session with a reference to it, describe it briefly and ask if it happens in your organisation. (This is not to be confused with raising it in order to demand to know whether people are not discussing stuff openly—such a confrontational approach would simply reinforce the undiscussable status of the undiscussability!)

Some of the articles listed below in *For further exploration* are generally readable and you might consider giving a copy to some key people in your organisation. It is likely that they will ring big-time bells with some people.

The purpose of all this is to raise consciousness. Once you have started to discuss undiscussability, it is much harder for people to avoid discussing it.

3 The learning organisation

Recent interest in 'knowledge management'[9] and 'the learning organisation'[10] have opened up another avenue of attack within the anti-learning organisation.

Knowledge management often focuses on capturing the tacit knowledge that resides within the organisation, the stuff that people know but isn't written down anywhere. This stuff is now known to be valuable to the point where people are trying to put a monetary value on it.

Making tacit knowledge explicit involves understanding how organisations learn. This creates the opportunity to raise Argyris's ideas as they relate directly to the quality of the organisational learning process employed.[11]

It is now respectable to talk about whether your organisation actually learns. In senior management forums, it may be fruitful simply to ask such questions as:

• How well do we learn from our mistakes and/or our successes?
• How do we know that we are learning from our mistakes and/or successes?
• Are we getting better at learning in this organisation?

Once again, this uses basic facilitation techniques to draw people into a discussion about things that are not normally discussed. Putting this stuff on the table is the first step.

For further exploration

Try some of the shorter and more accessible pieces by Argyris, such as his regular pieces in the *Harvard Business Review* (obtainable from http://www.hbsp.harvard.edu) or elsewhere.

If one or other makes sense to you, try spreading copies around to colleagues and use them as the basis for a discussion.

- C. Argyris, 'Empowerment: the emperor's new clothes', *Harvard Business Review*, May–June 1998, pp. 98–105.
- C. Argyris, 'Good communication that blocks learning', *Harvard Business Review*, July–August 1994, pp. 77–85.
- C. Argyris, 'Overcoming organizational defenses', *Journal for Quality and Participation*, March–April 1992, pp. 26–28.
- C. Argyris, 'Teaching smart people how to learn', *Harvard Business Review*, May–June 1991, pp. 99–109.

EMOTIONS AT WORK   25

Life at work is not usually considered in terms of emotional
extremes. Emotion is supposed to be left at home, a part of us
that belongs to our private non-working lives, generally
considered unsuitable for the workplace. But emotion is so
much a part of us that it is almost impossible to keep it out of
the workplace.

At one extreme, we have the emotional states associated
with success. Many people can nominate situations at work
when everything went just right for them. The daring few
might even describe such experiences as a time of happiness.
And happiness is relatively rare at work. What makes for a
happy work experience?

At the other extreme, we may encounter situations that are
profoundly disturbing and even frightening. One example of
this is when managers behave badly, whether it is an act of
bullying or some other form of inappropriate behaviour. Bosses
behaving badly can create profound unhappiness for everyone
else at work. What to do when a manager goes off the rails?

What can we do to influence emotional situations?

Background

For many people, one of the greatest things about being at
work is the opportunity to work with others. At its best, the
experience of working with others to achieve an objective is
very rewarding. But often such 'team experiences' are less than
satisfactory, when teams just muddle through and barely
succeed or fail altogether.

Happiness and teams

Most deliberate efforts to create superior team performance
fail. It seems that the high-performance team owes more to
serendipity than it does to planning. The study of high-
performance teams is a relatively recent affair. While work
groups have been studied formally ever since the US National
Training Laboratory was set up in the late 1940s, field studies
are still relatively rare, largely because of the difficulties of
studying teams in action. The presence of an observer affects
the team's performance and controlling all relevant variables is
almost impossible.

The research that has been done has thrown up much contradictory data, and even a cursory review of the literature suggests that there is still much debate about methods and virtually no agreement on theory. Once you move beyond the facile 'orming' stuff derived from Tuckman's well known model of the stages of group development (forming, storming, norming, performing),[1] there is almost no accepted explanation of how a high-performance team evolves. (I'm assuming here that it does evolve, although even that is debatable and debated.)

Indeed, the debate has been so vigorous and so unproductive that I am starting to wonder whether there is a more fundamental problem than just the difficulty of studying teams in action in a natural setting. Maybe we have been looking for explanations of the high-performance phenomenon in the wrong places. Maybe it is less to do with group psychology, team dynamics and team design and much more to do with something altogether more personal.

While from a managerial perspective we focus (naturally enough) on the outputs of the high-performance team, the other side of the benefit coin is personal satisfaction: the buzz you get when you work with others in a focused way and overcome a difficult challenge. And this is a highly personal experience, so personal in fact that the individuals in the team have considerable difficulty in explaining just what it felt like.

I have asked hundreds of team members to describe their experiences when they were participants in high-performing teams. Their answers have a sameness about them that is a bit unnerving: excitement, achievement, fun, satisfaction, exhilaration, making a worthwhile contribution, facing a difficult challenge.

For something that may well be a peak experience in employees' working lives, the descriptions of the experience are quite banal. One interesting variation is that frontline employees often nominate non-work examples of high-performance teamwork (for example, community groups, religious organisations, sports teams) while managers typically nominate work-dominated examples.

What is striking about all this, however, is that behind these banal descriptions there clearly lies a deeply moving experience that the words fail to capture adequately. Only the occasional team member has the courage to use words that are very unmanagerial, such as: 'It was the happiest work experience of my life' or 'It was a deeply satisfying part of my job'.

Flow and work satisfaction

All this makes me think that the explanation for the power of teams to motivate people has something to do with the general phenomenon of *human happiness*, rather than with some specific and special aspect of group dynamics.

Fortunately, considerable headway has been made in the state of our knowledge about human happiness. One of the best theorists in the field is Mihaly Csikszentmihalyi—best because, like most good theorists, his theorising is based on a wealth of data, gathered over many years.

Csikszentmihalyi is Professor of Psychology at the University of Chicago and is best known for his theory of *flow*, an unusually modest name for a theory that has considerable explanatory power in terms of what happens to us when we have peak experiences.[2] Flow includes what athletes call 'being in the zone', what artists might call 'aesthetic rapture' and what mystics refer to as 'ecstasy'.

Flow is the highly focused and concentrated state of consciousness that accompanies a sense of effortless achievement. It is a peak experience of deep satisfaction that results from the attainment of a goal. It happens when we strive for a worthwhile but difficult result and make it.

Flow fits comfortably with what happens in high-performance teams. It echoes the descriptions of the team experience: sense of achievement, difficult task, coordinated effort, urgent need to succeed, exceptional teamwork.

Csikszentmihalyi's studies suggest that flow happens when:

1 there are clear goals every step of the way;
2 there is immediate feedback on actions taken;
3 there is a balance between challenge and skill level;
4 action and awareness are intermingled;
5 the mind is focused;
6 there is no fear of failure and an absence of self-consciousness;
7 The activity has become an end in itself.[3]

Interestingly, Csikszentmihalyi's research suggests that, although people do experience flow at work, it happens more frequently for most of us during active leisure and hobby activities. It is least likely to happen during passive leisure activities such as watching television or snoozing on the couch.

It may well be the case that the formation of a team to tackle a project provides a structure for Csikszentmihalyi's flow prerequisites. By setting up a team, we are creating the right conditions for flow to happen. Teams that fail often lack this set of conditions (lack of clear focus, misunderstood goals, task too difficult or too easy, the team receives no feedback on how it is doing, etc.); successful teams are almost always provided with these conditions.

This would explain why some of the variables in team performance that we thought would make a difference (such as personality, technical skill level, previous team experience and leadership) actually don't make any difference at all.

Rather than looking at high-performing teams as first and foremost a group experience, maybe we should consider it an experience that allows the individuals in the team to undergo a 'flow' experience. We could then select the members of a team on the basis of their likelihood to fulfil Csikszentmihalyi's flow prerequisites.

For example, we might poll all potential members with such questions as:

1 Do they understand the goals of the team task?
2 Do they think the goals worthwhile?
3 How will they measure the team's achievements?
4 Will the tasks stretch their abilities?
5 Can they reflect on their actions as they undertake them?
6 Can they cope with failure?

All this makes the process of establishing and composing a team much more difficult. But by doing so we might increase the incidence of exceptional team performance from a rarity to a frequent occurrence. And that would make a lot of people happy.

When the manager is the problem

At the other extreme, what makes a lot of people unhappy is the behaviour of senior management.

The growing trend towards teamwork in many organisations raises the question of how to handle those situations where one member of a team (or possibly a whole team) behaves in ways that are disruptive to the organisation. This question becomes very pointed when the team member is a senior manager.

In one example, a large retail organisation agreed that strategic focus and teamwork at the top was the way forward after a period of stagnation. Unfortunately, one senior manager's style of behaviour seemed to contradict this, with autocratic and hostile behaviour towards colleagues and peers, as well as subordinates. The CEO's intervention amounted to no more than occasional remarks about the need for greater teamwork. Morale plummeted, other senior staff left the organisation, quickly followed by the senior manager in question, leaving a major and painful talent gap in the organisation.[4]

The CEO had failed to handle his 'moment of truth' by dealing with this admittedly difficult situation. The choice of acting decisively or walking away from an awkward task can be a defining moment for any leader. Unfortunately, there are few places a top executive can go for advice or training in how to handle 'moments of truth'. Experience is the usual proving ground, and role models may be few and far between.

'Bad' behaviour by managers can run counter to the professed values and principles of the organisation. In the extreme, it can damage the organisation. When senior management behaviour goes off the rails and starts to hurt the organisation and its people, top executives need to intervene early and handle these 'moments of truth'.

'Moments of truth' are inherently awkward. It is likely that the other party is a person of considerable experience and standing, and mishandling the situation carries considerable risk in the short term. However, in the long term, the consequences of doing nothing may be much greater, even disastrous.

Managing bad behaviour
So, how do you tell a senior manager that he or she suffers from the behavioural equivalent of bad breath? Very, very carefully!

1 Plan carefully—execute flawlessly   In one situation, the CEO took action in relation to a senior manager who continually interfered in areas outside his expertise.[5] First, the CEO carefully developed a series of probing questions designed to evoke descriptions by the senior manager of the contentious situations in which he had been involved. Next, the CEO convinced the senior manager to get feedback from others including peers and an independent executive coach about the impact of his personal approach. Third, the CEO got agreement to a timetable of follow-up meetings to resolve the issue.

By using a planned and deliberate strategy, the CEO made a pathway of steps that led him through the process of dealing with the issue. The senior manager concerned did modify his behaviour to the extent that it lessened the impact of his style.

2 Address issues head-on and put teeth into the solutions In another case, the CEO was required to deal with continual conflict between a super-analytical R&D manager and the intuitive-thinking head of marketing.[6] She first used an executive coach to involve both in feedback about their personal styles. She then brought them together to discuss the results of that process. Next, she allocated them a joint assignment that could only be completed successfully if they worked together; she attached significant bonuses for successful cooperation.

This type of approach avoids the common crisis-like meetings that involve mutual criticisms about attitudes and beliefs.

3 Set clear behaviour expectations Leaders who set clear expectations about both outcomes and behaviours are following a known recipe for success. The leader needs to paint a detailed and descriptive picture of what is acceptable and what is not. They need to get understanding of these rules as well as initial acceptance to adhere to them. If subsequently any manager or team member breaks these rules, there is little room for excuses or evasions.

4 Encourage open discussion If the behaviour of the top leader is antagonistic to open discussion, a CEO may need to take the lead and seek feedback (usually anonymously) from others in the senior team about the leader's behaviour. This takes courage and opens the individual up to critical observations. The cost of not doing so is the risk of being isolated from what is happening in the larger organisation. Further, the process of gaining feedback from subordinates sets a precedent for others and encourages the top leader to become a role model in the organisation.

5 Accept and exploit the paradoxes of leadership

Leadership is inherently a paradoxical role. Leaders must be decisive and inquisitive, fiercely individualistic but team players, tough but open-minded, visionary but humble. These contradictions are simply part of the job. The effective leader brings a balance to these opposites and accepts that they may never be truly reconciled.

Managing 'moments of truth' will call on this balancing ability more than most other situations. The executive's choice is to deal with them and learn, or ignore them and fail.

The two extremes under discussion (happiness when things are going well and unhappiness when managers behave badly) are only two examples of how emotions inevitably enter into the workplace. It seems that no matter how hard we try, we will not be able to keep the affective side of us from influencing what happens at work.

Maybe we had better open the door and acknowledge that emotions are a workplace issue.

Guidelines

1 Plan the intervention

When people behave inappropriately, it often becomes the manager's responsibility to take action. If such intervention is to succeed, it will need to be planned. The alternative (making it up as you go along) usually results in unforeseen outcomes.

One of the problems is that many managers handling such situations tend to store stuff up until it leads to an explosion of accusations to the other party. So plan what you intend to do when handling such difficult situations.

2 Prepare the ground

Part of the planning involves preparing for the various discussions. Each step is about being able to respond to fairly predictable reactions from the other person. It involves gathering as much information as possible.

First, you need to be able to explain why the issue matters (to counter the response that it is not important). Second, you need to be able to explain what happened (to counter denial).

And, third, you need to be prepared for an emotional reaction (to handle anger or other emotions). Each of these steps requires information, and each needs to be handled with some tact (see the case studies above). But before anything else, it requires a willingness on the part of the manager to deal with the situation.

3 Execute consistently

More than just dealing with the one situation, the issue of inappropriate behaviour by others in the workplace needs to be handled consistently by the organisation as a whole.

In too many cases, the inappropriate behaviours are tolerated until a certain point is reached, whether that is determined by some disciplinary code or just by someone 'having a gutful'. Often, a lot of damage has been done by this time and the issue has to be dealt with in an explosive or tense atmosphere.

When it comes to inappropriate behaviour, intervene early and intervene often.

For further exploration

If you want to tackle the subject of emotion at work in some depth, you could try a special issue of the following journal:
• *European Journal of Work and Organizational Psychology*, 1999, Volume 8, Number 3.

It covers a range of topics such as 'The neglect and importance of emotion at work' and 'Emotion at work: to what extent are we expressing, suppressing, or faking it?' These are academic contributions (and I mean that as a compliment), which means that you won't necessarily find easy prescriptions for what to do about emotional issues at work.

Leadership

LEADERSHIP: A PRACTICAL APPROACH

Many organisations consider leadership to be a critical issue. It is generally considered a vital precondition for organisational success that an organisation be well led. At the same time, leadership capability has become a personal issue for many managers because it is now a common requirement for career progress.

The problem is that we know little about leadership, despite the many mighty tomes that have been devoted to the topic. More insidiously, as we do find out bits and pieces about leadership, some do not like what is found.

The debate as to what leadership is will continue for as long as managers and organisations promote the need for leadership. What practical things do we know about leadership?

Background

The problem with leadership is that we don't understand it. This tends to handicap rational discussion. Moreover, it significantly hampers our ability to make sense of something that is generally deemed important to government and business. Fortunately, this has not held back the consulting industry, which has thrived amid (and possibly because of) this confusion. Sheer ignorance is unlikely to constrain the consultant whose business thrives on delivering leadership programs.

What is leadership?

Most of what is said about leadership derives from one of two views:
1 leadership as trait;
2 leadership as behaviour.

The first view, *leadership as trait*, may be compared with the notion of beauty—that is, you either have it or you don't. Like beauty, it is hard to define but, like pornography, we know it when we see it. According to this perspective, you are born with the potential for leadership, but it does take some experience in the field to bring out this potential.

The second view, *leadership as behaviour*, may be compared to good manners—that is, it can be acquired through dedication, learning and practice. You get better at it over time. After a while leadership becomes second nature, so much so that you are no longer aware of it even as others comment on your effortless ability.

Experience is important to both views, with one needing it to bring out the potential, the other to make it habitual through practice. But that is largely where the similarities end. Certainly, the consequences of these two views are both significant and significantly different.

Leadership as trait

If leadership is a trait, then those who do not have 'it' need not bother to apply for leadership positions.

The problem with this approach is that we do not (yet?) know how to measure 'it'. This has not prevented researchers from trying to measure 'it', but most models of leadership traits are not very convincing. Possibly the best researched (and at the same time the most unpopular) is the theory developed by Elliott Jaques.[1] His work has the unique distinction among theories of leadership of being rooted in some of the world's largest longitudinal studies, spanning more than fifty years. Most people hate the findings.

Jaques' model (known as *Stratified Systems Theory*) suggests that we are born with clear limitations as to how far up the leadership tree we will go. Lack of developmental experience may hold us back, but no amount of experience will make us go further than our natural propensity will allow. Jaques and his colleagues developed a testing process to measure this limit so that organisations could know who (and who not) to spend their leadership development money on.

Those who fell into the 'not' category were rarely happy about this. Organisations that applied Jaques' ideas (in Australia, Westpac and CRA were big fans ten years ago) soon had minor staff rebellions on their hands as even those who had 'for promotion' stamped on their foreheads confessed to not much liking the idea. Those who carried the stamp 'not for promotion beyond this point' were even less happy and many left the organisation. Jaques' ideas languish but, unlike almost any other theorist, he can actually point out the research that backs his ideas.

There are some softer versions of the *leadership as trait* perspective, most of which revolve around the idea that some people are better suited to leadership positions than others. Social egalitarianism demands that the basic notion be soft-soaped so as not to upset people too much. Suitability is therefore judged on a bundle of criteria of which psychological traits are but one.

For example, in selecting those who are to be fast-tracked for leadership development, the talk is blandly about potential, abilities, suitability and aptitude. In reality, all these words are code for *trait*, even where the methods for assessment are rather dubious. The preferred method is a combination of task-based tests (for example, completing an in-basket exercise involving decisions that leaders might make, or participating in a simulation that calls for such judgments) and psychometric tests (for example, the Myers-Briggs Type Indicator or 16PF).

The problem with this approach (known in the trade as *assessment/development centre*) is that the task-tests simply measure existing abilities (that is, what you can do now). Only the psychometric tests are truly predictive. But the question is: What do they predict?

The claim is that in general we know the psychological characteristics that make a person suitable for leadership roles. But much of this research is highly questionable. For example, for reasons of ease of access, much of the research to validate various leadership models based on psych tests took place in the armed forces. The resulting leadership model is therefore typically skewed towards such things as action-orientation and emotional resilience. Good stuff if you are a general leading the troops into battle, but of questionable relevance to running organisations such as schools, shops and factories.

In the end, the psych-based stuff is still highly selective. *You're in or you're not.* And that brings us back to the egalitarian problem, which explains why the popular media loves nothing better than to poke fun at the use of psychometric tests in recruitment and promotion. The tests inevitably smack of preference and advantage. Never mind that most are carefully validated and that it is the nearest predictive tool we have to indicate what people are likely to be able to do in what are, after all, highly selective positions of leadership. Leadership is fundamentally an elitist notion.

Leadership as behaviour

> *If leadership is behaviour, then there is hope for everyone (and everyone will hope).*

The other approach is not exactly without its problems, not least of which is that we don't know which behaviour is in the leadership mode and which is not. Naturally, into this breach between need and ignorance has stepped the consulting industry with everything from personal coaching to packaged leadership training solutions.

Meeting the need for leadership development is big business. One of the most thriving—and, some might say regrettably abiding—examples is the Stephen Covey phenomenon. It is hard to describe this without swooning at the sheer size, audacity and industriousness of what is a complete industry in its own right. Based on the two biggest selling leadership books of all times (*Principle Centred Leadership*[2] and, especially, *The Seven Habits of Highly Successful People*[3]), Covey has expanded his eclectic leadership and self-management theories in all manner of directions. (Do you have your copy yet of *How to Develop a Family Mission Statement?*[4])

Possibly, what Covey has done is to make the mirage of leadership (and the benefits and rewards that come with it) appear accessible to all those who want it. Just do the things that leaders do and you too will be a leader. Copy the behaviour and that's all there is to it. Do first things first and sharpen your saw, and you're half-way to becoming a success. Just ignore those little gnawing doubts that you're actually not good enough to be a leader and just do it. This is the Nike route to leadership. But does it work?

It is hard to judge just what sort of impact this is having in the workplace. Simply buying the book, and others like it, may comfort some people that they are doing something about their leadership development needs. Those who actually read the books may be influenced by what is largely very sensible advice on how to behave sensibly.

But is today's workforce showing more highly developed leadership capabilities? And how do you measure this anyway?

Measuring leadership

One attempt to make all this a bit more measurable arose out of the idea that, if you want to know about leadership, maybe you should ask the followers. After all, it is a bit hard having one without the other. Most of these approaches now go under the name of '360-degree feedback' or 'multi-rater feedback'. That is, subordinates (along with peers, bosses and others) provide feedback through questionnaires as to how well leaders do what they are supposed to do.

Possibly the best and most serious of these tools is the *Leadership Practices Inventory*[5] developed by James Kouzis and Barry Posner in the 1980s. The inventory was developed from extensive research and based largely on people's observations about what leaders actually do in the workplace. It is a pragmatic approach that neatly sidesteps the issue of *What is leadership?* and focuses on *What do leaders do?* The findings are modest, pointing largely at the behaviours exhibited by good leaders as opposed to managers. It does not identify behaviours that are unique to good leadership, but points out behaviours that, if exercised more often, would make people better leaders. The book describing their approach, *The Leadership Challenge*,[6] is refreshingly down-to-earth and readable.

If, after all this, you do want to read something sensible about leadership itself, John Kotter's writings provide an elegant introduction. Kotter casts the distinction between leadership and management in terms of *systems of action*. That is, they are distinct but complementary. In contrasting the two functions, Kotter brings out a range of interesting observations and challenging conclusions without falling into the trap of building elaborate models. The following statements are from his article, *What Leaders Really Do*:[7]

- *Most . . . corporations are over-managed and under-led.*
- *Management is about coping with complexity . . . leadership is about coping with change.*
- *Leadership complements management; it does not replace it.*

In the face of this continuing uncertainty, what can we say about leadership that is practical? We get bombarded with stuff about leadership that is either academically sound but incomprehensible or heavily loaded with overt commercial agendas ('buy my instrument') and/or the hidden personal agendas ('buy my values system') of the author. All this is only worsened by the uplifting case studies that paint a picture of heroic leadership appropriate to saving small defenceless nations from large aggressive neighbours.

So let's tackle this from another angle: *When it comes to leadership, what works?*

Some debatable issues

Before we can get really practical, we have to clear the decks of some issues that get in the way of being practical. This is the stuff that continues to be debated without being resolved. Let's acknowledge these thorny questions and then move on.

Question 1: Are leaders born?

Answer: Who cares? Even if we ever do find out whether nature is more important than nurture (or vice versa), right now we don't know. So why not pick the option that is most practical. Let's assume it is all nurture. That is, let's assume that anyone can lead. If we turn out to be wrong, at least we had a go. If we turn out to be right, then we did the right thing. It feels a lot more empowering if we assume we all have some capacity to become a leader.

Question 2: Is leadership different from management?

Answer: Who cares? Does it really matter whether we call this stuff management or leadership? Surely, what matters is what we do and how we do it? Whether you call it management or leadership, it's always about working with people to get things done. Those who wrote about management at the beginning of the last century did not bother separating leadership from the rest of the managerial challenge. Writers such as Henri Fayol and Mary Parker Follett happily incorporated leadership into management.

Question 3: Is leadership found only at the top of an organisation?

Answer: Who cares? The real answer is probably in the negative, but if you feel a driving need to believe that only people in senior roles in an organisation lead, be my guest! Most people can provide examples of leadership behaviour across the whole of the organisation, and some of the most uplifting examples of leadership come from settings that have nothing do with the world of paid work. It seems sensible to assume that anyone anywhere can lead at any time.

Question 4: Is leadership about being heroic or inspirational?
Answer: Go away! It's hard enough having a discussion about leadership without getting into the even more complex area of exemplary heroic behaviour. All those case studies from history about great leaders do not help very much when we're trying to figure out what people can do in their workplace. All those inspirational quotes from Churchill or Gandhi or Mandela about leadership make good desk-calendar fodder but they don't really help when we're trying to figure out the practicalities of leadership in everyday situations.

Question 5: Can leadership be learned?
Answer: Don't know, but let's assume it can be. If we assume the opposite, then we are left powerless to do anything. It seems sensible to assume that we can, if for no other reason than it makes me feel better to believe that. As Alfred Lord Tennyson put it: 'to strive, to seek, to find, and not to yield' which seems somewhat more positive than 'we're all buggered'.

The *what* and *how* of leadership

So, our working hypothesis then is that anyone can lead, regardless of their genetic inheritance, their upbringing, their organisational role or the size of their pay cheque.

Righto, what's next? Well, we need to agree on the *what* and the *how* of leadership. The first is relatively easy and the second relatively difficult.

The *what* of leadership can be summed up in many ways, and it has been. This is about what leaders *do*, and that has been studied intensively over the years. It is stretching it a little to say that a consensus has emerged, but there is a lot of common ground about what comprises the behaviour of leading, and some key words appear in much of the recent writing on leadership.

Leaders do three key things better and more often than others:
1 Leaders set direction.
2 Leaders make it easy for others to follow.
3 Leaders encourage others when they do contribute.

Most of us do some of this some of the time. People acknowledged by others as good leaders do it more often, more appropriately and more thoroughly—not necessarily lots better, just a bit better.

Almost any definition, description or formalised theory or model of leadership contains these three elements. Most have more bells and whistles (for example, about visions, rewards, values and modelling the way) but we will stick to the practical basics. Leadership is about

- setting direction
- easing the way
- encouraging others.

Now for the *how* of leadership. This is the tricky bit. It does seem that some people do the leadership thing better than others. This is about style, timing and context. For example, there is a right time and a wrong time to talk to others about the direction you want to move in. When the payroll staff is desperately trying to complete the payroll late on a Wednesday afternoon, it's probably not the best time to have a conversation with them about the future direction of the organisation.

The thing about leadership that makes many people think it is different from management is the element of *volunteering*. This line of thought suggests that management is about *directing people* to do things and leadership is about *inviting and encouraging* people to do things. Leaders make people want to do things. And some people have a personal style that suits that way of working and some do not (see Chapter 4).

But that only means that some people find it easier to lead and others find it harder. It does not mean you can't do it because you do not have the right style. You can change your style to some extent by changing the way you do things. I don't mean wholesale change but small and incremental changes that take you away from directing towards inviting a contribution.

You can start with the direction thing. Ask people what they think the right direction forward is. Make it a point to seek out their views. Then, when you do identify what the direction will be, they have a different view of it because of their involvement in the process. People support what they help to create.

Finally, there is the matter of context. This could get really murky, but here goes. First, there is the national cultural context. You may have noticed that Australians are different from other people around the world. We have certain characteristics that make us unique, just as do other national cultures. But while we recognise the unique elements of other cultures (and stereotype them), we are less able to see our own. And, of course, these cultural traits are part of the scenery in any Australian workplace.

There have been a couple of attempts to capture our cultural traits but in my view the most comprehensive and useful has been the work of Cultural Imprint Pty Ltd[8] (conducted with their major sponsors Australian Quality Council, Telstra, Westpac and Sydney Electricity). In a series of studies, John Evans and his colleagues have provided us with a rich array of data, imagery and conclusions about what it means to be a leader in Australia.

Some of the broad conclusions are that, to be an effective leader in Australia, you need to:
• care about what you do;
• support your followers;
• be consistent;
• stick to your principles;
• think of others.

The study teases out each of these to show what they mean in practice. It helps to explain, for instance, why imported ideas like 'Employee of the Month' schemes and American leadership training programs generally fail in Australia.

Cultural context is not just national, however, but also organisationally specific. To be considered a leader in your organisation means something different to what it would be in another organisation. You still provide direction, make it easy to follow and encourage your followers, but it translates into specific actions differently. In a highly entrepreneurial organisation, a sudden change in direction is no big deal. In an organisation that values consistency of purpose and efficiency of process, changing direction needs more care and thought (see Chapter 16).

And, finally, context is also individually specific. This is where an approach such as Ken Blanchard's *situational leadership* comes into its own.[9] People at different stages of development in terms of competence and confidence need to be led (or managed—it blurs again) differently. As Ken says, different strokes for different folks. (Does anyone know an Australian version of that? My Australian cultural imprint is playing up whenever I use that phrase.)

So that is the practical approach to leadership. Do the three key *whats* of leading (provide direction, make it easy and encourage others) but keep in mind the *hows* such as style, timing and context.

Guidelines

1 Provide direction

Leadership implies that you are taking people somewhere. Be very clear about what and where that place is. Be prepared to describe it to others in terms that they can understand and buy into.

It does not necessarily mean 'vision' but it does mean 'direction'. It certainly does not mean 'trust me'.

You have to be prepared to provide detail. And if there are bits you are not sure about, say so. Paint the picture.

2 Make it easy to follow

People who are expected to follow you are entitled to know what will happen tomorrow.

These 'first steps' towards the direction in which you are taking them should be small steps, steps they can take with confidence. This will avoid resistance (which is based on fear of the unknown) and inertia.

Paint a picture of how life will be different for them, not when the change journey is completed, but tomorrow.

Those who follow you want to know where you are taking them but, even more importantly, they want to know how their life will be different tomorrow. Help them to understand that and they will come with you.

3 Encourage others

The journey will have its hiccups.

To prepare for those times, pay close attention to what people are experiencing along the way. Talk with them and listen. Try to pick their concerns before they have to raise them with you. Encourage them through the rough bits.

For further exploration

If the psychopathology of leadership interests you (that is, the thin line between being a leader and being mad), try:

- M.F. R. Kets de Vries, *Leaders, Fools, and Imposters: Essays on the Psychology of Leadership*, Jossey-Bass, San Francisco, 1993.

If you see leadership as a relationship challenge as much as an action challenge, try the gentle, almost poetic observations of Max Depree:

- M. Depree, *Leadership is an Art*, Australian Business Library, Melbourne, 1989.

If you see leadership as a mantle of responsibility rather than a licence to command, try Peter Block's approach:

- P. Block, *Stewardship: Choosing Service over Self-interest*, Berrett-Koehler, San Francisco, 1993.

BEYOND HEROICS

Leadership is promoted mainly through the popular literature on the subject. This is a little unusual. Most other aspects of organisational behaviour are driven by academic research (for example, Robert Kaplan's development of the Balanced Scorecard) or developments in leading organisations (for example, GE creating renewed interest in the continuous improvement tool, *Six Sigma*).

A recent search on the subject 'leadership' at Amazon.com generated 7604 titles. This suggests that it is not unfair to characterise leadership publishing as an industry in its own right. It makes leadership different from most management fads, where one book and one guru is enough to launch a fad. Leadership is in a different class, a class all of its own. Leadership is way beyond fad status.

All of which makes it difficult to get back to basics. Some writers are trying to redefine the field away from instant self-help and 'heroic' models of leadership. They seek to move the leadership debate towards informed self-insight and personal growth. However, it is the instant solutions that sell well in the bookshops.

Are we being sold leadership?

Background

Writings on leadership continue to flourish, seemingly without quenching the thirst of their readership. The sheer quantum demands some explanation. In 1990 one researcher cited more than 3000 modern studies of leadership.[1] Historical material (Greek, Roman, Judaic, Chinese, Islamic, Icelandic, Renaissance, etc.) would easily double that. The last ten years may well have added as much again, especially taking into account the ease of self-publication now offered by the Internet. Leadership literature is big business.

What explains the attraction of the genre? It ranges broadly from didactic tomes written by academics to biographical accounts and autobiographies (ghost?) written by those who consider themselves worthy leaders.

The leadership fantasy

The attraction seems to have little to do with its impact in the real world. Despite many decades of the production and consumption of this material, there has been no noticeable increase in the calibre of leadership evident in the workplace. Many argue that, if anything, the opposite is the case and that leadership is now talked about more than it is practised.[2]

We probably need to reframe the question regarding why so much is published on leadership. An alternative (and possibly seditious) frame of inquiry is that those who expect the literature on leadership to have any impact are falling prey to an enormous fallacy—that is, that the purpose of writings on leadership is to enable the readers to become better leaders. Instead, it may well be that the opposite is true. Maybe the real purpose of the leadership literature is to prevent people from becoming leaders without them finding out that this is its purpose.

What we are facing here is a literary commodity that is being consumed by its readers in much the same vein as other forms of fictional literature. Any suggestion that these scribblings have some application in practice must be treated with suspicion, given the sheer volume. After all, if the leadership literature had any practical aspect to it, such as a technical manual or how-to handbook does, then clearly the demand would have been sated at some point. Even Harley-Davidson can sell only so many technical manuals for any one of its types of motorcycles.

The books on leadership are probably more like that small percentage of sales that Harley-Davidson makes to people who do not own a bike but buy the technical manual anyway. Such readers love the idea of owning a Fat Boy bike but for one reason or another (lack of money; lack of courage; lack of a driver's licence; mother/father/husband/wife won't let you, etc.) they don't actually own one.

Those who buy books on leadership are like this minority. They buy (there is evidence that a significant number of people buy but never read what they buy) because they are indulging in a fantasy. The act of purchasing a book on leadership suggests an aspiration to be worked towards, not by any realistic means (such as actually acting like a leader) but by the vicarious means of experiencing someone else's experience, whether in a biographical manner or a directly didactic form.

The leftover artefacts of this fake experience end up gracing the home office bookshelf like tourist junk attesting to travel experience. But the leadership trip was never taken, the experience never had and the expertise never acquired.

The fantasy is based on a number of fallacies, chief among them that leadership is reducible to some behavioural formula that can be emulated by others. It assumes, for example, that successful leaders knew what they did and why they did it. Few real leaders have ever claimed this. Even those who are persuaded by the money to share their experience with others, either by writing the book or hitting the speakers' circuit, are more likely to claim that leaders follow their heart and act intuitively.

Further, it assumes that others can change their behaviour to be like that of successful leaders. Behaviour change is difficult at the best of times and change that is based on admiration from afar of some putative role model is unlikely to last past the first Monday morning business meeting.

Some of this is driven by the current era of discontinuous change in which the identity of the individual becomes less secure as the world changes ever more quickly. This insecurity feeds not only the publishing world but also the peculiar world of the speakers' circuit and the current gargantuan appetite for seminars and workshops. Whole industries thrive on feeding this insecurity and they make a good buck from it. Few of those involved stop to think that it may all be pointless, and that no amount of accumulation of information will increase their leadership capabilities. No one with a vested interest is likely to point this out to these hapless consumers.

On careful reflection, it seems that the only difference between leadership literature and, say, romantic fiction is that the readership is aware of the fantasy in the latter and not in the former.

Is there another way? Well, we could try to lower the leadership bar by redefining it in a slightly more achievable way. Instead of elevating it (by publishing all those books on heroic leadership), let's tone it down and position leadership as something that many people, if not all people, can do. *Let's make leadership ordinary.*

Leadership through diplomacy

One way of doing this is to find a different metaphor to describe leadership. For example, Manuel London suggests *business diplomacy*[3]—an approach to leadership based on explicit values such as treating others with respect, doing good and being kind while still seeking to add value and make profit. Doing business in the globalised world of the twenty-first century will demand a different approach from the 'winner-take-all' philosophy still prevalent today. Achieving business success in a variety of cultural settings requires the capacity to base actions on universally acknowledged principles and values. Being good, doing good, and making money are not mutually exclusive goals, and a diplomatic style of management can achieve all these goals.

Principled leadership involves the application of ethical values. Business diplomacy is a practical way of adhering to fundamental principles while still achieving business objectives. It is especially useful in situations where there is considerable conflict and disagreement because the stakes are high.

Principled leadership is not a new concept and is similar to the Japanese notion of *kyosei* (working for the common good) or the Hebrew concept of *tikkun olam* (making the world a better place). It also has many similarities with Buddhist ideas of goodness, well-being and getting along with each other. Another recent and more individualistic interpretation is provided by Stephen Covey's *Principle Centred Leadership*.[4]

Business diplomacy is a way of applying these concepts in Western cultures which are typically more confrontational and competitive. The essence of the technique is to apply tact to all situations and seek the common ground that will satisfy all parties. This involves a lot of hard work to understand the positions of others, their needs, their moods and their interests. It requires a great deal of strategising and planning.

The approach is especially difficult but also especially necessary when the stakes are high. It requires a high degree of mental discipline and toughness, persistence and patience, and the ability to control your own feelings. It is quite contrary to the instinct to 'crash or crash through' that characterises the thinking and behaviour of many business people.

While the techniques of business diplomacy can be learned, management training and development typically focuses more on competitive processes around gaining advantage. In tough business situations, such as negotiations or takeovers, the expectation of others is that the tough-guy attitude will prevail. A diplomatic approach may even be interpreted as a sign of weakness.

A skilful business diplomat will consider a range of strategies and use a variety of tactics to create successful outcomes. The tactics may involve varying degrees of risk for the diplomat but will always be positive in moving towards a win–win solution. Conservative tactics include the use of shuttle diplomacy to obtain consensus, establishing decision rules and round-table discussions. More risky tactics include explicit announcements of preferred outcomes, coopting dissenters and announcing tentative decisions.

The application of business diplomacy involves two types of goals:

1 *Process goals*—such as working together cooperatively, avoiding coercion and threat, communicating constantly, remaining flexible and being open to new ideas.
2 *Outcomes goals*—such as making consensus decisions, ensuring stability, fostering positive relationships and achieving positive outcomes.

Business diplomacy will not work in all situations. If other participants are intransigent and uncommunicative, then diplomacy may fail. Nevertheless, the business diplomat perseveres if only to leave open future possibilities for negotiation. Even intransigent parties may eventually return to the table. Specific tactics for dealing with intransigence include withdrawing gracefully, adopting a 'wait-and-see' attitude, changing the environment and letting diplomacy evolve over time.

A modest but effective approach

There are many ways to make diplomacy more effective in an organisational setting. They include:

1 Explicitly state the values underlying the diplomatic way of doing business so that everyone is clear about the preferred way of operating. Evaluate people's contribution on the extent to which it lives out the principles being espoused. Build the values into processes such as promotion, recruitment, performance appraisal and reward systems.
2 Require leaders to demonstrate principled leadership and business diplomacy, especially in their interactions with others in the organisation.
3 During business activities, check with participants that the process being used is in accordance with the principles of business diplomacy. Observe proceedings with a view to the

'how' as well as the usual 'what' and 'why'. Comment on the extent to which the principles and values of business diplomacy are being enacted.

4 Accept mistakes and failures but learn publicly from them the lessons for future success. Avoid the excesses of superiority and arrogance in applying principled leadership.

5 Let diplomacy become a way of life as much as a way of doing business.

6 Manage crises diplomatically by looking for small gains and minimising resort to power tactics. Evaluate progress as much on process as on outcomes.

Business diplomacy is only one approach among many that offer an alternative to the 'all conquering hero' model of leadership. It is modest but not necessarily simple. If you are successful at it, no one will offer you a publishing opportunity or invite you to become a guru.

But you will have made a difference, and will have done it in the real world.

Guidelines

1 Practice

Find something in the list of suggestions made by London that you can try in your workplace.

Write it down in behavioural terms—that is, in the form of something that you can do. Then find opportunities to put it into effect and see what happens.

Make a note (maybe in your diary) about what happened when you tried it. Keep experimenting with it until you have conquered it as a technique.

This does not sound very sophisticated as a learning technique but it's actually very powerful.

2 Practice

Repeat (1) above with another technique.

3 Practice

Repeat (1) above once more with another technique.

It won't get any sexier but putting small steps in place does work!

For further exploration

Manuel London wrote the book on feedback. Others have done so as well, but London's approach is one of the most practical that you will find:

- M. London, *Job Feedback: Giving, Seeking, and Using Feedback for Performance Improvement (Series in Applied Psychology)*, Lawrence Erlbaum, Hillsdale, 1997.

One of his latest books zeroes in specifically on how you can use self-insight to enhance your leadership capabilities. This book explores how leaders obtain and then use self-knowledge for personal and career development. It shows how leaders can help themselves and the people they work with to understand themselves, and become more self-determined people through such techniques as feedback and coaching. The book stresses the need for accurate self-understanding, explaining the meaning of internal strength and resilience for self-regulation.

- M. London, *Leadership Development: Paths to Self-Insight and Professional Growth (Series in Applied Psychology)*, Lawrence Erlbaum, Hillsdale, 2001.

For more details on how to make business diplomacy work, try:

- M. London, *Principled Leadership and Business Diplomacy: Values-Based Strategies for Management Development*, Quorum Books, London, 1999.

LEADERSHIP WITH INTEGRITY

28

No matter which writer you consult or which consultant you read, 'management' always loses out to the more charismatic and inspirational option of 'leadership'. Leadership is good. That is one of the key mantras to emerge from the 'leadership versus management' debate of the last twenty years.

To test this observation, you only have to cast its opposite into the world: 'Leadership is bad'. That is so obviously the wrong thing to say in business that it instantly proves the original proposition. And yet we know that there are many leaders out there in business who do damage just to satisfy their own ego. Their worst excesses are usually covered up, and in many cases the organisation simply does not know how to deal with a leader gone wrong.

There is an antidote to all this and that is to restore the rather old-fashioned notion of integrity as a desirable managerial characteristic. Look at any modern list of management 'competencies' and it is likely that you will find much that is about technocratic capabilities and little about what our parents used to call 'character'.

Why has leadership integrity declined?

Background

Typically, leadership is distinguished from management by means of contrast. Where management is about getting things done right, leadership is about getting the right things done. Where management directs, leadership inspires. Here's how John Kotter summarises the difference:

> *Leadership and management are two distinctive and complementary systems of action. Management is about coping with complexity, whereas leadership is about coping with change. Firms manage complexity first by planning and budgeting. By contrast, leading a firm to constructive change begins by setting a direction, thus developing a vision of the future along with strategies for producing the changes needed to achieve that vision. Management develops the capacity to achieve its plan by organising and staffing. The equivalent leadership activity is aligning people—that is, communicating the new direction*

to those who can create coalitions that understand the vision and are committed to its achievement. Management ensures plan accomplishment by controlling and problem solving. For leadership, achieving a vision requires motivating and inspiring. Leaders keep people moving in the right direction by appealing to basic but often untapped human needs, values, and emotions.[1]

In other words, leadership is a higher-purpose activity than mere management. The abilities needed to be a leader are different from, and by implication, sexier than those needed to be a manager. Describing management as a complementary activity is mere mealy-mouthed obsequiousness. Let's face it: leadership is better.

What is implicit in all this is that leadership is essentially a benign activity, with leaders working for the good of the organisation and all its stakeholders. It suggests an almost moral dimension to the task, one that involves a calling to a higher plane, certainly higher than mere management. Virtually all modern musings on leadership follow this angle, whether they discuss *transformational leadership*[2] or *doing the right thing*.[3]

The dark side of leadership

All this ignores the dark side of leadership, the side of the leadership equation that thrives on the power that comes with the role. This Darth Vader side is about self-aggrandisement, abuse of power, narcissism and self-deceit. This side reflects the psychopathology of leadership, where the combination of neurotic personality and personal power creates social and business disasters.

Not much of the dark side of leadership makes it into the learned writings on leadership. It is generally glossed over in the roseate tracts on how to inspire followers. But ignoring it won't make it go away. Many workers are only too aware of the boss who is a complete egomaniac or neurotically obsessed with irrelevant detail. In the workplace, the dark side of leadership is a reality. Even the popular press reflects this reality through cartoons about the workplace (for example, Dilbert[4]) and through satirical works on life at work (for example, Robert Townsend's *Up the Organisation*[5]).

One of the few writers to take this topic seriously is Kets de Vries whose delightfully titled *Leaders, Fools and Imposters: Essays on the Psychology of Leadership*[6] is actually a bit of a hard read unless you're into Freudian-style psychoanalytical theory in a big way (see Washbush and Clements[7] for a readable overview).

Essentially, Kets De Vries characterises various aspects of the dark side of leadership, focusing on those tendencies that reinforce a less-than-balanced approach to the role. Some of these include:

- **Mirroring**—the tendency to see yourself as your followers see you and the need to satisfy the perceptions of those followers. This may encourage leaders to take actions designed to shore up their image rather than serve the needs of the organisation.

- **Narcissism**—a distorted view of self that leads to intolerance of criticism, unwillingness to compromise and the tendency to surround yourself with sycophants. Such tendencies draw people to positions of leadership in the first place, but then may also lead them to take actions based on a distorted view of business realities, at some cost to the organisation.

- **Emotional illiteracy** (alexithymia)—the inability to acknowledge and understand the emotional side of life. People with this tendency appear controlled, structured and dispassionate, all of which makes them good candidates for leadership positions. At the extreme, however, such people lack the emotional ability to empathise, connect with others or deal constructively with conflict.

- **Fear of letting go**—the inability to accept that you are no longer suited to the position you occupy, driven largely by the need to maintain position and power. This is likely to lead to a determination to succeed at all costs, which may well be seen as admirable leadership behaviour. At the extreme, however, it leads to counterproductive behaviour. One example is what is known as the *Talion Complex,* where fear of reprisals by others when the position of power is abandoned in the future drives the leader to irrational behaviour, such as culling the talent from the next generation of leaders. This is designed to make the incumbent irreplaceable.

All of which is not to say that the leaders in our organisations are mad. Some, no doubt, are. (We may even fall prey, in our idle moments, to suspecting that our immediate 'superiors' belong in an entirely different institution from the organisation they now lead.) What this discussion reminds us of, however, is that a notion such as leadership is inextricably linked to the whole 'people thing'. Leadership is not just something that comes into this world wholly formed and good. Rather, it sparks from a number of human characteristics, each of which is capable of leading to productive or unproductive behaviour when judged from the organisational perspective.

If all this sits uneasily with those who make their living from leadership education, then they are only fooling themselves. Leadership can be evil, not just in history or politics but also in the modern organisation. Worse, there is not much we can do about it. Those who are capable of examining their own foibles are probably not the ones we have to worry about. Those who are not capable of the required degree of introspection are unlikely to be persuaded by those who 'teach' leadership.

What we can do is maintain some perspective on the notion of leadership, and not get carried away by the claimed need for inspirational styles and charismatic personalities. It is always dangerous to put things on pedestals. Leadership is no exception.

Integrity, trust and credibility

The opposite profile to the mad-and-bad leader is that of leaders who fulfil their role from a perspective of *integrity*. Integrity is generally acknowledged as a critical ingredient of effective leadership; it is usually defined as *congruence between what is done and what is said*. In many workplaces, it is very difficult for managers to match their words with their deeds (behavioural integrity), especially when organisations are going through major change and managers have only limited control over events. Ironically, such periods of transformational change demand that leaders be seen as having integrity if they are to lead effectively.

The perceived divergence between managerial words and deeds has been growing over recent years. This pattern is probably driven by the constant adoption of new management techniques and approaches. The accelerating use of fads and fashions in management practice increases the risk that what is said by managers (for example, 'We will empower our people') does not match what is done (for example, the imposition of more and more control systems).

All this is happening at a time when many organisations are going through a period of transformational change, often driven by planned change programs. The need for organisations to reinvent themselves ever more frequently is a logical response to a period of intense local competition and furious global change. But it takes its toll on the managers who have to manage such change programs.

Put the two together—a perception of declining integrity and the impact of major organisational change—and you have a recipe that effectively undermines the credibility of managers. Today, many managers are seen as untrustworthy or lacking in credibility. Those who espouse the latest management fashion are treated with scepticism, cynicism or outright hostility. At a time of change, this will undermine their ability to lead others through the change.[8]

Transformational leadership is the process of leading others through major change. While there are many different definitions and descriptions of the process, all theorists agree that it calls for *a high level of trust between the leader and the led*. Trust is a complex concept, but is generally seen as involving a belief that the trusted party will do the right thing, a willingness to be vulnerable to the actions of the trusted party and an assumption of competence. All these elements come back to the issue of behavioural integrity. The best way to undermine trust between two people is for one to perceive the other as not doing what they say they will do.

Credibility is also based on behavioural integrity. While it differs from trust (a manager can be credible but not be trusted), it shares the same basis of demanding a match between words and deeds. Therefore, if behavioural integrity declines, both trust and credibility decline.

Consistency

So why this decline in behavioural integrity? Once again, the rapid adoption and abandoning of new management practices (fads/fashions) has been identified as a major cause. For example, by 1982, 90 per cent of Fortune 500 companies were using quality circles; by 1988, 80 per cent of them had dropped the practice.[9] Similar figures apply to other fads.

The adoption of a fad increases the risk of a decline in the perceived behavioural integrity of managers. The fad is often adopted to create a planned change in organisational practice.

Change is precisely the time when the risk of a decline in behavioural integrity is at its greatest. Precisely when managers need to be seen as behaving with integrity, they are at the greatest risk of getting it wrong. Just when managers need it most, they stand to lose it!

Further, since managers are only people after all, they are unlikely to realise that their perceived integrity is declining. Various psychological mechanisms encourage and drive humans to believe that they behave consistently with their intentions. Inconsistencies between words and deeds are glossed over, and a consistent managerial self-image (albeit a false one) emerges over time.

All of the above may go some way to explaining the growing divergence between what managers say and what they do. This is not to say that new management practices should be avoided or that major change should be abandoned. But it does mean that managers need to recognise the risks inherent in both options, and obtain effective feedback on whether their words and deeds are aligned. We are dealing with matters of perception and only feedback from others can tell us how we are perceived.

For a long time managers have been exhorted to 'walk-the-talk'. It is time for managers to also 'talk-the-walk'.

Guidelines

1 Match talk to walk

Credibility is a precious possession for any manager. It is not a trait, but more like a reputation.

Credibility is acquired over time by being seen by others to do what you say you will do. Over even more time, this evolves into integrity—that is, being seen by others as a person who matches deeds and words.

Be aware that others judge you constantly and your credibility (and along with it their view of your integrity) can go up or down depending on what you do.

2 Ask others whether you're matching talk and walk

Being aware of the issue is one thing; being accurate in your perception of your credibility is another. The problem is that your own perception does not count very much here. What counts is the view of others.

Telling yourself that you are credible and are seen as a person of integrity by others may be no more than wishful thinking. You need to do a reality check to be certain (although many managers do have quite accurate perceptions of how they come across to others). The only way to do that is to ask others whether they see you as credible. A multi-rater (360-degree) feedback survey can do this or even just a conversation with someone you trust to tell you the truth.

3 Encourage others to be credible

The above applies to others as well. By setting an example, you are leading the way. But maybe there is more you can do to encourage others to think about their own behavioural integrity. If acceptable to others, give them feedback about how you perceive them in terms of credibility in the workplace.

This may form part of some kind of development exercise, especially if they are your staff. Lead by example.

For further exploration

Integrity is a topic that is not much discussed in the management literature. Funny thing, that! If you go looking for material on integrity, your search is most likely to return stuff about 'data integrity' in computer systems. Lots of material on that! (It's ironic that we are more concerned about the integrity of our data storage devices than about the behavioural integrity of our managers.)

The following articles at least tackle the issue head on and provide food for thought as well as guidance for action. The authors suggest that leaders can and should be held accountable for enhancing the intangible strategic asset of integrity capacity in order to advance organisational excellence. They define 'integrity capacity' and frame it as part of a strategic resource model of sustainable global competitive advantage.

- J. Petrick and J. Quinn, 'Integrity capacity as a strategic asset in achieving organizational excellence', *Measuring Business Excellence*, 5(1), 2001, pp. 24–31.

The next article discusses honesty and integrity as the basic principles of leadership. It defines leadership excellence as something beyond mere technical competence, and argues that successful leaders continually demonstrate honesty and integrity as an essential element of their professional fabric. Lack of commitment to these fundamental principles renders all other managerial skills meaningless. Scarnati offers a sound philosophy that increases the probability for long-term success and professional fulfilment. The article includes quotes from contemporary and historical leaders.

- J. Scarnati, 'Beyond technical competence: honesty and integrity', *Career Development International*, 2(1), 1997, pp. 24–27.

The final article is based on interviews with the chief executives of seven large firms. The authors suggest that integrity is the critical executive behaviour that leads an organisation to achieve outstanding performance. Integrity is reflected in a consistency of personal values, daily actions and organisational goals that encourages the successful resolution of conflict and business dilemmas.

- J. Badaracco and R. Ellsworth, 'Leadership, integrity and conflict', *Management Decision*, 30(6), 1992.

Managing
yourself

THE TRAP OF 'EMOTIONAL INTELLIGENCE' **29**

In the leadership debate, any new theory that offers the hope of clarity and simplicity is likely to fare well. A new theory about leadership comes along every few years, shines brightly for a while before settling down to being just another little star in the firmament of management theories.

Emotional intelligence is following this well worn path. It provides almost a case study of how to launch a management fad, satisfying all the basic requirements of the type. It seems destined to last no longer than other fads (one academic has calculated the average management fad lasts 7.2 years) and the jury is out on whether it will leave a lasting impression.

Is 'emotional intelligence' the way to more effective leadership behaviour?

Background

There is a tide in the affairs of management writing which if taken at the flood leads on to greatness. Or so it seems in the world of management fads. The art of creating 'the next big thing' in management is a bit like getting a rocket off the ground: it's all about timing and spin. A grand example is *emotional intelligence.*

The rise of emotional intelligence

While others have a legitimate claim to its parenthood, the idea of emotional intelligence is now firmly associated with Daniel Goleman. His books, *Emotional Intelligence*[1] and *Working with Emotional Intelligence,*[2] have just about muscled the competition out of the way in claiming pre-eminence in the field.

A sure sign of this pre-eminence is, of course, the publication of a *Harvard Business Review* article. One duly appeared in late 1998 under the title, 'What makes a Leader?'[3]

Goleman suggests that there are five components of emotional intelligence (EI):

1 **self-awareness**—recognising and understanding your moods and feelings, and appreciating their impact on others;
2 **self-regulation**—controlling disruptive impulses;

3 motivation—a desire to work for intrinsic rewards and pursue goals with persistence;

4 empathy—understanding other people's emotional makeup;

5 social skill—managing relationships and associations by finding common ground with others.

Having a high EI means understanding your own and other people's emotional makeup well enough to move people in the direction of accomplishing your goals.

In his article, 'What makes a Leader', Goleman argues that effective leaders are alike in one crucial way—they all have a high degree of EI. Especially at the upper levels of organisations, EI is what makes the difference. Without it, a person can be highly trained, very clever and brilliantly creative, but he or she will not cut the mustard as a great leader.

In terms of the fundamental concepts put forward by Goleman, this is hardly ground-breaking stuff. Many would recognise its components as reminiscent of Dale Carnegie, Chris Argyris, Eric Berne, Stephen Covey and many others. However, it provides an interesting case study in how the not-so-original can become the one-and-only. The publication of the *HBR* article completes the traditional journey of management ideas from a good kernel or clever summary to all-round panacea.

Goleman's timing is impeccable. The mood in management thinking is swinging away from one-minute prescriptions to an acceptance of complexity; from rational modes of thinking to learning to live with paradox and chaos; from singular solutions to multiple perspectives. Reinvigorating the notion of the affective domain of the brain and applying it to an organisational setting in the midst of all this management turmoil and confusion is a stroke of near genius. Spin and timing!

Managing the non-rational

The reality, of course, is that the idea of management as a partly non-rational activity has always been there. Being able to work with that aspect of the management job wasn't called 'emotional intelligence' but it existed. It was called interpersonal intelligence or empathy or character or even just feeling.[4]

Even the term 'emotional intelligence' predates guru Goleman.[5] In fact, going back a few generations (not something generally encouraged in management thinking), there is an enormously rich tradition of writings on this subject including Rousseau, Kant, Goethe, Nietzsche, Freud, Kierkegaard, Merleau-Ponty and Foucault. But this tradition has simply not touched modern management thinking.

About the only exception is Henry Mintzberg, the well known writer on strategy, who has argued for most of his published life that the non-rational aspects of strategising are as important as the rational ones. For a man celebrated for works like *The Rise and Fall of Strategic Planning*,[6] it is ironic that he actually pans most approaches to strategic planning as ineffectual. His concept of *emergent strategy* (that is, making it up as you go along) has provided the post facto justification for many a managerial decision.

Goleman has brought this non-cognitive side of human nature back into the limelight, by relying not on philosophy but on neurological research. After all, in the cynical world of management you can hardly quote a philosopher as your spiritual forebear. Better find something hard-nosed like neurological research.

So recent brain research makes the Goleman prescription (is it too disingenuous to summarise it as 'Be nice'?) acceptable to generations of managers brought up on a diet of hyper-rationality. Goleman has come up with an action plan that addresses the well documented phenomenon of *cognitive bias* in our thinking.[7]

Thankfully, at last, we will be able to do something about all those tortured workplace relationships out there in the real world. If Jack Nicholson asked, as the Martians invaded, 'Why can't we all just get along?' then Goleman has the answer to how we can do it.

But there is a catch.

As Goleman observes in his closing paragraph in the *HBR* article:

It is fortunate, then, that emotional intelligence can be learned. The process is not easy. It takes time, and, most of all, commitment. But the benefits that come from having a well-developed emotional intelligence, both for the individual and for the organisation, make it worth the effort.[8]

Now there's an invitation to consulting nirvana. The learning process is time-consuming, requires expert assistance and, if it doesn't work, it's your fault, not the consultant's.

Try changing your attitude

To find something a little more practical than EI, you might care to re-examine what sits behind managerial behaviour in the workplace: *attitude.*

Any leader can increase their effectiveness by addressing areas that involve changes in attitude rather than by developing new skills. Like increasing emotional intelligence, changing attitudes is not easy, but it is something each individual can do if they want to, and without the assistance of a consultant.

For example, consider the following straightforward approach, suggested by Dennis Stratton:[9]

1 Decide what you want
Many managers view themselves as problem solvers, which tends to lead to a mode of working that closely resembles crisis management. Instead, change your perspective to focus on longer-term outcomes. Clarity about outcomes will make it much easier to communicate your purpose to others. Such clarity can be achieved by asking such simple questions as:
- What do I want?
- How will I know when I have it?
- What do I need to do now to get there?

2 Be honest
There is not enough honesty in most organisations. Covering up mistakes is common, as is not telling the truth, often in the mistaken belief that it will protect people. Try a total honesty policy, especially about what is working and what is not, regardless of who it is directed at—your boss, your peers or your direct reports. Honesty will enable you to pick up signals about issues much more easily before they become a crisis.

3 Express yourself
While moving to a position of greater responsibility involves many changes, it should not lead to changes in your basic self. Many managers feel pressured to act differently once they gain promotion. Yet most of the respected leaders we can think of behave today in the same way as they did before their elevation.

Be yourself, be real and tell it like it is.

4 Take risks

In a changing world, always doing what has worked before is not necessarily the best strategy. It is sometimes important to deliberately push your own envelope and move out of your usual comfort zone. Deliberately upsetting your own peace of mind by tackling risky projects will pay off in the long run. The risks may be measured and controlled, but it is almost impossible to learn without incurring some element of risk.

5 Participate fully

Managers are frequently required to do things that are boring or humdrum, such as going to meetings. No matter what you may think, others will pick up on whatever attitude you bring to such tasks. You therefore need to find value in whatever activity requires your involvement and focus on exploiting that. This sort of 'positive thinking' approach is not necessarily easy (especially first thing on a Monday morning!) but it does work, as many well known leaders testify.

6 Take personal responsibility

In any organisation there are many things outside your control but this should not be taken as an invitation to think like a victim. Instead, find a means to influence the situation so that at least you have some impact. If a problem occurs despite your best efforts, look for a way to avoid it happening again. If someone else makes a mistake, look for ways and means to help them correct the situation. Leaders typically accept responsibility even when others are in fact responsible. It is part of the leadership role.

7 Create partnerships

More and more organisations value collegial and cooperative ways of working. Few now openly express admiration for 'command and control' styles of management. This means that, to get things done, managers must rely more and more on their influencing skills rather than their authority. You can increase your influence simply by developing more partnership arrangements with others in your organisation.

Make alliances; build relationships; develop mutual obligations. Collaboration has been shown to be the most effective form of collective action in the long term.

8 Commit fully

Once you've decided what it is you want to achieve (and, surprisingly, few managers can articulate what it is they want to achieve), work towards it with all your might. People respect someone who can describe a goal and then is seen to work towards it. Contrast this with people's opinions of a manager who simply goes through the motions. People can easily tell the difference between a manager who complies and a leader who commits. This is a personal matter but it will affect how others perceive you.

In the leadership debate, Stratton's advice is somewhat novel in that he focuses on *attitudinal change* rather than skills or aptitude. While the advice itself is not rocket science, it is to the point, based on practical actions, and within the province of any manager to carry out. It simply requires a bit of intelligence and application. The 'emotional' side will look after itself.

Guidelines

1 Assess your attitude

It's very hard to assess your own attitude but almost no one else can do it for you (unless you want to bring your life partner into this!).

Reflect on the mindset (the collective expression of your attitudes) that you bring to work. Some bits will be positive; some will be negative.

Start with the negatives. Identify one particular habitual view that you often fall prey to (for example, that the only way to get a job done right is to do it yourself) and consider how you might change this to a more positive version (for example, that each job is a chance for someone else to learn how to do something they could not do before).

If this sounds a bit 'touchy-feely' to you, so be it. That's what changing attitudes is all about.

Think about the feelings you bring to work. If you think others don't notice your feelings and the attitudes that come with them, you're just fooling yourself.

2 Pick something, anything

Stratton's list makes a good starting point for doing some things a little differently.

Review the list and find areas of strength and areas of weakness. Look for opportunities at work that play to your strengths. It will enhance your reputation. But also look for opportunities that will give you a chance to practise getting better.

It doesn't matter where you start as long as you start.

3 Interpersonal skills

Much has been written about how to improve interpersonal skills. Not all of it appeals to everyone.

If Goleman does the trick for you, fine. If not, shop around for someone who does, whether it is Eric Berne, Norman Peal or Dale Carnegie. All have something to offer and their reputations would not have lasted this long if a large number of people had not benefited from reading their advice.

For further exploration

Sometimes the oldies are the goodies. Self-development has a long and honourable tradition and the best of the books on this topic probably laid the foundation for business-oriented publishing. The following are three of the best in the field.

- Dale Carnegie, *How to Win Friends and Influence People*, Simon & Schuster, New York, 1999 (first published in 1937).
- Norman Vincent Peale, *The Power of Positive Thinking*, Ballantine Books, New York, 1996 (first published 1953).
- Eric Berne, *The Games People Play*, Penguin, Harmondsworth, 1964.

Each one has an established track record in helping people understand how other people tick and how they themselves tick. Just dip into them and see if it makes sense.

THE UNCERTAIN PROFESSION **30**
OF MANAGEMENT

In the early 1900s, according to the *Oxford English Dictionary*, management meant 'the use of contrivance, prudence or ingenuity for effecting some purpose; often in an unfavourable sense, implying deceit or trickery'.

If this has changed at all—and some may argue that it has not—it is probably due to the efforts of Frederick Taylor, Henri Fayol and Mary Parker Follett. These three led a deliberate and determined effort to 'invent' management as a disciplined activity, or at least to rescue it from those who were responsible for giving it the bad press suggested by the *OED*.

As industry emerged from the period of owner-led capitalism and moved towards managerial capitalism at the end of the nineteenth century, a perceived need to clean up the management act emerged. Unfortunately, not much has happened since those early thinkers.

What progress has the profession of management made?

Background

Most professions either have a long and largely honourable history (architecture, engineering, law) or were able to carve out a legitimate role more recently using science as a backbone (medicine, chemistry, physics). Management clearly did not have the first (see the *OED* definition) so its founding theorists turned to the scientific model.

This was not without its problems, largely because there was no science that could be applied to the emerging activity of professional management. Therefore, the necessary science was invented.

A science or a philosophy?

Frederick Taylor was first and took the obvious step of dubbing his pronouncements 'scientific management'. At the time, this breathtakingly ambitious phrase was readily accepted, to the point that in 1908 the Harvard Business School announced that Taylor's approach was the new standard for modern management and reorganised its courses around his theories. Thus, Taylor effectively founded the MBA.

Taylor's science was extremely dubious, even by the standards of the day. The language he used makes it clear that he was seeking to 'discover' laws of management. Only occasionally did he admit that he was 'developing' theory. The work is sprinkled with terms drawn from engineering but the actual data is scant and suspect. Rather, he adopted a declarative tone that makes challenge both difficult and an affront to common sense. When he is challenged, a detailed explanation of his method[1] shows a number of assumptions that inevitably lead to his desired conclusion.

Henri Fayol supported Taylor in most things, but argued that the great man's works could be supplemented by developing a set of principles. His method relied not at all on science but on codification of presumed knowledge. Fayol was fascinatingly single-minded in his reliance on charts, tables and lists. His statements were categorical, as illustrated by the following selection from *General and Industrial Management*,[2] first published in French in 1916:

- 'All activities to which industrial undertakings give rise can be divided into . . . six groups' (p. 3).
- 'Good planning calls for six essential traits' (p. 50).
- 'Organisations have sixteen "managerial duties"' (p. 53).
- 'Seven qualities are desirable for higher management' (p. 73).
- 'Managers who command should have eight characteristics' (p. 97).

Fayol is best remembered for his reduction of management to five functions:

1 Planning
2 Organising
3 Commanding
4 Coordinating
5 Controlling.

This list is still taught to management students today and the words have become an indelible part of the language of management. Not a bad feat, considering that it has no discernible foundation in fact. Not until Henry Mintzberg had the bright idea of following a handful of managers for a few days with a stopwatch in 1968 (his findings were published in the *Harvard Business Review* in 1976 and much reprinted since) did we realise that Fayol was just making it up as he went along.

Where Taylor offered method, and Fayol a set of principles, Mary Parker Follett gave the world the first *philosophy* of management. She drew on psychology, political science, philosophy, history, economics and social work to create an approach or attitude to the managerial role. She attempted to legitimise her views by drawing on her many interdisciplinary sources. Like Taylor, she used anecdotes to illustrate her arguments; like Fayol, she sought to capture the essence of the managerial situation.

Follett is most like today's authorities on management, most of whom know better than to suggest 'laws of work'. She relies on persuasive argument and polemical statements rather than hard evidence. To this extent, she set the benchmark for the management writers that came after. Why bother with hard facts if you can convince them with a good argument? Virtually every best-selling management textbook has followed this prescription. (An exception may be Peter Senge's *The Fifth Discipline*,[3] rumoured to be the best-selling unread book ever; Senge is in the grand tradition of Fayol.)

Follett's observations ring true largely because they are couched in generalities, appealing to common sense and heavily reliant on broad concepts. The following statements are from *Dynamic Administration*,[4] written in 1924:

- 'That centralisation and decentralisation are not opposed is . . . the central lesson for business administration to learn' (p. 80).
- 'The main problem of the workers . . . is how much power they can themselves grow' (p. 95).
- 'The essence of organisation is the interweaving of functions' (p. 149).
- 'The most important thing to learn about co-ordination is that it must begin at the bottom, not at the top' (p. 222).
- 'The success and progress of any business will depend largely on its ability to get his fullest contribution from every man' (p. 228).

These statements would not be out of place in a modern text. Nonetheless, they are assertions and observations, hardly the basis for a science that will enlighten and elevate the 'profession' of management.

The gap between theory and practice

So there you have the scientific backbone of management, the legacy of almost a hundred years ago. Its foundation rests largely on untested assertions and unproven conclusions. The foundation itself is polemical and declarative. The structure built upon it is comprised of impressive laws, principles and codifications, none of them disprovable. The whole looks almost like a proper building. And subsequent buildings have aped its basic features. But when you try to occupy it, most practising managers see the flaws only too clearly.

This account may go some way towards explaining the growing gap between management theory and practice. What we know to be management 'best practice' is not being practised. What we know works in management is not being applied by managers. Even if we accept that management is a practice (and not a science), those elements that by any rigorous standard we can claim to 'know' are not being used by the practitioners.

If this were true in any other field, it would be scandalous. If doctors did not apply what was known to work, they would be struck off the medical register and prevented from practising. When engineers fail to adhere to what is known to work, they may be prosecuted for negligence, especially if buildings collapse as a result. Even those practitioners working in the Dark Arts, such as psychology, are expected to adhere to professional standards of practice. But when managers fail to do what is known to work, there are no consequences.

This is curious. There are many more managers in the world than there are doctors. Managers generally outnumber the technical experts, especially as so many technical specialists are also managers. In any one organisation, you will find many technical experts, often in quite specialised fields. But you will find hordes, indeed swarms, of managers. They are everywhere. And while a technology-driven shakeout in the 1980s saw a relative decline, recent surveys show an upturn in their numbers.

So, as the gap between 'good practice' and 'actual practice' widens, its impact grows as the number of managers in the world continues to proliferate. Most newly appointed managers must wonder where the 'accepted practices' are, especially if they come from a technical background where that notion is the basis for professionalism.

Strangely, lack of knowledge is not always the problem. There are many management practices that have been clearly shown to have 'better ways', if not 'one best way'. But despite the best efforts of academics and others, the knowledge does not translate into action. This leads to considerable frustration on their part.[5]

Ignoring good practice—an example

One example of just how big the gap is comes from the management activity called 'staff selection', an activity that many managers are involved in simply because picking staff for jobs is a core managerial activity. Over many years, research has shown that a structured approach to the selection process is far more effective than a less formal approach.[6] Effectiveness is easily measured by the eventual success of the person in that job. The effectiveness of different means of selecting people for jobs is easily tested because it is a relatively easy process to measure and compare. The research literature has demonstrated beyond any reasonable doubt that structuring the selection process by techniques such as behavioural descriptive interviewing (BDI)[7] will roughly double your chances of picking a candidate who will be successful in the job.

Using BDI is not complex. Essentially, the interviewer asks the candidate questions about what they have done in certain situations in the past or what they would do if faced with such situations. These situations should reflect aspects (skills, attitudes, knowledge, etc.) that are required to do the job well. It helps if all candidates are asked the same questions. Study after study shows that this is what the 'science' of staff selection is about. Do these things and you will significantly improve the chance of picking the right person.

But BDI isn't used. Not only do managers not do it, specialists paid to bring expertise to the selection process (for example, human resources managers or even recruitment consultants) do not practise BDI. In a few cases, managers have been trained to use BDI, by doing a course designed and provided by a consultancy that has created a proprietary version of it such as the well known Targeted Selection®.[8] But even then, the company that paid for all that expensive training tends to lose focus after a few years and forgets to reinforce the need to stick to BDI principles in selection interviews. Managers soon revert to their unstructured habit of making it up as they go along.

It is not just a case of not knowing what to do or never having learned how to do it. Ignorance is not the explanation. Even though most formal management education programs still suffer from large doses of irrelevance, the role of providing management knowledge has been filled to some extent by a variety of other sources, predominantly through management training programs. (By the way, how many professions do you know where people are appointed first and then trained for the job?)

If this is bigger than simple ignorance, then we face a dilemma. Can managers be trained? Some evade this issue by saying that we train dogs but we develop people. However, the issue is not about the long-term development of managerial capability but the short-term application of effective practice.

Maybe the training is at fault, through failing to get the knowledge across effectively? Again, not true because, in the practice sessions built into the training (and immediately afterwards), trainees show that they can apply the technique. It is only when they're back in their traditional roles on the job that the newly learned practice slowly fades.

Maybe there are institutional barriers that prevent its application? Unlikely. For example, in the above mentioned area of staff selection, there are few barriers that prevent managers from doing what they like. In many other cases (for example, 'empowering' others), you may well be able to cite in-built and ingrained constraints that prevent new learning from being practised. But not so with what managers do in the interview situation. They rule the roost in that interview room.

Maybe managers don't want to do it differently. Maybe you can make the horse drink in the training room but not in the interview room. Perhaps so, in some cases, but most participants in training are volunteers, not conscripts. They come to learn and most are eager to do so. It simply does not make sense that they would consciously undermine themselves by not applying what they have learned, knowing that it is the most effective way to do what they are paid to do.

How to get the best managers

What is left is the most worrying explanation of the lot: that changing managerial behaviour is far more difficult than our training experts admit; that to get someone to behave differently requires more than just the knowledge, the skill and the motivation to do what should be done; that people are in fact highly unlikely to do anything different even when they could do so, and probably should do so, and know they should do so.

So maybe the fundamental model is wrong, the one that makes us pick managers from among those who are successful in their current job. We usually select beginning managers from among those who are most successful in their 'line' job. The best teachers become principals; the best mechanics become maintenance supervisors; the best insurance clerks become managers of that section.

Are there alternative ways of doing selection? One idea is to pick managers on the basis of managerial potential. A bit of this already happens through mechanisms such as Assessment/Development Centres where high-potential candidates are put through structured exercises and psychological tests in order to assess their capabilities. Where the purpose is selection, they are usually called 'Assessment Centres'; where it is done for development reasons, it is usually called a 'Development Centre'. This sort of process is much relied upon by larger organisations but it is an expensive option and takes a bit of a toll on the applicants—two or three days in the hands of a team of psychologists will test anyone's fortitude.

Another option is to pick managers from a pool of managers employed to be managers from first entry into the organisation. This is something that is rarely done now but it was very common in the past, with large companies employing 'trainee managers'. Recently, this idea has had a bit of a bad press because it has become an excuse to employ young people on low wages while holding out the hope of a managerial career. But providing you can overcome some youthful suspicion, it is still a good idea to consider.

Or maybe the workers should pick the managers. This model is emerging in a faint sort of way from the use of self-managing teams. Such teams often select their own leader, although it is by no means universal even in organisations that use self-managing teams.

Or maybe we abolish the managerial role altogether and look for different ways to get managerial tasks done. This is a bit like rotating household chores that nobody really wants to do. Whatever the best answer, training managers after we have put them into a managerial job may not be an answer.

Abolishing the managerial role would at least save us the trouble of trying to professionalise a set of activities that seems quite resistant to standardisation and codification.

For the time being, it seems unlikely that the management role will disappear so the debate on what comprises the role will no doubt continue. Maybe the best that we can hope for is that the debate will eventually become a little better informed as to its historical roots.[9]

Guidelines

1 Read something

It may be worthwhile re-examining how you are keeping yourself up to date with management ideas and practice. This may well involve keeping up to date with stuff that was published many years ago.

Look for material that focuses on techniques (the 'how-to' stuff) rather than the big-picture material on ephemeral topics such as leadership, empowerment or organisational culture.

If you want to explore the big issues, read anything, anything at all by Peter Drucker (see *For further exploration*). If you want the more practical stuff, try any of the big three in management journal publishing: The *Harvard Business Review*, the *California Management Review* and the *MIT Sloan Management Review*.

2 Apply something

Try to apply an idea that you have not tried before. Experiment with something that seems like a good idea at the time (that's your defence if it goes pear-shaped) and see what happens.

Hopefully, by now, you will have come across something in this book that looks like a good idea. If it's in this book, someone else will have tried it before you and made it work.

3 Selection

If you are involved in selecting people, whether for promotion or recruitment, review whether you and your colleagues are using 'best practice' techniques. That is, are you using structured interviewing techniques such as behavioural descriptive interviewing? At the very least, structure the interviews so that you are asking the same questions of all the candidates. Do a course such as Targeted Selection®.

For further exploration

Management is one of the few fields where a single thinker both dominates the current scene and is generally acknowledged to do so by his peers. Peter Drucker is a prophet in his own land. He has contributed for more than sixty years to developing and deepening our understanding of a field of practice that has affected (directly or indirectly) all those who work.

Any Drucker bibliography is so extensive that it can be hard to decide where to start. One way to get around the bewildering quantity of his published work is to dip into the 'samplers' that are now starting to appear. One of the best is:

- *The Essential Drucker: In One Volume the Best of Sixty Years of Peter Drucker's Essential Writings on Management*, Harperbusiness, New York, 2001.

The earliest piece, *Management by Objectives and Self-control*, written in 1954, demonstrates Drucker's clarity about key issues and the impact of his writings. For example:

Each manager, from the 'big boss' down to the production foreman or the chief clerk, needs clearly spelled-out objectives [that clarify expected contributions] to the attainment of company goals in all areas of the business.

Another approach is to try his collection of *Harvard Business Review* articles (no one has published more) in:

- N. Stone, (ed.), *Peter Drucker on the Profession of Management*, Harvard Business Review Book Series, Harvard Business School Press, Boston, 1998.

HBR articles are usually an excellent introduction to larger works by an author, and this collection is no exception.

THE IRRATIONALITY OF MANAGEMENT

31

Rationality is one of the cornerstone beliefs of modern management. Most of what is done by managers is done in the belief that their actions are rational and serve rational purposes. To a large extent, such beliefs go without question—in itself not a very rational act, but probably forgivable in an era of overwork for the employed. Managers rarely sit back and question the rationality of what happens in organisations. Most don't have the time and many don't have the inclination.

Questioning the rationality of management is usually met with the argument that any action that supports the purpose of the organisation is inherently rational. A hasty afterthought may lead to the suggestion that it should be ethical as well, but that is usually preceded by the almost apologetic 'of course'.

But things are not necessarily this clear-cut. There is simply too much evidence that organisations sometimes do dumb things down and that managers sometimes behave irrationally.

Is management a rational activity?

Background

Management is a goal-directed activity. The goal-directed explanation of what constitutes rational behaviour is very much in the modern management tradition. It may well be linked (causally?) to the rise of capitalism in the Western tradition, which, through its spread around the globe over the last two hundred years, has become a dominant ideology.

This rapid spread may well suggest that management is a naturally goal-directed activity. Indeed, 'goal rationality' (as one of the earliest writers on the subject of management, Max Weber, called it) is usually held up as the paradigm of rationality. In fact, it is only one version of rationality. It is not even the version most closely associated with the practice of management over the four thousand or more years that it has been recorded, described and prescribed. It is just the latest and current version and possibly one whose time is limited.[1]

Rationality, goals and values

It is sobering to consider that the oldest known complete text in the world is a management primer. Or maybe it is enough to drive the average manager to drink to recall that in 2700 BC someone took the trouble to explain the tasks of management to wannabe managers. *Instruction of Ptah-hotep*, probably written by a vizier to King Issis, was used to instruct students in the Egyptian scribal schools in how to become good administrators.[2] It was a management bestseller, at least in the sense that it continued to be used for many hundreds of years. This feat is comparable to Stephen Covey's whose books simply refuse to leave the bestseller lists, although it only seems as if Covey has been around for hundreds of years.

Among many others, there are two aspects of this first management book that stand out. First, its style is that of an instructional text written in the form of advice to the reader. This stylistic form continued to dominate the field of management writing until supplanted in the nineteenth century by the tradition of scientific management, when the tone changed from 'this is good advice' to 'this is what is true'.

Second, its advice is remarkably modern in content. Or maybe the sage observations of today's management theorists are strangely ancient: 'If thou be a leader, as one directing the conduct of the multitude, endeavour always to be gracious, that thine own conduct may be without defect'.[3] Or 'walk-the-talk', as we say nowadays. It kept the Egyptian kingdom well managed for some millennia.

Now, this kind of advice is intended to get people to do the right thing. And 'right' in this context does not just mean effective or efficient—it also means ethical. Until the rise of 'scientific management', all management writing had such a moral dimension to it, to a greater or lesser extent. Max Weber, who gave us the description 'goal-rational' (*zweckrational*), as applied to social actions, also wrote about 'value-rational' (*wertrational*), its less glamorous cousin, which focuses on the extent to which an action is in accordance with an ethical, religious or aesthetic principle.

Where goal-rationality is about ends, means and effects, value-rationality is about the rightness of an action as measured against some specific value. However, having articulated the concept, Weber appears almost pleased to concentrate on the seemingly more scientific notion of goal-rationality. Thus, we live with his legacy today.

But let's be fair: we can't blame it all on Weber. He capped a tradition of progressive uncoupling of the notion of rationality as 'that which works' from 'that which is right'. The language of the ancient Greeks did not even allow them to separate the two—the word '*logos*' comfortably embraces both. However, by the time the Romans got hold of the idea (*ratio*) it had become an act of human reason, still with strong normative overtones but separate from what is naturally right and proper.

The rot set in with the Enlightenment. Rationality became a matter of method, of precision and of accuracy. For the likes of Descartes, rationality promised a technical process for progress, and progress was deemed good. Utility was its handmaiden, and society became something to be organised.

From this point on, Western philosophy (the driver behind capitalism and its chief vehicle—the modern organisation) was lost to the siren songs of positivism and empiricism. Value-based decision making was banished to the realm of the non-rational or, even worse, the irrational.

Do the right thing or do the thing right?

The sum of all this cogitation is that it explains the current moral predicament of the average manager on the St Kilda Road tram when deciding what to do in any given situation. The external expectation (as urged by the prevailing ideology of goal-rationality) is to do what is most efficient, effective or economic. The inner self, however, may urge an action that is right because it is based on some moral principle.

The strength of the external driver may lead to feelings of irrationality in wanting to do the right thing, as well as doing the thing right. To want to make a decision that is morally based is almost to disqualify yourself from the role of management. To lead with such views at a job interview would be sheer lunacy.

But compare all this with the reality of the sales volume of management books by Stephen Covey. If Covey stands for one thing, it is leadership behaviour based on moral principles. I have observed ordinary Australian managers wave his books in the air with a deep-felt gratitude that is nothing short of overwhelming. As one manager said: 'At last, someone who understands my daily dilemmas'. In fact, Covey satisfies a deep spiritual need, and his writings fill a dimension that has been missing from the workplace for many years.

Both *Principle Centred Leadership*[4] and *The Seven Habits of Highly Successful People*[5] have sold by the mega-truckload and allowed Covey to charge a reputed A\$70 000 per appearance (slightly cheaper if it's by video link-up). His franchised global chain of leadership development centres is possibly the single most successful enterprise in the history of management training. You don't achieve all that on the basis of a temporary fad.

Covey has tapped a deep well, one that is shared by millions of managers as they consider the meaning of their work and realise that the goals of their organisation may be, and possibly should be, judged by a standard other than the goals of their organisation.

All this guarantees Covey his place in the pantheon of management thinkers. His ideas are singularly unoriginal (as he readily admits), and drawn from a broad sweep of history, but they are the ideas for these times. The author of *Instruction of Ptah-hotep* would not have wanted it any other way.

The trap of superstitious learning

Bringing a moral purpose to work is not the only non-rational thing managers do. Like all other people they also behave non-rationally in other areas. Learning is one such area. The learning behaviour of people is not just non-rational, it can be irrational.

Behaviourist psychologist B.F. Skinner first demonstrated much of this in the 1940s. As Skinner watched his little pigeons in their experimental boxes, he noticed something. Among other tricks, he had taught them that, if they pecked a red button, they would receive a food pellet. After a while, the pigeons would peck the button even if the food pellet did not always appear. In fact, the pellet could appear intermittently and still the pigeons would peck away. This behaviour backed up his famous Stimulus–Response Theory of Learning.[6]

Every now and again, however, a pigeon would do something a little unusual, such as scratch its beak with one claw or move its neck in a circular motion. If, at that precise time, a pellet appeared, they would instantly repeat the behaviour. It was as if the little pigeons believed that their unusual behaviour had induced the feeding mechanism to disgorge a food pellet.

This happened often enough for Skinner to give the phenomenon a name: *superstitious learning* (a belief that a random event, unconnected causally to a subsequent event, did in fact cause that subsequent event to happen).

Pigeons are not the only animals to engage in this type of 'learning'. Humans are also susceptible to this attribution fallacy. When Papua New Guinean villagers observed during World War II that the construction of airfields by Allied soldiers invariably led to the arrival of aircraft filled with supplies, they took to building airfields, long after the war was over. The planes didn't come but it took a long time for the 'cargo cult' belief to die out.

Little pigeons and tribal villagers aside, the phenomenon is rarely mentioned. Yet it seems to offer an explanation for a wide range of managerial behaviour. For example, in business, we draw up budgets in the hope that their creation will lead to the achievement of our performance goals. And when the targets are achieved, we readily take the credit.

The notion of cause and effect is based on the need to establish reasonable links between the two. We must know that there is a link, not just believe it so. And we can only be said to know something if, in addition to believing it to be true, it is in fact true and we have reasonable evidence for it. It is that last bit that gets us into trouble: reasonable evidence.

Our inclination towards learning superstitiously often leads us to accept a dramatically lower standard of proof than we might accept otherwise. This is driven partly by a need to keep things simple. A nicely linear cause-and-effect explanation will easily win out over alternatives that are complex, uncertain and ambiguous. So we readily convince ourselves that we have the right explanation by the tail and act accordingly.

And, like the pigeons and the villagers, once convinced it is very hard for us to be unconvinced. The evidence needs to mount up in great stacks before we will abandon our beliefs. An almost unreasonable standard of evidence is needed before we abandon our beliefs.

When experience isn't enough

Why should any of this matter to managers? Because, if the theorists and researchers are right and learning (whether individual or organisational) is the critical difference between success and failure in business, then the trap of superstitious learning can easily bias you towards eventual failure.

Ironically, this mechanism is often driven by success. The CEO who made the 'right call' in terms of a strategic decision will readily assume the ability to repeat that success. Confidence in their recipes for achieving success leads to overconfidence. Emerging signs of a wrong decision then leads to a search for 'other factors' rather than a fundamental questioning of the original logic: the decision was not wrong—it just wasn't implemented well, or it was under-resourced, or people didn't try hard enough. The more successful the CEO, the less likely that failure is their fault!

Most of this is well researched if not well publicised. Case studies show over and over again that admitting failure is hard for most managers, and plainly impossible for some. Experiments show that those who initiate a policy decision will attribute its failure to causes other than the policy itself, while those who have no ownership of the policy can see its failings more clearly.[7]

As the ability to learn faster and better than your competitors becomes a 'distinctive capability', 'core competence' and 'competitive advantage', beware the manager who relies solely on the University of Hard Knocks:

Experience is often a poor teacher, being quite meagre relative to the complex and changing nature of the world in which learning is taking place . . . Learning from experience involves inferences from information. It involves memory. It involves pooling personal experience with knowledge gained from the experiences of others . . . Even highly capable individuals and organisations are confused by the difficulties of using small samples of ambiguous experience to interpret complex worlds.[8]

We need to believe in the rationality of management but, as both moral management and superstitious learning show, there's more to management than being rational.

Guidelines

1 Managing morally

Although this side of management will never make it on to the boardroom agenda, managers do bring a moral dimension to their work. It is unlikely that this will ever be celebrated or acknowledged.

Nevertheless, for many it is there and it is a real part of their life at work. How this expresses itself can only ever be a personal choice. For some, it revolves around doing work that is of real value to the community. For others, it's about how they interact with those around them.

Either way, it's your business.

2 Learning superstitiously

The tendency to superstitious learning is part of our humanness.

It is unlikely that we will ever be able to separate our rational side from the more irrational aspects of our thinking. (I presume somewhere in the dim past there was some survival value in this type of thinking—maybe 'believing' is a better word.) But when it takes one of the more extreme forms such as those described above (for example, CEO infallibility) then it needs to be considered.

It is in the best interests of the organisation for its senior managers to behave rationally.

I recommend a healthy dose of cynicism (or at least scepticism) about your personal impact on organisational success. No manager is indispensable or infallible.

Roman emperors needed a slave standing next to them to remind them of their mortality. Hopefully, you won't have to go to that extreme.

3 Being irrational

There are times when rationality seems a bit overrated.

Much of our thinking, our decision making, our judgment making and our beliefs are hunches and best guesses, dressed up for public consumption as rational. Things were always thus.

At the end of the day, there is still much that falls within the scope of management that is unclear, imprecise and uncertain. Maybe it will always be so. But at least you can shine a rational torch in some areas, maybe with a little help from this book.

Please do so in the knowledge that no one can ask you to do more than that. If that means there are a lot of places left that are dark, dim and even mysterious, that's modern management for you. Enjoy!

For further exploration

Business books suggesting that management might be an irrational activity (as described above) are not good for business, so there are not a lot of them about. People want to buy books that reduce the complexity of the business situation to simpler and more comprehensible states. The last thing that most managers want is to hear the argument that some of what they do on a daily basis is not rational.

One writer who has tackled an area of frequent irrationality in business is Henry Mintzberg (see Chapter 11). Henry focuses his attention on planning issues, and in his research he found clear examples that many managers do not plan, they make things up as they go along. What's more, he found it to be very effective strategy for dealing with planning issues. Henry called this approach 'emergent strategy', and for some managers it is actually liberating to discover that what they have been doing for years without admitting it is actually a sound approach. By naming it, Henry has given all of us permission to do it. For more on this, see:

- H. Mintzberg, *The Rise and Fall of Strategic Planning*, The Free Press, New York, 1994.

For irrationality in our leaders, try the following (also discussed in Chapter 28).

- M.F. R. Kets de Vries, *Leaders, Fools and Imposters: Essays on the Psychology of Leadership*, Jossey-Bass, San Francisco, 1993.

And if you really do want to know more about the role of irrationality in management, the following journal devoted two issues to a symposium on the subject.

- *The Journal of Management History*, Volume 5, Numbers 1 and 2, 1999.

Fascinating reading, but don't let your boss catch you reading this sort of stuff—she might get the wrong idea!

WHAT IT TAKES TO SURVIVE AS A MANAGER 32

Managers spend a lot of time looking after the people they work with, but they rarely look after themselves as well as they should. Usually, this is to do with pressures caused by time and workload. But there are also other factors at work in managers' general reluctance to do some self-maintenance. These factors might include arrogance ('I don't need to get better'), fear ('Maybe I can't get better') and ignorance ('I don't know how to get better').

And yet in the highly competitive environment of today's organisations, regular maintenance and the occasional overhaul are vital if you are to remain as effective as you can and need to be. So finding the time to invest in your best asset (you) is important, especially if you have more than just survival on your mind.

How can managers survive in a competitive work environment?

Background

Surviving in today's competitive world is as challenging for managers as it is for the organisations in which they work. While the worst of the downsizing boom may be over, there is a continuing threat of Darwinian selection hanging over every manager: organisations want the best. So how do you survive against the competition? Which factors make the difference in the career jungle?

Career survival factors

All downsizing exercises (under whatever name) ultimately come down to a choice between which people stay and which people go. A survey of over 5000 managers asked respondents to nominate those factors that mattered in career survival. Although twenty factors were most frequently nominated, further research suggested that only ten were absolutely critical.[1] These ten factors comprise the critical pieces in the success puzzle. They are:

1 excellent performance record;
2 communication skills;

3   interpersonal skills;
4   personality factors (for example, enthusiasm);
5   technical skills/staying current;
6   significant work experiences/assignments;
7   ability to stay 'cool';
8   ability to make difficult decisions;
9   power;
10 having a mentor/sponsor.

As some of these factors overlap, they reduce to roughly six areas in which managers need to display competence.

1 **Performance record**—the critical element here is recency. Outstanding performance is remembered only until the next performance hurdle. Consistency is critical, therefore, if you are to have a good track record. Yesterday's successes matter only if they are repeated today and tomorrow. And, for managers, this means the performance of a group of people, not just their own personal achievements. It is difficult to be seen as successful if the unit you manage is not.

2 **Communication skills**—the ability to keep people informed and on side regardless of context. Lean organisations, global organisations, virtual organisations, team-based organisations—all these demand higher levels of communication skills than ever before. If you are not working on improving your communication skills today, then you know where you will end up in the career race tomorrow.

3 **Interpersonal skills**—the basis for all management roles, especially as the technical element becomes less important and the people management element gains prominence. This aspect is rarely taught in formal education programs and our informal education is usually limited to interacting with those who are similar to us—our friends and family. Thus limited opportunities to learn come our way, and it is easy to assume that you are performing as well as anyone in the area of relationships. You almost need to go out of your way to experience situations in which you will be challenged in order to develop better and different skills in dealing with others. Ignoring this area of personal development because it is 'touchy-feely' only identifies you as a potential has-been.

4 **Personality aspects**—the factors that are most difficult to change but which can be managed. Start off with gaining an

understanding of what makes you tick and an appreciation that others may march to the beat of a different drum. This will lead to all-round greater understanding and possibly to ways of managing those aspects of your personal approach that are least effective in an organisational setting. You will never become a 'different you' but you may learn to make the best of your strengths and minimise the impact of your weaknesses.

5 **Technical skills, experience and power**—all related to what you do in practice. These three factors are connected by what you are able to do in your job, and all are interrelated. Your technical expertise may gain you new experiences and these in turn add to your skill levels. All this adds up to a degree of power you have that derives from your technical competence.

6 **Staying cool, making decisions, and having a mentor/sponsor**—all elements of the action-orientation that is still the preferred model for the successful manager. Decision making is almost the hallmark of management and this ability needs to be executed in a cool, objective and detached manner. It always involves an element of risk and requires the maturity to accept the responsibilities inherent in the management job. That maturity comes from reflection, and often through conversations with others who can guide that reflection—mentors.

Interestingly, managers, to a greater or lesser extent, can influence all these factors. They are within the reach of all managers to manage. In a sense, it comes down to whether you can be bothered to actively manage your own career or prefer to place your faith in random selection. Darwinian theory suggests the latter is a high-risk strategy.

Can you be nice and still succeed?

On the other hand, maybe we make too much of the populist version of Darwinian strategy. The business environment is often described as 'dog-eat-dog' where competition and winning are the key words. But is it necessary to be ruthless, aggressive and even brutal just to succeed? Or is it possible to be nice and still succeed in business? Most recent research (from sociobiology to management research) suggests that the advice to care for your fellow employees is well founded. However, there are also some contradictory findings. Possibly the most profitable course of action is to appear to be nice but to be mean and ruthless behind the scenes.

Traditionally, the words used to describe life in the modern organisation draw on jungle analogies with an emphasis on doing whatever is necessary to survive. This contrasts sharply with the words now used by senior executives which emphasise that it is important to create a 'caring and sharing' work environment that nurtures and supports employees.

There are many examples of organisations that actually live out those values and some have acquired a reputation for being a 'great place to work'. However, in many organisations what is said by top management and written in corporate 'value statements' does not tally with people's stories about what the organisation is really like. Is the 'caring' talk just hot air and PR waffle?

Altruism and business

Over the last twenty years, the notion of the caring company has become an urgent ideal for many. J. Willard Marriott (the legendary founder of one of the world's largest hotel chains) was one of the first managers to articulate this goal as being good for business: 'You can't make happy guests with unhappy employees'. It certainly helps if employees at least mean it a little bit when they wish their customers a nice day.

Management writers such as W. Edwards Deming and Tom Peters have long advocated that business does not have to be a cut-throat and ruthless competition. Recent research in sociobiology suggests that being nice pays off in the long run. A sophisticated model created by two academics[2] demonstrates that a strategy of 'indirect reciprocity' (helping others without any direct gain or return) is very successful in Darwinian terms: the nice guys survive!

The assumption behind the model is that being nice gives you a good reputation and being nasty gives you a bad reputation. In the short term, the nasty behaviour gets results; in the long term, it leads to failure. As the intelligence level of the creatures in the model is increased, the niceness strategy is increasingly successful. In the model, humans in particular do very well by being nice rather than nasty.

In real nature, there are many examples of nice behaviour on the part of animals that survive very successfully. For example, the Arabian babbler (of the ornithological variety) is well known for its random acts of generosity. Ethologists have yet to determine exactly why altruistic behaviour pays off for this bird and for many other species. Altruism is part of the human condition.

Does altruism work in the world of business? There is some evidence to suggest that companies need to be tough to survive. For example, research from the Warwick Business School (UK) suggests that the link between employee satisfaction (presumably high in nice companies) and profitability is a complex one. In fact, one piece of research suggests that the relationship is inverse: the higher the level of employee satisfaction in a chain of retail stores, the lower the level of profitability.[3]

Before managers pull on their jackboots, it should be noted that the profitable stores were also the larger stores with many more customers, more supervisors and generally busier than the smaller (but happy!) stores.

In surveys, most employees express their belief that their jobs are getting tougher, harder and more stressful. Ferocious competition has led to many management tactics that have made corporate life a matter of survival: re-engineering, downsizing and de-layering have created a 'survivor syndrome' where the command to be nice brings only hollow laughter.

Managers have been driven to look after their own interests first. The bearer of 'pink slips' one day may be the recipient the next day. A continual state of turmoil in many organisations has led to varying degrees of mistrust, cynicism and fear among the managerial groups. Accordingly, being nice to your staff moves down the list of priorities.

No doubt senior executives do mean it when they exhort their managers to put people first. But, at the same time, the working environment for many organisations has grown tougher and meaner. Pressures are increasing from customers, competitors and shareholders. These demands can be quite contradictory and ever more immediate, leaving even less room for acts of altruism.

In the end, most organisations do aspire to be good places to work. But the reality is that many fail in this aspiration.

What, therefore, is the best strategy for the individual manager to pursue? Research may suggest that the most effective approach is to be seen to be nice and accept the benefits that this impression brings, but behind the scenes behave in a ruthless, mean way.

For most managers, it is far simpler just to do what they feel is right. This may well be one case where the research data is not morally worthwhile.

Guidelines

1 Spot the weakness

When it comes to your ability to survive, the lists provided above enable a quick-and-dirty piece of self-analysis. Where are your strengths? Where are your weaknesses?

By the way, there's not much point fooling yourself when you're doing this type of analysis, so be honest; if you're not sure, ask other people for their opinion of you.

Maybe something stands out as an aspect that really is an area of weakness for you. Reflect on how you could develop additional skills in that area. Attend a training program. Do some reading. Get advice from someone who is good at it.

Experiment with doing some things differently.

2 Put yourself in a different situation

One of the most confronting, but also fastest, ways to develop new capabilities is to transport yourself to a different working context.

The first few months in any new job is the time when you learn the most. You can replicate that experience by deliberately putting yourself into a new situation. For example, you can volunteer for a project that is significantly unrelated to the work you do at the moment. Or you can do volunteer work with a non-profit organisation. Or you do a 'sabbatical' with another organisation in another industry.

As long as you move out of your comfort zone, it is almost inevitable that you will learn new things.

3 Remaining true

In the end, most of us find it difficult to be other than what we are. It creates too much stress and just feels wrong. So rather than take too much notice of what research or writers say about how to succeed in business, it is usually a more effective strategy to start with what *you* think matters.

It's quite handy to have an 'inner voice' that you can turn to in times of need to check whether what you plan to do is the right thing. It's fast and it's effective.

As someone once suggested, if you're wondering whether a proposed action is the right thing to do, ask yourself whether you would be happy telling your grandmother what you did and why.

For further exploration

Self-development is the backbone of the world of business publishing. The very first books aimed at business people were about how to improve yourself. So there is something like eighty years of published material to draw on. Picking a few out of all these thousands is a bit hazardous, so the short list that follows is entirely personal. The items are on the list because I like them and I'm the author so I get to pick! They are not in any special order, as I couldn't decide which was the best—let your mood guide you.

- W. Bridges, *Transitions: Making Sense of Life's Changes,* Perseus Publishing, Cambridge, 1980.
- M. Buckingham and C. Coffman, *First, Break all the Rules: What the World's Greatest Managers do Differently*, Simon & Schuster, New York, 1999.
- S. Sample, *The Contrarian's Guide to Leadership,* Jossey–Bass, San Francisco, 2001.
- J. Badaracco, *Leading Quietly,* Harvard Business School Press, Boston, 2002.
- J. Fox, *How to become CEO: The Rules for Rising to the Top of any Organization,* Hyperion Press, New York, 1998.
- R.N. Bolles, *What Color is your Parachute? A Practical Manual for Job-Hunters and Career-Changers,* Ten Speed Press, Berkeley, 2001.
- R. Tedlow, *Giants of Enterprise: Seven Business Innovators and the Empires They Built*, HarperCollins, New York, 2001.
- R. Bramson, *What your boss doesn't Tell You until it's too Late: How to Correct Behaviour that is Holding You Back*, Simon & Schuster, New York, 1996.
- J. Gabarro and J. Kotter, *Managing your Boss,* PDF Download, Harvard Business School Press, Boston, 2002.

Acknowledgments

Earlier versions of some of the material in this book have appeared in:

- *Business Review Weekly*
- *The Manager Online*
- *Management Today*
- *Management Summaries*
- *The Heart and Soul of Leadership* (Management Today Series, McGraw-Hill 2002)

Notes

Chapter 1   Trust in the workplace

1 B. Malinowski, *Argonauts of the Western Pacific: An Account of Native Enterprise and Adventure in the Archipelagoes of Melanesian New Guinea*, Waveland Press, Prospects Heights, 1984.

2 K. Ryan and D. Oestreich, *Driving Fear out of the Workplace*, Jossey-Bass, San Francisco, 1991.

3 D. Reina and M. Reina, *Trust and Betrayal in the Workplace*, Berrett-Koehler, San Francisco, 2000.

4 E. Marshall, *Building Trust at the Speed of Change: The Power of the Relationship-based Organisation,* Amacom, New York, 1999.

5 O. Williamson, 'Calculativeness, trust and economic organization', *Journal of Law and Economics*, 36, 1993, pp. 453–86.

6 A. Giddens, *The Consequences of Modernity*, SUP, Stanford, 1990.

7 M. Korczynski, 'The political economy of trust', *Journal of Management Studies*, 1(37), 2000, pp. 1–21.

8 D. Robertson, 'Trust, loyalty, risk and revenge: leadership challenges in healthy organisations', *Training Journal*, July 2000, pp. 12–14.

Chapter 2   Empowerment

1 H. Metcalf and L. Urwick (eds), *Dynamic Administration: The Collected Papers of Mary Parker Follett*, Pitman, London, 1941.

2 R. Wright, *Non-zero: The Logic of Human Destiny*, Vintage, New York, 2001.

3 Metcalf and Urwick, as above.

4 P. Graham, *Mary Parker Follett—Prophet of Management: A Celebration of Writings from the 1920s,* Harvard Business Press, Boston, 1996.

5 K. Blanchard and S. Johnson, *The One Minute Manager,* Berkley Books, New York, 1983.

6 K. Blanchard, J. Carlos and A. Randolph, *Empowerment Takes More Than a Minute*, Berrett-Koehler, San Francisco, 1996.

7 R. Semler, *Maverick*, Arrow, London, 1994.

Chapter 3   Workplace satisfaction

1 J. Pfeffer, *The Human Equation*, Harvard Business School Press, Boston, 1998.

2 A. Kohn, *Punished by Rewards*, Houghton Mifflin Co., Boston, 1999.

3 M. Buckingham, *First, Break all the Rules*, Simon & Schuster, New York, 1999.

4 Buckingham, 1999.

5 Buckingham, 1999.

6 Buckingham, 1999.

Chapter 4   Discretionary effort

1 C. Handy, *The Age of Paradox*, Harvard Business School Press, Boston, 1995.

2 C. Handy, *Gods of Management: The Changing Work of Organizations,* Business Books, London, 1991.

3 C. Handy, *Age of Unreason*, Harvard Business School Press, Boston, 1998.

4 C. Handy, *Beyond Certainty: The Changing Worlds of Organizations*, Harvard Business School Press, Boston, 1998.

5 M. Weisbord, *Productive Workplaces*, Jossey-Bass, San Fransisco, 1987.

Chapter 5   Feedback

1 D.F. Baker and M. R. Buckley, 'A historical perspective of the impact of feedback on behaviour', *Journal of Management History*, 2(4), 1996, pp. 21–33

2 D.A. Wren, *The Evolution of Management Thought*, John Wiley & Sons, New York, 1987.

Chapter 6   Shared goal setting

1 E. Berne, *The Games People Play*, Penguin, Harmondsworth, 1964.

2 T. Harris, *I'm OK—You're OK*, Cape, London, 1973.

3 K. Blanchard and S. Johnson, *The One Minute Manager*, Berkley Books, New York, 1983.

4 B. Posner and J. Kouzes, *The Leadership Challenge*, Jossey-Bass, San Fransisco, 1995.

5 M. LeBoeuf, *How to Motivate People*, Sidgwick & Jackson, London, 1986.

6 C. Argyris and D. Schon, *Organizational Learning II*, Addison-Wesley, Reading, 1996.

Chapter 7 Measuring performance

1 K. Cameron and R. Quinn, *Diagnosing and Changing Organisational Culture*, Addison Wesley, Reading, 1999.
2 *Dictionary of Business*, Oxford University Press, Oxford, 1996.
3 R. Kaplan and D. Norton, *Balanced Scorecard: Translating Strategy into Action*, Harvard Business School Press, Boston, 1996.
4 www.unpan1.un.org/intradoc/groups/public/documents/aspa/unpan002075.pdf
www.som.cranfield.ac.uk/som/cbp/BScorecard.html

Chapter 8 On-the-job training

1 L. Baird, P. Holland and S. Deacon, 'Learning from action', *Organisational Dynamics*, 4(27), 1999, pp. 19–31.

Chapter 9 Problem solving

1 J. Hammond, R. Keeney and H. Raiffa, 'The hidden traps in decisionmaking', *Harvard Business Review*, September/October 1998, pp. 47–58.

Chapter 10 Decision making

1 P. Drucker, 'The effective decision', *Harvard Business Review*, Jan–Feb 1966.
2 M. Balle, 'Transforming decisions into action', *Career Development International*, 6(3), 1998, pp. 227–32.
3 T. Grundy and R. Wensley, 'Strategic behaviour: the driving force of strategic management', *European Management Journal*, 17(3), 1999, pp. 326–34.
4 ibid.
5 T. Grundy and R. Wensley, *Harnessing Strategic Behaviour: Why Personality and Politics Drive Company Strategy*, Financial Times Management, London, 1998.

Chapter 11 Planning versus strategising

1 H. Mintzberg, 'The manager's job: folklore and fact', *Harvard Business Review*, July–August 1975.
2 H. Mintzberg, *The Rise and Fall of Strategic Planning*, The Free Press, New York, 1994.
3 ibid., page 321.
4 ibid., page 159.
5 E. Chung and C. McLarney, 'When giants collide: strategic analysis and application', *Management Decision*, 3(37), 1999, pp. 233–47.

Chapter 12 Scenario planning

1 www.business2.com/articles/mag/0,1640,35945,FF.html

2 J. Coates, 'Scenario planning', *Technological Forecasting and Social Change*, 65, 2000, pp. 115–23.

3 P. Schwartz, *The Art of the Long View: Planning for the Future in an Uncertain World*, Doubleday, New York, 1996.

4 J. Coates, op. cit.

5 A. Wright, 'Scenario planning: a continuous improvement approach to strategy', *Total Quality Management*, 4(11), 2000, pp. 433–8.

6 D. Mercer, 'Robust strategies in a day', *Management Decision*, 35(3), 1997, pp. 219–23.

Chapter 13   Structure and performance

1 R. Hale and P. Whitlam, *Towards the Virtual Organisation*, McGraw-Hill, London, 1997.

2 H. Voss, 'Virtual organization: the future is now', *Strategy & Leadership*, July/August 1996, p. 12.

3 C. Barnatt, 'Virtual organisation in the small business sector: the case of Cavendish Management Resources', *International Small Business Journal*, July/September 1997, p. 36.

4 D. Nadler and M. Tushman, 'The organization of the future', *Organizational Dynamics*, 1(28), 1999, pp. 45–60.

5 Nadler and Tushman.

6 Nadler and Tushman.

7 Nadler and Tushman.

Chapter 14   The internal resource advantage

1 A. Sloan, *My Years with General Motors*, Doubleday, New York, 1964.

2 M. Porter, *Competitive Strategy: Techniques for Analyzing Industries and Competitors*, The Free Press, New York, 1980.

3 M. Porter, *Competitive Advantage: Creating and Sustaining Superior Performance,* The Free Press, London, 1985.

4 Resource theory is still largely confined to journals:
- J. Barney and M. Hansen, 'Trustworthiness as a source of competitive advantage', *Strategic Management Journal*, Winter 1994 (Vol. 15).
- D. Collis, 'A resource-based analysis of global competition; the case of the bearings industry', *Strategic Management Journal*, Summer 1991 (Vol. 12/Special Issue).
- J. Fahy, 'The resource-based view of the firm', *Journal of European Industrial Training*, 2(24), 2000, pp. 94–104.
- S. Maijoor and A. van Witteloostuijn, 'An empirical test of the resource-based theory: strategic regulation in the Dutch audit industry', *Strategic Management Journal*, July 1996.

- D. Miller and J. Shamsie, 'The resource-based view of the firm in two environments: the Hollywood film studios from 1936 to 1965', *Academy of Management Journal,* June 1996.
- C. Pringle and M. Kroll, 'Why Trafalgar was won before it was fought: lessons from resource-based theory', *The Academy of Management Executive,* November 1997.

5 G. Hamel and C. K. Prahalad, 'Core competence of the organization', *Harvard Business Review,* May–June 1990, pp. 79–91.

Chapter 15   Cultural diversity

1 F. Trompenaars and C. Hampden-Turner, *Riding the Waves of Culture,* McGraw-Hill, New York, 1998.

2 J. Gilbert and J. Ivancevich, 'Valuing diversity: a tale of two organisations', *The Academy of Management Executive,* 1(14), 2000, pp. 93–106.

3 C. Hampden-Turner and F. Trompenaars, *Building Cross Cultural Competence: How to Create Wealth from Conflicting Values,* Yale University Press, New Haven, 2000.

4 Trompenaars and Hampden-Turner, as above.

Chapter 16   Organisational culture

1 M. Herskowitz, *Man and his Works,* Knopf, Westminster, 1948.

2 T. Peters and R. Waterman, *In Search of Excellence,* Harper & Row, New York, 1982.

3 T. Deal and A. Kennedy, *Corporate Cultures: The Rites and Rituals of Corporate Life,* Addison-Wesley, Reading, 1982.

4 W. Ouchi and A. Johnson, 'Types of organizational control and their relationship to emotional well-being', *Administrative Science Quarterly,* 23, 1978, pp. 292–317.

5 D. Pheysey, *Organizational Cultures: Types and Transformations,* Routledge, London, 1993.

6 I. Briggs Myers, *Introduction to Type: A Guide to Understanding your Results on the Myers-Briggs Type Indicator,* Center for Applications of Psychological Type, Gainesville, 1998.

7 G. Hofstede, *Culture's Consequences: Comparing Values, Behaviours, Institutions, and Organizations across Nations,* Sage, Thousand Oaks, 2001; F. Trompenaars and C. Hampden-Turner, *Riding the Waves of Culture,* McGraw-Hill, New York, 1998.

8 R. Harrison, 'Understanding your organization's character', *Harvard Business Review,* 3, 1972, pp. 119–28.

9 C. Handy, *Understanding Organizations,* Penguin, Harmondsworth, 1976.

10 E. Schein, *Organizational Culture and Leadership,* Jossey-Bass, San Francisco, 1985.

11 P. Hawkins, 'Organizational culture: sailing between evangelism and complexity', *Human Relations*, 4, 1997, pp. 417–40.

12 V. Vaisnys, 'Managing culture for strategic success', *Strategy & Leadership*, 6/28, 2000, pp. 35–8.

13 ibid.

Chapter 17   Renewal and innovation

1 R. Ashkenas, 'Real innovation knows no boundaries', *The Journal for Quality and Participation*, 21(6), 1998, pp. 34–7.

2 ibid.

3 M. Croft, 'Time to nurture creativity', *Marketing Week*, 12 November 1998, pp. 40–2.

4 M. Corso and S. Pavesi, 'How management can foster continuous product innovation', *Integrated Manufacturing Systems*, 11(3), 2000, pp. 199–211.

Chapter 18   Enduring organisational structures

1 T. Peters and R. Waterman, *In Search of Excellence*, Harper & Row, Sydney, 1982.

2 J. Collins and J. Porras, *Built to Last*, Century, London, 1995.

3 J. Lipman-Blumen and H. Leavitt, 'Hot groups with attitude: a new organizational state of mind', *Organizational Dynamics*, 4(27), 1999, pp. 63–73; J. Lipman-Blumen and H. Leavitt, *Hot Groups: Seeding them, Feeding them, and Using them to Ignite your Organisation*, Oxford University Press, Oxford, 1999.

4 ibid.

Chapter 19   Work design

1 H.M. Parsons, 'What happened at Hawthorne?' *Science*, 183(8), March 1974.

2 G. Dalton, 'The collective stretch', *Management Review*, December 1998, pp. 54–9.

3 ibid.

4 ibid.

5 ibid.

Chapter 20   Self-managing work teams

1 For example, R. Semler, *Maverick*, Warner Books, New York, 1993, and J. Katzenbach and D. Smith, *The Wisdom of Teams,* Harvard School Press, Boston, 1993.

2 R. Carroll, 'The self-management pay-off; making ten years of improvements in one', *National Productivity Review*, 4(19), 2001, pp. 61–7.

Chapter 21   Consultants

1 *Consultants News*, Kennedy Information, http://www.kennedyinfo.com

2 ibid.

3 A. Payne, 'New trends in the strategy consulting industry', *Journal of Business Strategy*, 7(1), 1986, pp. 43–55.

Chapter 22   Change management

1 E. Kübler-Ross, *On Death and Dying*, Macmillan, New York, 1969.

2 C. Steiner, 'A role for individuality and mystery in "managing" change', *Journal of Organizational Change Management*, 2(14), 2001, pp. 150–67.

3 I can't recall where I first came across these principles, but it was many years ago. To the original author, my apologies, appreciation and the promise of a future acknowledgment.

Chapter 23   Management and metaphors

1 K. Lewin, *Field Theory in Social Science*, Tavistock, London, 1963.

2 G. Morgan, *Images of Organization*, Sage, Beverly Hills, 1986. For more examples, see:

- R.D. Stacey, *Complexity and Creativity in Organizations*, Berrett-Koehler, San Francisco, 1996.
- R.G. Eccles and Nitin Nohria, *Beyond the Hype: Rediscovering the Essence of Management*, Harvard Business School Press, Boston, 1992.
- K. Devlin and D. Rosenberg, *Language at Work*, CSLI Publications, Stanford, 1996.
- R.C. Hill and M. Levenhagen, 'Metaphors and mental models: sensemaking and sensegiving in innovative and entrepreneurial activities', *Journal of Management*, 21(6), 1995, pp. 1057–74.
- J. March and H. Simon, *Organizations*, 2nd edition, Blackwell Press, Oxford, 1993.
- I. Nonaka and T. Yamanouchi, 'Managing innovation as a self-renewing process', *Journal of Business Venturing*, 4(5), 1989, pp. 299–315.
- L. Smirich and C. Stubbart, 'Strategic management in an enacted world', *Academy of Management Review*, 10, 1985, pp. 724–36.
- S. Srivasta and F. Barrett, 'The transforming nature of metaphors in group development: a study in group theory', *Human Relations*, 41, 1988, pp. 31–64.
- K.E. Weick, *Sensemaking in Organizations,* Sage Press, Thousand Oaks, 1995.

3 R. Seel, 'Organizational change', *Organizations & People: Successful Development*, 7(2) May 2000, pp. 2–9.

4 ibid.

5 ibid.

Chapter 24   Discussing the undiscussable

1 P. Senge, *The Fifth Discipline*, Doubleday, New York, 1994.

2 www.actionscience.com/argbib.htm

3 C. Argyris, *Flawed Advice and the Management Trap: How Managers can Know when they're getting Good Advice and when they're not*, OUP, Oxford, 1999.

4 C. Argyris and D. Schon, *Organizational Learning II*, Addison-Wesley, Reading, 1996, p. 90.

5 C. Argyris, 'Teaching smart people how to learn', *Harvard Business Review*, May–June 1991, pp. 99–109.

6 Argyris and Schon, op. cit.

7 ibid.

8 ibid., p. 249.

9 For example, see T. Stewart, *Intellectual Capital: The New Wealth of Organizations*, Doubleday, New York, 1997.

10 P. Senge, *The Fifth Discipline*, Doubleday, New York, 1994.

11 Argyris and Schon, op. cit.

Chapter 25   Emotions at work

1 B. Tuckman, 'Developmental sequence in small groups', *Psychological Bulletin*, 63(6), 1965, pp. 334–99.

2 M. Csikszentmihalyi, *Beyond Boredom and Anxiety: Experiencing Flow in Work and Play*, Jossey-Bass, San Francisco, 2000.

3 ibid.

4 W. Henge, 'Managing moments of truth', *Management Review*, 87(8), pp. 56–60.

5 ibid.

6 ibid.

Chapter 26   Leadership

1 E. Jaques, *Requisite Organization: The CEO's Guide to Creative Structure and Leadership*, Cason Hall & Co, Arlington, 1989.

2 S. Covey, *Principle Centred Leadership*, Simon & Schuster, London, 1992.

3 S. Covey, *The Seven Habits of Highly Successful People*, Simon & Schuster, London, 1989.

4 S. Covey, *How to Develop a Family Mission Statement,* Covey Leadership Centre (audio cassette), 1996.

5 J. Kouzes and B. Posner, *The Leadership Challenge*, Jossey-Bass, San Francisco, 1996.

6 ibid.

7 J. Kotter, 'What leaders really do', *Harvard Business Review*, May–June 1990.

8 Cultural Imprint, *Leaders in Australia*, Cultural Imprint, Melbourne, 2000.

9 K. Blanchard, et al., *Leadership and the One Minute Manager*, Morrow, New York, 1985.

Chapter 27   Beyond heroics

1 B.M. Bass, *Bass and Stogdill's Handbook of Leadership*, The Free Press, New York, 1990.

2 V. Newman and K. Chaharbaghi, 'The study and practice of leadership', *Journal of Knowledge Management*, 4(1), 2000, pp. 64–73.

3 M. London, 'Principled leadership and business diplomacy', *Journal of Management Development*, 18(2), 1999, pp. 170–92.

4 S. Covey, *Principle Centred Leadership*, Simon & Schuster, New York, 1992.

Chapter 28   Leading with integrity

1 P. Kotter, 'What leaders really do', *Harvard Business Review*, May–June 1990.

2 B.M. Bass, *Handbook of Leadership*, The Free Press, New York, 1990.

3 W. Bennis, *On Becoming a Leader*, Addison Wesley, Reading, 1989.

4 See, for example, the IT section of *The Age* newspaper, published in Melbourne.

5 R. Townsend, *Up the Organisation*, Coronet, London, 1971.

6 M.F.R. Kets de Vries, *Leaders, Fools and Imposters: Essays on the Psychology of Leadership*, Jossey-Bass, San Francisco, 1993.

7 J. Washbush and C. Clements, 'The two faces of leadership', *Career Development International*, 4(3), 1999, pp. 146–8.

8 T. Simons, 'Behavioral integrity as a critical ingredient for transformational leadership', *Journal of Organisational Change Management*, 12(2), 1999, pp. 89–104.

9 ibid.

Chapter 29   The trap of 'emotional intelligence'

1 D. Goleman, *Emotional Intelligence*, Bantam, New York, 1995.

2 D. Goleman, *Working with Emotional Intelligence*, Bantam, New York, 1998.

3 D. Goleman, 'What makes a Leader?', *Harvard Business Review*, November–December 1998.

4 A. Etzioni, *Character Building and Moral Conduct: The Spirit of Community*, Crown, New York, 1993; M. Hoffman, 'Empathy, social cognition, and moral action', in W. Kurtines and J. Gerwitz (eds), *Handbook of Moral Behaviour and Development*, Lawrence Erlbaum, Hillsdale, 1984.

5 P. Saloyev and J. Mayer, 'Emotional intelligence', *Imagination, Cognition and Personality*, 9, 1990, pp. 185–211.

6 H. Mintzberg, *The Rise and Fall of Strategic Planning*, Prentice Hall, New York, 1994.

7 D. Knights and G. Morgan, 'Corporate strategy, organizations and subjectivity: a critique', *Organization Studies*, 12(2), 1991, pp. 251–73.

8 D. Goleman, *Harvard Business Review*, 1998, op. cit.

9 D. Stratton, 'Leadership with attitude; eight winning strategies', *Industrial Management*, 42(1), 2000, pp. 20–3.

Chapter 30   The uncertain profession of management

1 For example, the full page footnote on page 60 in F. Taylor, *The Principles of Scientific Management*, Dover, Mineola, (1911— reprinted 1998).

2 H. Fayol, *General and Industrial Management*, Davis S Lake Publishing, Belmont, 1916 (1987 edition).

3 P. Senge, *The Fifth Discipline*, Doubleday, New York, 1990.

4 M. Parker Follett, *Dynamic Administration*, Pitman, London, 1973 (drawing on papers written in 1924).

5 See, for example, articles such as F. Herzberg, 'One more time: how do you motivate employees?', *Harvard Business Review*, January–February 1987.

6 J.M. Barclay, 'Employee selection: a question of structure', *Personnel Review*, 28(1/2), 1999; L. Di Milia and M. Gorodecki, 'Some factors explaining the reliability of a structured interview system at a work site', *International Journal of Selection & Assessment*, 4(5), 1997.

7 J.M. Barclay, 'Improving selection interviews with structure: organizations' use of "behavioural" interviews', *Personnel Review*, 30(1), 2001, pp. 81–101.

8 Targeted Selection®: www.ddiworld.com

9 E. O'Connor, 'Lines of authority: reading the foundational texts on the profession of management', *Journal of Management History*, 3(2), 1996, pp. 26–49.

Chapter 31   The irrationality of management

1 M. Rutger, 'Be rational! But what does it mean?', *Journal of Management History*, 5(1), 1999.

2 B. Gunn, *Instruction of Ptah-hotep and the Instruction of Kegemni: The Oldest Books in the World*, John Murray, London, 1906.

3 ibid.

4 S. Covey, *Principle Centred Leadership*, Summit Books, New York, 1991.

5 S. Covey, *The Seven Habits of Highly Successful People*, Simon & Schuster, New York, 1989.

6 B.F. Skinner, '"Superstition" in the pigeon', *Journal of Experimental Psychology*, 38, 1948, pp. 168–72.

7 B. Staw and J. Ross, 'Commitment to a policy decision: a multi-theoretical perspective', *Administrative Science Quarterly*, 23, 1978, pp. 40–64.

8 D. Levinthal and J. March, 'The myopia of learning', *Strategic Management Journal*, 14, 1993, pp. 95–112.

Chapter 32   What it takes to survive as a manager

1 J. Simonetti, 'The key pieces of the career survival and success puzzle', *Career Development International*, 4(6), 1999, pp. 312–17.

2 M. Lynn, 'Can nice guys finish first?', *Management Today*, February 1999, pp. 48–51.

3 ibid.

INDEX

Page numbers in **bold** type refer to main entries

MANAGEMENT
TODAY

The Australian Institute of Management's national monthly magazine
Management Today keeps you in touch with all the issues that matter –
leadership, globalisation, strategic thinking, e-management and much more.
It is Australia's only magazine focusing on the profession of management
and is a 'must read' for managers at all levels.

A free subscription to *Management Today* is one of the many bonuses
of AIM corporate and personal membership. However, additional or new
subscriptions are available for $55.00 (GST included) per year (ten issues
including postage and handling).

Please return by
post ...
fax (07) 3832 2497 ...
phone (07) 3227 4888 ...

or visit our website www.aim.com.au

and follow the links to *Management Today*.

WHAT'S
HAPPENING IN
MANAGEMENT
TODAY?

SUBSCRIBE

AND FIND OUT.

YES! I WANT TO SUBSCRIBE TO MANAGEMENT TODAY.

name _____

address _____

☐ please bill me

☐ please find enclosed a CHEQUE or MONEY ORDER
(payable to Australian Institute of Management Qld & NT)

tel ( )_____ fax ( )_____

email _____   **$55**

☐ Visa ☐ Diners ☐ Bankcard ☐ Mastercard

☐ Amex   Amex ID number _____

cardholder name _____

card/account number _____

expiry date _____   signature _____

Delivery Address
PO Box 200
SPRING HILL QLD 4004

Management Today
Australian Institute of Management
QLD & NT
Reply Paid 200
SPRING HILL QLD 4004